Japanese Economic Development

**This book is to be returned on or before
the last date stamped below.**

The Nissan Institute/Routledge Japanese Studies Series

Japanese Economic Development

Theory and Practice

Penelope Francks

London and New York

First published 1992
by Routledge
11 New Fetter Lane, London EC4P 4EE

Simultaneously published in the USA and Canada
by Routledge
29 West 35th Street, New York, NY 10001

Reprinted 1993

British Library Cataloguing in Publication Data
Francks, Penelope 1949–
   Japanese economic development: theory and practice.
   (The Nissan Institute/Routledge Japanese studies series).
   1. Japan. Economic conditions
   I. Title II. Nissan Institute of Japanese Studies 330.52
   ISBN 0–415–04100–7
   ISBN 0–415–04101–5 pbk

Library of Congress Cataloging-in-Publication Data

Francks, Penelope, 1949–
   Japanese economic development: theory and practice / Penelope Francks.
   p. cm. – (Nissan Institute/Routledge Japanese studies series)
   Includes bibliographical references and index.
   1. Industry and state – Japan.   2. Agriculture–Economic aspects–Japan.
3. Japan–Industries. I. Title. II. Series.
HD3616. J33F73 1992
338.952–dc20   91–12622
                                                                      CIP

Contents

Tables

General Editor's Preface

Now that we are in the 1990s, most would agree that Japan is a nation of absolutely first rate significance. The successes of the Japanese economy and the resourcefulness of her people have long been appreciated abroad. What is new is an awareness of her increasing impact on the outside world. This tends to produce painful adjustment and uncomfortable reactions. It also often leads to stereotypes based on outdated or ill-informed ideas.

The Nissan Institute/Routledge Japanese Studies Series seeks to foster an informed and balanced – but not uncritical – understanding of Japan. One aim of the series is to show the depth and variety of Japanese institutions, practices and ideas. Another is, by using comparison, to see what lessons, positive and negative, can be drawn for other countries. There are many aspects of Japan which are little known outside that country but which deserve to be better understood.

How relevant is the early modernising experience of Japan to less developed areas of the world today? Given the intrinsic importance of this subject, surprisingly little thoughtful work has been written about it hitherto. Not only Japan specialists and scholars researching Third World countries, but even economic historians and development economists, have an unfortunate tendency to talk past each other. In fact, however, as Dr Francks cogently argues in this pioneering book, despite historical, cultural and technological differences of time and place, the Japanese modernising experience has much to offer states for whom Western development models and prescriptions have been found wanting.

In parts of East and Southeast Asia the Japanese model is already influential. Elsewhere, disillusioned with Western blueprints, castigated by dependency theorists and neoclassical economists alike, leaders of contemporary developing states could do worse than to examine, critically and constructively, the path taken by the first non-Western nation to build a world-class economy.

J.A.A. Stockwin

ix

Acknowledgements

This book is in the main the product of solitary communion with printed works and the word processor and my debts are therefore of the broad kind, to those who have provided me with the stimulus, the time and space, and the moral support required to write it. It has its origins in a course I have taught for a number of years at the University of Leeds and inasfar as it is comprehensible at the same time to both economists and students of Japan, it owes much to the expressions of interest and/or puzzlement of successive generations of my students. My colleagues in the Department of East Asian Studies have borne with me, covered for me and made sure I kept my nose to the grindstone. I am grateful to Professor Arthur Stockwin for continued support and some helpful comments on the text, and to my fellow British-based economic historians of Japan, Janet Hunter of the London School of Economics and Kaoru Sugihara of the School of Oriental and African Studies, as well as to other members of the group on the Teaching of Japanese Economic and Social History, for reassuring me that the book needed to be written.

Finally, thanks as always to Richard, without whom my arguments would lack logic, my prose such style as it has, and my projects their purpose.

Note
Japanese personal names are given in the Japanese order, that is, family name first, except in the cases of those who write in English. English versions of Japanese company names are given where these are widely used. The glossaries are designed to serve as crash introductions to the terminologies of Japanese economic history and development economics. Those unfamiliar with either field might find it helpful to glance through them before reading the book.

General introduction

This book represents an attempt to apply to the historical case of Japan some of the ideas and theories produced in recent years in the field of development economics. To both sets of readers at which it is aimed – those studying Japan and those studying economic development – this might appear an odd enterprise: after all, Japan today is quite obviously very far from being a developing country. On the one hand, those engaged in analysing and trying to understand her economy and society might wonder why they should burden themselves with a new set of theories and jargon, not of apparently direct relevance to the economic giant that Japan now is. On the other hand, development economists, only too familiar with the poverty and inequality pervading much of the developing world, might ask how the processes which, over the past century or so, have generated the rich, technologically sophisticated and relatively equal society of contemporary Japan could possibly contribute anything to an understanding of the mechanisms of development and underdevelopment in Asia, Africa and Latin America today. Some justification is therefore required to explain why students of Japan and students of development should get to know one another through the analysis of the experience of the first non-Western society to become economically developed. If nothing else, all might bear in mind that there are those alive in Japan today who have experienced the whole process of economic development, from peasant farming to the high-tech miracles of the present day, in their lifetimes. In this respect at least, Japan still remains unique in the modern world.

It would clearly be appropriate to begin with some sort of definition of the field of theory and practice which we shall be using. However, it has to be said that for some years now development economics, and the wider area of development studies of which it forms a major part, have been diagnosed as suffering from an identity crisis which makes such definition difficult.[1] The 1960s and early 1970s were the boom years of development economics when a steady stream of theories, controversies and empirical research was emerging from newly-formed development studies centres and when practitioners of the subject saw the influence of their ideas spreading through the planning agencies and aid organisations promoting development in the Third World. Since then, however, disillusion has set in. In the real world of developing countries, despite often impressive rates of economic growth and the implementation of many of the policy proposals of the dominant schools of thought in the field, poverty and inequality, even in places famine, remained for all to see, amid the increasingly divergent experiences of the great variety of Third World states. Meanwhile, in the academic world, the theoretical justification for distinguishing a sub-set of 'developing countries' according to particular features of their economic, political and social structures was being undermined by the revival of 'neo-classical' approaches which stressed the significance of market forces, as against 'structural' or institutional factors, in explaining the speed and pattern of economic change. Developing countries can no longer be unambiguously defined according to certain common characteristics and significant numbers of those working in the field have come to believe that economic actors operate according to broadly similar principles regardless of the environments, institutions and social structures around them. In such a situation, what justification can there be for devoting a book to the application of the somewhat disarrayed body of development-economics theory to the individual case of that most successful once-developing, now developed, economy, Japan?

In answer to this, I would argue that students of Japan should in fact be among the first to appreciate the value of development studies as a body of comparative knowledge and analysis devoted to the processes which, more than anything else, have revolutionised Japanese lives over the past two hundred years. Despite its 'crisis', development economics, in the form of the application of economic reasoning to the enormous and multifarious sub-set of the world's economies which differ significantly from those of the standard North American or Western European model, continues to be widely practised and is, in this sense at least, thriving. With the demise of any generally accepted theoretical consensus about development, however, the detailed experiences of individual countries or regions have come to receive much greater attention. In this situation, as those of us who work on Japan know only too well, there is a danger that the effort to acquire sufficient knowledge of a society's language, history and culture to be able to make the attempt to describe and explain its processes of development can all but obliterate the capacity to work with general theories or a comparative framework, both on a practical level, given the constraints of time and recognised academic specialisations, and from an intellectual and emotional point of view. Yet the Japanese case illustrates particularly vividly the ease with which a society can become categorised as unique and inexplicable if efforts are not made to relate its experience to the theories and issues which concern students and scholars of other areas and disciplines. The loss of potential understanding which this represents, not to mention the wider dangers of such isolation, are obvious. The body of development-studies knowledge therefore remains as a vital means of interrelating experiences of economic change in widely different historical and cultural environments, thereby generating the comparisons and contrasts without which studies of individual societies become esoteric and pointless.

Nonetheless, as this suggests, it is difficult enough to relate to one another individual cases from within the contemporary Third World. How much more so, then, in the case of comparisons with historical examples such as that of Japan, whose period of economic development is here taken as stretching from the mid-nineteenth century to the 1950s. With the exception of some of the 'stage theorists' of the immediate post-World War II period, development economists have only rarely used the economic history of presently-developed countries as a source of examples for development theories, and, vice versa, economic historians working on Europe or North America have not in general applied to their material the theories devised to explain development processes taking place today. There are academic and institutional reasons for this – economic historians and development economists use different kinds of data, inhabit different university departments, and so on – but it can also be argued that the direction taken by much thinking about development in the 1960s and '70s made the past experience of now-developed countries seem in many respects irrelevant to the problems confronting now-developing ones.

The essential cause of this lay in the fact that, for the dominant schools of thought within development studies over much of the post-war period, the key factor conditioning the experience of the developing world was the prior existence of already-developed countries. At the extreme, it was argued that the forces generated by the developed capitalist 'centre' of the world economy made long-term successful economic development in the Third World 'periphery' impossible. But more broadly, throughout the spectrum of development studies, the choice of issues and theoretical stance tended to be predicated on the assumption that the major problems and potentials facing developing countries arose from their relationships with the industrialised economies. It was this that made essential state intervention to regulate dealings with the outside world and to protect and plan for the growth of infant industries in the face of developed-country competition. It was the structure of the world economy, shaped by the demands of advanced countries for the products and markets of their former colonies, which determined the cultivation patterns and institutional organisation of Third World agriculture, and it was also in the advanced industrial sectors of the developed world that there lay the technical and organisational keys which would unlock the productivity of Third World labour and make available the consumer goods now so widely advertised to the people of developing countries through the network of mass communications.

As a result, the body of development theory, as it had emerged by the mid-1970s, seemed to have little relevance to study of the economic history of those countries which had industrialised before the nations of the world could clearly be divided into the developed and the underdeveloped. Of present-day industrialised countries, two, though, could be picked out as having begun and successfully pursued a process of economic development in a world already so divided. One of these was the Soviet Union, which, despite its untypical size and resource base and the European roots of much of its culture and political organisation, served as perhaps the single most important development model for much of the Third World after World War II; the other was Japan. However, it required the Japanese economic miracle of the late '50s and '60s to alert mainstream scholars and students of development to the significance of Japan's economic past.[2] By that time, the tools of non-Marxist analysis of development had been substantially refined and it was these which were utilised to construct what came to be known as the 'Japanese model of economic development'. This depended heavily on 'dual economy' theories of industrialisation, which portrayed development as essentially a process of inter-sectoral (agriculture–industry) movement of labour and capital. Japan was a key example used by Fei and Ranis (1964), for example, in the construction of their famous two-sector model, and studies of inter-sectoral movements of labour and capital, and of the means whereby 'surplus labour' was utilised, dominated the work of those who began, in the 1960s, to apply 'modern' methods of economic analysis to Japan's past.[3] The relevance of development theory to Japan, and of Japan to development theory, was widely accepted in these kinds of study and in work on Japan's 'modernisation' more broadly.

From an academic development-studies point of view, therefore, Japan represented a relevant example of a developing country, as it had come to be defined by the 1960s, that is, as an economy changing within a world in which industrialised countries already existed, with all that that implied as to the functions of the state, the potential of imported industrial technology, the role of agricultural resources, and so on. Outside the academic world too, and especially with her emergence in the 1960s as a major economic power, Japan began to appear as a potent and significant model to the governments and peoples of a number of developing nations.[4] Here Japan's appeal lay less in the timing and economic nature of her development process and more in her characteristics as an Asian nation. She was the first, and for a long time the only, country to break the Western monopoly on successful long-term industrialisation, the first rice-cultivating society to become industrialised, and of course a nation with Chinese-based cultural, philosophical and social traditions which apparently bore much closer resemblance to those prevailing elsewhere in Asia than did those of Europe. The specifically 'Japanese' characteristics of Japan's industrialisation thus began to receive much more attention as offering perhaps a different model of development in areas such as industrial organisation, the functions of the state, rural economic and social institutions and so on, and one more appropriate than that based on Western theory and practice.

It was within this sort of atmosphere that I, as a development economist, first came to study Japan. Since then, however, the world has changed. In development studies, the confident belief in development planning and modelling has been undermined, at first by the doubts raised by structuralist, neo-Marxist and dependency-school theorists as to the possibility of real development within the present structures of the world economy and of developing countries themselves, and then by disillusion with the powers of the state to intervene to promote development and the consequent revival of 'neo-classical' or 'free-market' theories. The developing world itself has changed and the divergent experiences of individual developing countries, highlighted by the success of the East Asian Newly Industrialising Countries, have cast doubt on the validity of many general development models. Furthermore, as Japan has become an economic superpower with her political and economic feet firmly planted in the camp of the Western industrialised world, her relevance as a model to much of the Third World has come to seem more remote and her role, from the point of view of developing countries, appears to have shifted to one as aid-donor, foreign investor, progenitor of multinational companies and general economic imperialist, resembling much more closely that accorded to the developed countries of the West.

Meanwhile, however, work on Japan's economic past has proceeded apace and with the recognition of Japan's place in the world economy and the growth of Japanese Studies in the West, a much more detailed understanding of Japanese economic history has become possible. Since the mid-1970s, a considerable amount of research on a range of aspects of Japan's agricultural and industrial history has been published and the underlying picture held by economic historians of her industrialisation process, its speed and phasing, its interrelations with the world economy and its political ramifications, has changed significantly. The increasing complexity of this picture, combined, on the development-studies side, with the lack of any clear consensus about development theory, has meant, however, that few attempts have been made to consider its relevance to the wider pattern of development experience as it is now being analysed in development-studies work.[5] Hence, important studies of Japan, particularly at the micro-economic and institutional level, which challenge widely-held beliefs about her economy and which provide valuable examples of the experience of development outside the Western world, remain accessible only to those with the scope to devote considerable time to the acquisition of the Japanese background, thereby risking, unless they are very strong-minded and thick-skinned, the loss of much of their comparative perspective.

This book is thus an attempt to make such work more accessible and at the same time to provide those who study Japan with one possible comparative framework within which to consider Japanese experience. Those hoping, on the other hand, to be presented with a new 'Japanese model' or the latest 'key to Japanese success' should however be warned that they are likely to be disappointed. Since development economists themselves have lost faith in development models that are easily generalised, and in-depth study of Japan should, if nothing else, undermine belief in any single key to 'understanding the Japanese', the most that can be aimed for is to draw out the 'family resemblances' between the experience of Japan and that of other developing countries and to examine and test, against particular aspects of the Japanese case, some of the many new concepts and empirical results coming out of development studies in recent years.

In view of this, it has been necessary to select, as topics for consideration, those areas where the directions of work on Japanese economic history and on present-day development processes most clearly intersect, within the constraints of the author's own interests and competence. These intersections seem to me to fall into the three broad categories around which the three parts of the book are organised. Each part begins with an introduction to the theoretical and practical issues which have concerned development economists in its particular area, before going on to look at the relevant Japanese experience. Part I considers the interrelated issues of development strategy, particularly as regards economic relations with the outside world, and the role of the state in planning and directing development in 'late-developing' economies. The shortcomings of the state-led import-substitution industrialisation strategies pursued in many parts of the developing world, especially when contrasted with the export-oriented success of the Newly Industrialising Countries of East Asia, have given rise to advocacy of less government intervention and freer trade policies. Meanwhile, although much has been written, or assumed, about the role of the Japanese state in initiating and promoting development, much has also come to light in recent years to cast doubt on the degree of planning and the efficacy of the state's actions in the Japanese case. Part II looks at the rural economy during the industrialisation process in the light of, on the one hand, the growing recognition of the significance of long-term changes in agriculture and 'traditional' industry for an understanding of the nature of Japan's development and, on the other, the increasing importance attached by development economists to agricultural development and hence to the analysis of 'peasant' farming. Finally, in part III various aspects of the process of importing and adapting industrial technology and industrial organisation are examined and the emergence and developmental significance of a number of 'peculiarly Japanese' institutional phenomena are analysed.

As a result of this process of selection, many areas of development experience, for example as regards trade (except in relation to overall development strategy) and finance, receive inadequate attention, either because little emphasis has been placed on them as yet in recent research on Japan or because they lie outside the micro-economic and institutional areas in which, it seems to me, the most interesting work in both development studies and Japanese economic history has been taking place. In addition, some development issues, particularly those relating to poverty, inequality and the overall distribution of the costs and benefits of industrialisation, which I would like to have been able to cover in greater detail, have proved difficult to analyse satisfactorily in view of the absence of historical data on such topics.

Throughout, the focus of the work is on the micro-economic level and the reader will find that the broader description and analysis of Japanese development is interspersed with more detailed case-study material designed to illustrate the range and variety of experience among the institutions, social groups and individuals who constituted the actors in the play of economic forces. Part I, which takes the state as its starting point, is designed to give some degree of chronological outline at the national level for those generally unfamiliar with the course of Japan's modern history, and macroeconomic overviews of particular issues are presented here and there. A number of broadly macro economic histories of Japan are already available,[6] however, and any economist-readers who find themselves lost are asked to refer to these. I have tried to keep statistical material and tables to a minimum as these are generally off-putting to non-economists, but summary tables of relevant statistics are included in places and more comprehensive macro-statistical data are quite easily accessible in a number of widely available works (e.g. Ohkawa and Rosovsky 1973; Ohkawa and Shinohara 1979). Sources and references have been confined almost exclusively to English-language material. It would be a task of an altogether different magnitude to bring the ever-growing volume of Japanese-language economic-history work into the present framework. Finally, as with any topic-based historical study, a certain amount of cross-referencing and repetition has been unavoidable. I hope that users of the book will feel that the broader comparative insights thus made possible, and the scope opened up for the use of Japanese examples within topic-based development-studies courses, will compensate for this.

What follows is, unashamedly, an attempt to kill two birds with one stone and to thread a difficult path between two bodies of knowledge, two kinds of methodological approach and two terminologies. The result may appear unsatisfactory to both establishments but, on the one hand, it is all too easy, given the nature of the sources they use, for students of Japan as a social, cultural or linguistic entity to be unaware of how the experience of the country they study compares with that of other countries, and the techniques of another discipline have to be applied to remedy this. Equally though, students of development cannot usefully consider Japan, perhaps the single most important example for an understanding of development processes in the contemporary world, without reasonably accurate information about it, couched in terms which they understand but reflecting the details of specialist research. If this book can go some way towards bridging this gap, it will have served its purpose.

Part I
Development strategy and the role of the state

1 Introduction

Ever since the impact of the first industrial revolution on the economic and political relationships of the world became apparent, the conscious promotion of national economic development has been seen as one of the prime responsibilities of government and a major aspect of the role of the state in society. From the point of view of the 'state' itself, and of the interests which maintain a particular structure of political power and organisation, economic development provides the means of establishing military strength and national independence and, more widely, it enables the demands of the population for higher standards of consumption and welfare to be met. As increasing numbers of Third World countries have become independent, their governments have espoused economic development as a major national goal, and the analysis of the methods adopted to try to achieve it, that is to say of development strategies, has become one of the most significant areas of concern for development economists.

For the majority of developing-country governments, development has been seen as synonymous with industrialisation. Only an economy based on the manufacture of industrial goods could provide the resources for military and economic independence, generate the higher levels of productivity which improved living standards would require, and create a trading structure free of dependence on unstable exports of primary products. Hence the strategies pursued have essentially aimed at developing a modern industrial base, and the problem facing governments has been that of increasing and/or redirecting savings and investment flows to that end. Given the prior existence of already-developed countries and the state of underdevelopment in which Third World countries found themselves, state intervention which altered the conditions facing domestic investors and entrepreneurs was seen as the only means whereby such a redirection of resources could be achieved. Moreover, under such conditions it was difficult to see how key industries could grow up if they had to compete, either at home or in export markets, with the products of similar industries in already-developed countries, and the selection of industries to promote, along with the choice of the methods to be used to assist them, was inextricably bound up with the nation's trading relations with the outside world. Hence, development strategies have come to be classified according to both the scope of state intervention and the nature of trade policy.

The methods adopted by developing-country governments in pursuit of their development strategies have of course varied widely. At one extreme lie those countries in which the state, for political and ideological as well as economic reasons, took over ownership of the means of production to a substantial degree and drew up more or less comprehensive plans for the allocation of resources between investment and consumption and between different industries. Such planning also of necessity required a high degree of insulation from the fluctuations of the international economy and trade relations with the outside world (at least the market-economy parts of it) tended to be kept as limited as possible. The governments of the majority of developing countries, however, have not intervened to this extent, sometimes for reasons of ideology but also because of limits to the resources and degree of control available to them, and have simply tried to guide the economy along the lines of 'indicative' plans by means of, for example, the provision of finance or subsidies for particular projects, thus leaving much more scope for market activity and private investment.

Nonetheless, there has been one generalised weapon widely used by a great variety of developing-country governments in their efforts to see modern industries established. This is the manipulation of exchange rates and controls over trade flows as a means of making profitable the domestic production of goods for which demand would otherwise have been met by imports. The removal of foreign competition, through tariffs which raise the price of imports or other kinds of trade control, would leave the domestic market open to local producers who could take the opportunity to set up production facilities, master new technology and, in the long run, achieve the lower production costs needed to compete with existing developed-country producers. The attempt to establish new industries in this way came to be known as the import-substitution industrialisation (ISI) strategy and it was commonly employed by Third World states in the 1950s and 1960s. The kinds of industries promoted and protected varied over time and place, with the planned

economies frequently giving priority to establishing heavy industry
and capital-goods production, while typical more limited ISI strategies
generally began by restricting imports, and hence promoting domestic
production, of consumer goods, in the hope that the foreign exchange
thus saved could eventually be used to import more sophisticated
capital goods.

The rates of growth achieved by both planned and more or less free-
market Third World countries pursuing ISI strategies were generally
acknowledged to have been initially, by historical standards, relatively
high. However, by the 1970s growth rates appeared to have stagnated
and many of the problems experienced by developing nations came
to be attributed to the pursuit of ISI strategies. The industries which
protection had encouraged tended to be those which produced the
'inappropriate' products demanded by the better-off sections of the
population, rather than those meeting the 'basic needs' of the
majority for food, clothing, shelter, and so on. They utilised the
relatively capital-intensive technology developed for such products
in the industrialised world and tended to rely heavily on foreign
involvement or imported capital goods, thus increasing rather than
reducing dependence on advanced countries. They did not generate
export income and hence were unable to offset the rising import costs,
for example of oil, which were driving many developing countries
heavily into international debt. Protection created vested interests in
the monopoly position of domestic producers in small home markets
and made it hard to reduce import controls or raise the relative
profitability of investment in other lines of production. Somewhat
similar kinds of problem emerged even in planned socialist economies,
as monolithic and inflexible planning authorities with vested interests
in particular industries became entrenched. In general, ISI strategies
seemed to have resulted in the creation of enclaves of high-cost,
capital-intensive industry producing for the urban rich, generating
little employment and creating little impact on the livelihoods of the
majority of the Third World's population.

For some, this experience served to show that it was indeed
impossible for developing countries to achieve independent industrialisation within the prevailing domestic and/or international economic
and political system and only revolutionary structural or institutional
change could bring it about. For others, it proved the futility of
attempts to interfere with the market, when well-meaning schemes
to allocate resources contrary to the dictates of competitive forces
resulted only in the choice of inappropriate technology, the failure
to generate employment, and the inefficient production of goods for

which demand did not exist at home or abroad. It was against this background that the test cases for ISI strategy were to emerge in the shape of the so-called Newly Industrialising Countries (NICs), most notably the East Asian 'Gang of Four' (South Korea, Taiwan, Hong Kong and Singapore). These countries, it was argued, had abandoned (or never adopted) ISI, dismantled the structure of protection and exchange-rate control, and encouraged industries which could profitably export their products at prevailing world prices. These policies were seen as the key to the rapid growth and development of the NICs in the '60s and '70s and represented, for a significant school of development economists, a new development strategy, christened Export-Oriented Industrialisation (EOI).

The rapid development achieved by the NICs made the idea of EOI strategy a highly influential one and even heavily planned economies such as the People's Republic of China set about introducing policies designed to promote exports. For the 'free-market', neo-classical economist, this apparent acceptance of the laws of the market meant the growth of industries utilising more appropriate, labour-intensive technology which generated a much more rapid expansion of industrial employment and of the market for domestically-produced food and consumer goods, and hence a more equal distribution of the growing national income, than ISI strategies had done (see eg Little 1982). Against this it has been suggested that NIC states, with some exceptions, have in fact been actively involved in the promotion of industry, sometimes through relatively subtle forms of assistance to exporters, sometimes through more obvious forms of protection of, for example, heavy industry, and it is difficult to argue that the promotion of exports is much less of an interference with free trade than the limitation of imports (White and Wade 1985). Hence the role played by the state in EOI strategies remains controversial.

There is, however, a third approach to the categorisation and analysis of the state's role in economic development and this makes use of the concept of the 'developmental state' employed by Chalmers Johnson in his study of Japanese industrial policy (Johnson 1982), and subsequently by others. According to Johnson, in Japan (and by extension, following other authors, in other East Asian developmental states) the role of the state conforms neither to the liberal Anglo-American tradition, under which the legitimate functions of governments are in theory restricted to administering and policing the overall legal framework within which individuals freely compete with one another, nor to the ideologically-based practice of planned socialist economies, in which state ownership and management of the means of production are seen as desirable ends in themselves. In the East Asian developmental state, economic goals are paramount and based on a consensus behind the pursuit of industrialisation which it is the function of political leaders to create and maintain. The methods whereby these goals are to be accomplished, however, are not ideologically predetermined, and the task of devising the day-to-day ways and means of achieving them is largely left in the hands of the professional officials of the state, the bureaucracy. Under such a system, bureaucrats have the greater degree of power and status necessary to enable them to engineer, within the framework of vague and all-embracing laws, the kind of assistance they regard as likely to be most effective in the case of each particular industry, frequently through informal or unofficial channels. They are thus able to pursue different courses for each specific case and it may not be easy to categorise the overall results of their actions according to the classification of development strategies outlined above. It is possible to argue that the underlying basis of the bureaucrats' role in the developmental state lies in a Confucian heritage of ideas concerning the responsibility of the official for the welfare of the people. Be that as it may, as Johnson's study of the Japanese Ministry of International Trade and Industry shows, it is nonetheless only through appreciation of the particular historical experience and institutional practice of bureaucratic bodies that their role in the process of economic development can be understood and assessed.

The story of the role of the state in the economic development of Japan can therefore be taken as describing the emergence of the first of the East Asian developmental states, and many of the issues raised concern the part played by the economic bureaucracy in this process. However, the story has to be seen against the changing background of international and domestic forces which conditioned the role the state was able to pursue and the kind of strategy it was able to adopt towards, for instance, Japan's trading relations with the then-developed world. Given the commitment of the new government which came to power in 1868 to the goal of catching up with the industrialised nations, and the obvious success in the pursuit of that goal achieved by the time of the Pacific War or, even more, by the 1970s, it is easy with hindsight to discern the guiding hand of the state, selecting the right strategies and methods, and to look for lessons in that. Nevertheless, there were many trials and errors along the way, and many other forces both at home and abroad, including, for example, the activities of private Japanese entrepreneurs and investors, determining the course the economy took. Furthermore, although it is helpful to see Japan as the first nation successfully to pursue the NIC-style developmental-state strategy in which bureaucrats play a key role in the establishment of both export industries and a domestic heavy industrial base, the study of Japanese experience suggests that certain contradictions existed within such a strategy which were never resolved, which contributed towards the disaster of the Pacific War and which continue to plague Japan's external economic relations. Similarly, it has been argued that strategies like those of today's NICs are flawed by the same contradiction in that, if pursued and extended to their logical extremes, they too would generate the protectionist response which contributed towards Japan's involvement in real war in the past and her current increasingly bitter diplomatic and political conflict with her Western trading partners.

2 The state and early industrialisation

Japan's 'modernisation' has traditionally been said to begin with the event known as the Meiji Restoration which took place in 1868. Although couched in terms of a restoration of the power of the Emperor, what took place was in practice a kind of coup d'état, whereby the Tokugawa family, who had held the reins of central government for over two hundred years previously, was overthrown by a coalition of rival feudal lords and their retainers. What made these events of such profound significance, however, and more than a simple change of ruling group, was the fact that they took place within the context of, on the one hand, the forced opening up of the country to the influence of the Western industrial powers and, on the other, the increasing inability of the old regime to control internal economic and social change. While recent trends in the study of Japanese economic history have tended to emphasise the importance for Japan's development of the growth and change which took place during the preceding 250 years of Tokugawa rule, from the point of view of the state's role in development, the Restoration represents a highly significant break in that it brought to power a government which had to cope with these new forces and which, willingly or not, came to define and adopt new goals clearly aimed at the modernisation and industrialisation of the country.

Given their lack of knowledge of the outside world, the new leaders were not always able to define these goals very specifically, nor were they always clear and consistent as to what strategies or methods they should adopt to achieve them. Nonetheless, by the turn of the century, significant steps had been taken in the direction of industrialisation, and the essentially non-industrial, though commercially and agriculturally developed, economy of the Tokugawa period had been substantially changed by the growth and spread of factory industry. Moreover, the threat of domination, economic or military, posed by the Western powers had been avoided and indeed, by the time of the outbreak of World War I, Japan had herself defeated both China and Russia and had acquired her own colonial footholds on the mainland of Asia. In what follows we shall be considering the part played by the state in initiating and promoting this process.

THE STATE AND THE ECONOMY IN PRE-INDUSTRIAL JAPAN

At the Battle of Sekigahara in 1600, the samurai armies of a coalition of feudal lords, under the leadership of Tokugawa Ieyasu, inflicted on the armies of their rivals the final defeat in a long military and political campaign for control of the central government of Japan and the person of the Emperor. Ieyasu took the title of Shōgun (in effect, the Emperor's supreme military commander) and he and his successors set about creating a system of government under which the people of Japan were to enjoy unprecedented peace and prosperity for two and a half centuries. The period of the Tokugawa Shogunate, once regarded as a picturesque but basically static feudal age of grim samurai and impoverished peasants, leavened by the floating world of geisha and actors, is now more generally seen as the period in which the bases of many crucial elements in Japan's subsequent economic success were laid. Moreover, from the point of view of the role of the state in the economy, it can also be seen as a period in which local government officials came to play an increasing role in the economic development of the areas under their control. Although it was not until the Restoration that there was to come to power a central government committed to a programme of economic modernisation, those who were to lead and administer that programme had acquired their education and experience in a climate in which government officials had become increasingly obliged to take steps to promote strategic industries and ensure the economic welfare of the state.

The system of government developed under the Tokugawa Shogunate had in common with European feudal systems the central role of feudal lords (*daimyō*), who governed, on a largely hereditary basis, domains (*han*) of varying sizes granted to them by the Shōgun. The lord was entitled to tax away a share of the rice crop of the peasants who farmed the land of his domain. In return, he was responsible for the maintenance of law and order and in this he was assisted by his military retainers (the samurai) who, in the long period of peace, became civil servants and administrators. The Tokugawa Shōgun was in essence simply the greatest of these feudal lords, controlling and taxing the largest domain as his fief. Central government was thus a question of maintaining the allegiance of the other feudal lords, using the revenue of the Tokugawa lands to do so. This was achieved through control over the activities and movements of the lords and their retainers, including, for example, the well-known *sankin kōtai* system under which each lord was obliged to spend regular periods in the capital, leaving members of his family behind there as hostages to his good behaviour when he returned to his domain. In addition, there were controls on communications between domains and on the political activity (e.g. marriage alliances) of the lords and their families, monitored by an efficient system of spies and intelligence agents. Except in cases of extreme mismanagement or internal disturbance, however, taxation and administration within domains remained in the hands of the hereditary *daimyō*.

As had been the case with previous governments of Japan, the ideological basis of the system was provided by Chinese political ideas, in particular those of Confucianism, and the aim of the Tokugawa rulers was to create a society in which everyone had their place and their duties and responsibilities to those above and below them. This was reflected in the emergence of a class hierarchy in which the samurai became a hereditary, in theory military, caste, with the stratum of lords above them, and below them the peasantry, who pursued the reasonably honourable occupation of cultivation. Those not born into the samurai or farmer classes, such as merchants and craftsmen, were regarded, in this scheme of things, as of inferior social status and marriage across class boundaries was in theory prohibited. In the ideal world, the lords would rule, the samurai would preserve peace and order, and the farmers would cultivate the rice and pay the taxes on which all depended, under the benevolent guidance of the Emperor and his Shōgun adviser. Change would be unnecessary, but to help make sure that no disruptive influences entered the system from outside, strict prohibitions were enforced, from the early seventeenth century onwards, on travel overseas or contact with foreigners (e.g. missionaries), and the limited amount of foreign trade that took place was strictly controlled through Nagasaki, the only port of entry for foreign goods.

Unfortunately, however, in the long run all was not immutable. During the preceding period of civil warfare, the samurai, originally small-scale local lords and landowners, had become increasingly professional soldiers, separated from their landed interests, and after the establishment of peace this trend was reinforced as *daimyō*, intent on consolidating their control over their domains and preventing the emergence of any rival power bases, drew their samurai into the central castle towns from which they ruled their *han*. Thus, unlike the Chinese adminstrative class, the samurai lost their direct links with productive activity and came to live on the stipends of rice paid to them by their lords in accordance with their particular ranks and duties. In order to enjoy the fruits of town life, the samurai needed to convert the stipends they received from their lords, usually paid in rice, into cash, and for this they needed the services of merchants and financiers to whom in due course many became indebted. The growth of towns and of urban commercial activity, as well as the development of the communications network linking each domain with the Shōgun's capital, Edo (later renamed Tokyo), generated growing markets for agricultural goods and the manufactured products, such as textiles, demanded by the urban samurai and merchant classes, and both agriculture and rural and urban handicraft industry grew and developed in response (see ch. 8, p. 129).

As far as the central shogunal government was concerned, the gradual economic growth and change which resulted from its success in keeping peace and order created disruption and friction within the ideal system it had hoped to build. Much of the growth of income was taking place outside that system, in forms of economic activity which did not fall within the accepted tax net. Attempts were made to tax merchant income through forced loans and the granting of monopolies, and long lists of regulations were issued to try to oblige farmers to concentrate on producing taxable rice rather than untaxed commercial products. When such moves failed to turn the tide, all that remained was to try to extract more from the tax-paying farmers of the Tokugawa domains, but by the early nineteenth century it was becoming clear that the economic centre of gravity had shifted and the financial base of the Shōgun's government was no longer adequate as a means to maintaining its traditional control over the country, let alone, as we shall see later, to dealing with the external pressures on Japan to modernise.

The individual *daimyō* experienced on a smaller scale the same financial problems as the Tokugawa House. The rice stipends of their samurai, who were faced with urban living costs and the temptation to try to live up to the standards of the merchant classes, continued to represent a heavy burden on their treasuries, while their ability to increase tax income along traditional lines remained limited. They therefore began to seek new ways of raising revenue and cutting expenditure. Organising farmers to work on expanding irrigation networks and increasing the cultivable (taxable) area was one recourse open, but in many areas opportunities for such projects were exhausted by the late eighteenth and early nineteenth centuries. A number of *han* governments encouraged the cultivation of commercial crops within their domains and established government monopsonies in the buying of these crops in order to maximise domain revenue from them. Some *han* imported technology from other areas and encouraged their farmers to diversify into new commercial crops with loans and tax exemptions. Others employed import-substitution policies, banning imports into their domains of products whose cultivation they wished to encourage (Hauser 1974: 44–5). *Han* governments thus became increasingly involved in the production and trading of commercial crops, in competition with the established merchant classes.

The idea of *han* government involvement in the development of industry and agriculture was therefore well established in some areas by the time that, in the 1840s and 1850s, awareness of the need to be able to produce the products of modern industry for defence purposes intensified. Despite the ban on foreign contact, the desire to acquire knowledge of the outside world, and especially of the products of its technology, had grown stronger, and a number of *han*, as well as the Tokugawa government itself, had established schools at which samurai learned foreign languages, especially Dutch, and through this gained access to literature on modern technical and scientific subjects. Thus when, as we shall see in the next section, foreign ships began to appear in Japanese waters and it became a matter of urgency to be able to produce armaments to match theirs, it was the *han* governments, rather than private commercial interests, which possessed at least the beginnings of the necessary knowledge and skills. Saga *han*, required to provide guns for the defence of the port of Nagasaki, pioneered in the 1850s the development of modern iron smelting using Japan's first reverberatory furnace, built according to methods described in a Dutch book (Smith 1955: 4–5). A number of *han* in the south-west of the country, particularly Saga, Satsuma and Mito, whose samurai were to play leading roles in the Restoration movement, were involved, alongside the Tokugawa government itself, in the construction of modern ships, and by the time of the Restoration all *han* together owned ninety four Western-style ships, while the Tokugawa owned forty four (Smith 1955: 9). Various European engineers were hired to construct shipyards and furnaces and to train samurai workmen. Some *han*, under the continued financial pressures of their military expenditures, even sought to develop modern commercial enterprises, with, for example, Satsuma *han* setting up a relatively large-scale, steam-powered spinning and weaving mill with equipment purchased from and installed by Platt Brothers of Manchester (Smith 1955: 11). Tosa *han*, which was also involved in the anti-Tokugawa movement, had a special agency (*Kaiseikan* = Industry Promotion Agency) to supervise its enterprises, with branches in Nagasaki and Osaka (Wray 1984: 22).

Thus, when the new Meiji government came to power it inherited not only a certain number of industrial facilities, some of which were to provide the basis for the subsequent development of the industries concerned, but also a corps of civil servants with experience in the establishment of new industries using imported technology. The private sector, though commercially-orientated and in many ways innovative and dynamic, for example in developing rural consumer-goods industries, had been working within the limitations imposed by the Tokugawa system, and it was only the samurai-based *han* governments, particularly those most independent of and hostile to the Tokugawa government, who felt the need and incentive to try to develop new industries and who had, to some extent, the knowledge and resources to establish such enterprises. The Meiji state was to continue to fulfil a similar role in the economy, undertaking the investments and bearing the risks of establishing a number of modern industries. Nonetheless, as Smith (1970: 197–8) points out, the subsequent responsiveness of the private sector of the economy to the opportunities opened up after 1868 is inexplicable if it is assumed that the idea of the sole responsibility of the ruling 'official' class for innovations to improve the welfare of the people was universally accepted during the Tokugawa period. There is growing evidence of a belief among sections at least of the merchant and farming classes in the value and virtue of individual efforts to improve the economic and technological workings of agriculture and industry (Najita 1987). This was a belief fundamentally subversive of the ideology of the samurai-ruled state, but one whose acceptance, out in the non-official world, meant that, once the economic and social barriers of the Tokugawa system began to break down, members of the rural and urban landowning and handicraft-industry classes were to prove by no means unenterprising in the face of new opportunities.

THE WESTERN IMPACT AND THE ADOPTION OF THE GOAL OF INDUSTRIALISATION

Throughout its early history, Japanese state and society had had contact with, and been profoundly influenced by, the civilisations of China and Korea, but it was not until the middle of the sixteenth century that travellers from outside Asia first began to reach Japanese shores. It was then that shipwrecked European sailors and, in their wake, missionaries began to arrive in Japan and they remained long enough to introduce Christianity, subsequently to be largely wiped out by persecution and isolation, and the musket, in some ways a more successful import. After the imposition of the Tokugawa seclusion policy in the 1630s, however, foreign contacts ceased, apart from the trickle of imports through Nagasaki, and it was not until the 1840s that foreign vessels again began to appear in earnest off the Japanese coast. The world out of which these vessels came was, of course, one transformed, from that of the sixteenth-century explorers and missionaries, by the Industrial Revolution and the development of the techniques of industry and warfare which had occurred during Japan's two centuries of seclusion. The first ships to appear were those of Russian expeditions exploring the Pacific coast of their country opened up by the development of Siberia. They were soon followed by American ships and by British expeditions looking for new fields to explore after the conclusion of the Opium Wars and the acquisition of Hong Kong.

Although, as Moulder (1977) points out, China represented the main focus of interest for the Western powers, both commercially and militarily, in the Far East, Japan appeared as a convenient and strategic staging post, a port of refuge and perhaps a potential market and source of raw materials for those trading along the Pacific shipping routes. The foreign powers that had rediscovered Japan thus began to dispatch demands to the Shogunal government that ports be opened to their shipping and trade initiated. The appearance of armed and steam-powered shipping around Japanese harbours served to emphasise what certain sections of the ruling elite in Edo and elsewhere must already have perceived through their study of 'Dutch learning', that is that Japan could not hope to match the technological and military strength of the Western powers. Thus the Shōgun had ultimately no alternative but to accede, in 1854, to the demands of the American naval expedition under Commodore Perry for a treaty opening up certain Japanese ports to American ships. This was to be followed by a series of treaties with the various Western powers which gave foreign traders more or less unrestricted access to the Japanese market through the designated foreign trade ports.

These treaties paralleled the so-called Unequal Treaties which had imposed the Treaty Port system on China a little earlier, and by restricting the right of the Japanese government to control imports or levy tariffs ensured that domestic industries would have to meet the full flood of competition from the industries of developed countries. Foreign buyers began to acquire supplies of Japanese-produced raw silk and cotton, pushing up prices to levels with which domestic spinners and weavers could not compete. Before long, imported textiles and other goods began to appear and the Shōgun's government was powerless to restrict the inflow.

The disruptive effects of the country's sudden initiation into foreign trade had domestic political repercussions. The protests of those adversely affected by foreign competition, combined with general anti-foreign sentiment among sections of the samurai, compounded the already difficult situation of the Shogunate, faced with *han* governments becoming increasingly independent and hostile as they sought their own means to overcome their financial problems. The government found itself nonetheless powerless to respond to increasingly vocal demands that it do something to protect the country from the incursions of foreigners. It possessed neither the overall national control nor the financial resources to be able to resist the Western powers. Thus, as the 1860s progressed, the ever more rebellious south-western *han* were drawn together in an alliance, based on longstanding hostility to the Tokugawa House but fuelled by frustration at the Shogunate's inability to provide any resistance to the foreign threat and backed up by their own growing independent military strength. In 1867, their allied army marched on Kyoto and then took Edo, defeating the forces of the Shōgun the following year at a battle known as Toba-Fushimi. The powers usurped by successive Shōguns were declared to be restored to the new young Emperor and his advisers from the victorious south-western *han*, and in 1868 the Emperor ceremonially moved from the old Imperial seat of Kyoto to the newly-named Tokyo, marking the inauguration of the government thereafter to be known by the name chosen for the new reign, Meiji.

However, the coalition of forces which had successfully brought about the Restoration was by no means clear or unified as to its future aims or the methods by which Japan's independence and dignity were to be re-established. Several leading members of the new government remained essentially conservative in their outlook, seeing the Restoration as a means of reviving the declining prestige of the samurai and freeing Japan from the corrupting influence of foreigners. Others believed that Japan could only resist the Western powers by adopting their technology and, where necessary, their institutions and other aspects of their alien way of life. The debate between the two lines was carried out through the 1860s and 1870s by political and ultimately military means, ending in the triumph of the modernisers and the defeat in 1877 of the final rebellion of traditionalist samurai. However, the decision to try to industrialise cannot be seen simply as the result of the victory of a faction of new men, a number of whom had had experience of industrial projects and had also been on the receiving end of the power of modern Western technology in their former *han*. More significantly, from the point of view of our understanding of the development process, it was equally necessitated by the economic position the government and country found themselves facing in the second half of the nineteenth century.

The inability of Japan to resist the demands of the foreign powers rested in part, of course, on military weakness, and the recognition of this fact had already led the Tokugawa and other *han* to attempt to introduce Western technology into industries such as iron-smelting and shipbuilding in order to produce the armaments needed by a modern military. However, the problem of coping with the impact of the West went beyond this. In the first place, in a situation in which it had no control over the inflow of imports, the government found itself facing, from the late 1860s onwards, intensifying balance-of-payments problems, signalled by an outflow of the country's reserves of gold and silver. In the period between the signing of the Trade Treaties and the Restoration the market for exports of Japanese raw silk and silk cocoons had been large, as a result of an epidemic of disease among European silkworms which seriously disrupted the French and Italian sericultural industries. Furthermore, imports of consumer goods into Japan remained relatively limited while Japanese consumers only gradually became accustomed to and developed tastes for foreign goods. By the end of the 1860s, though, European silk producers, who manufactured in general a higher-quality product than their Japanese counterparts, had recovered and in addition imports of consumer goods were beginning to grow fast, so that the Japanese balance of payments was in deficit by 1868 and remained so until the 1880s. With no ability to stem the tide of imports at the borders, the only solution open was to try to develop domestic industries able to compete with foreign products at home and abroad.

In addition to this immediate balance-of-payments problem, moreover, the opening of the country to foreign trade also threatened wider economic and social problems to which the development of new industries appeared the only feasible solution. The influx of imported textiles and other consumer goods threatened to deprive large numbers of farm households of the income they had come to earn from side-employment in rural industries (see ch. 8).

The farm sector provided the bulk of the government's tax revenue in the decades after the Restoration and farmers needed the cash income they derived from side-employments to buy the commercial inputs, such as fertilisers, on which they were increasingly coming to rely. A number of the industries which the government was to seek to encourage, such as silk reeling and sugar refining, potentially provided employment for members of farm households. Furthermore, these industries, as well as those of more strictly military or balance-of-payments value, opened up possibilities for the employment, as white-collar staff or skilled workers, of members of the samurai class, who also, as we shall see, faced unemployment in the years after the Restoration.

Thus, to use Smith's words, 'After the treaties of 1858 and 1866 (the 'unequal' trade treaties), the challenge of the West was not primarily military, but social and economic; and it was this challenge that industrial policy had to meet' (Smith 1955: 35). As he goes on to show from the speeches and writings of a number of the Meiji leaders, the policy of developing industry was clearly and consciously seen as a means not just of increasing Japan's military strength but also of dealing with the pressing economic and social problems the new government was experiencing. Faced with the sudden opening up of the country to developed-country competition, and denied, by the superior military capacity of the Western powers, the option of protection behind trade barriers, the establishment of new industries which could compete with imports and raise export revenue appeared the only means of trying to deal with the emerging balance-of-payments and employment problems. Thus, just as the anti-Shōgun forces had used slogans, notably 'honour the emperor, expel the barbarians', to focus their goals, so now the decision was taken to try to mobilise the nation as a whole towards a new goal, characterised by a new slogan, 'enrich the country, strengthen the army'. The first requirement of the developmental state, a clearly defined goal, was thereby met. The next section will trace the new government's first tentative steps towards the policies which might achieve it.

ECONOMIC AND INDUSTRIAL POLICY IN THE LATE NINETEENTH CENTURY

When the Meiji government came to power in 1868, it faced a precarious situation and many demands on its resources of finance and expertise. In addition to the lingering fear of foreign invasion, civil disturbances continued throughout the following decade, as those adversely affected by the economic and social changes of the period protested. There was initially no effective system of national government or of military organisation and in order to create these the structure of *han* and Shogunal government had to be abolished and new systems of taxation, bureaucratic administration and military conscription established. This entailed the appropriation by the new government of the powers of the *daimyō* in their domains, and the abolition of the system of administration by the hereditary class of nobles and samurai. Thus, the social and legal distinctions between classes were declared to be abolished; the *daimyō* received state pensions in return for surrendering their rights to tax and administer their *han*, and the rice stipends of the samurai were commuted in the form of government bonds. A new system of local and national government was set up to replace the old *han* administrations and conscription into the new national army and navy was instituted. The former samurai were freed into the world to find what employment they could. This revolutionary programme, along with the defeat, by force on occasion, of the resistance to it, tied up the bulk of the government's resources in the years immediately after the Restoration and a large part of government revenue was thus committed even before thought could be given to assistance in the modernisation of industry and agriculture. First priority lay with the establishment of the macroeconomic and institutional basis for the modernisation programme, but, as resources permitted, the initial moves in the development of specific industrial policies also began to emerge.

The macroeconomic framework

In the situation which the new government faced, the most urgent task was clearly to place its revenue sources on a sound basis. Given that 80 per cent of the population remained rural dwellers and earned at least the major part of their livelihood from agriculture, the farm sector would for the forseeable future have to provide the bulk of tax revenue, as it had been doing for the *han* governments previously. It was clearly impractical for the new national government to collect tax revenue as rice from farmers, however, and whereas previously villages had been collectively assessed for tax purposes by the *han* governments, a modern system of payment by individual households in cash was plainly preferable for the new government. This would require title to landownership, hence tax-paying responsibility, to be clearly established and the government instituted a land survey which determined the landholdings of individual households within the villages. Once private title had been established, tax was payable in cash at a predetermined rate (3 per cent later reduced to 2.5 per cent) of the assessed value of the land. The impact of what was, in effect, a land reform on farm households themselves will be considered elsewhere (ch. 8), but it is unlikely that the new government took a higher proportion of farm incomes than had the previous *han* governments, although under the old system payments were more flexible, in relation to harvest conditions, and possibly easier to evade.

From the point of view of the Meiji government, the land tax created a stable source of revenue which was to provide a large proportion of government tax income until around the turn of the century. Other sources of revenue, such as taxes on businesses and individuals, issue of government securities, and so on gradually increased in importance, and a later chapter, chapter 6, will consider the significance of the land tax as a transfer of 'agricultural surplus' for the development of the industrial sector. What should be pointed out here, though, is that, as compared with the situation in most later-developing countries, the Japanese agricultural sector was sufficiently productive during the early stages of industrialisation for it to be possible to tax 30–50 per cent of agricultural income for the government's developmental and other expenses, and the system of administration and communications was sufficiently developed to permit its assessment and collection on a consistent basis.

It is also worth pointing out at this stage that one source of revenue of which the Meiji government made only sparing use was foreign borrowing.[1] Just as direct foreign investment by overseas companies in Japan remained limited, so government borrowing never in total amounted to a very significant proportion of revenue. The government did seek to raise loans in foreign money markets for certain specific purposes, particularly for expenditures connected with the Sino–Japanese and Russo-Japanese Wars around the turn of the century, but, by comparison with many modern developing countries, the scale of foreign debt remained small. The difference between revenue and expenditure, which was considerable in the early years of the government (Smith 1955: 74–5), was made up largely through the issue of inconvertible currency and other forms of (forced or voluntary) domestic borrowing.

On the expenditure side, in the early years after the Restoration, a large part of the government's ordinary revenue, almost half in 1867–75 (Smith 1955: 71), was taken up by a number of 'one-off' payments, including pensions to samurai before their stipends were commuted, expenditures for the suppression of internal rebellions, and repayments of the debts of the former *han* and Shogunal governments. Of what remained, around a third was consistently allocated to the army and navy, but despite the other pressing demands on its resources, the state still managed to allocate substantial sums to assist the development of industry. Smith (1955: 72) shows that, up to 1881, annual sums equivalent to a third of expenditure on the military were allocated to state capital investment in industrial projects alone, and other forms of expenditure, on for example roads and general infrastructure investment, loans to businesses, and so on, must also have contributed to the industrialisation drive. Smith argues that, under the circumstances, there could have been very little scope for allocating any more to industrial projects and the fact that as much was spent as seems to have been the case indicates the high priority placed on this goal.

All this however meant that, throughout the 1870s, the government continued to live beyond its means, financing its deficit largely by printing money. By 1880, the inflationary effects of this policy had produced a financial crisis. The value of the Treasury's reserves of gold and silver had halved over the preceding three years as rising imports (including government purchases of military and industrial equipment and expertise) had been financed in specie. The gold value of paper currency fell drastically and domestic prices rose fast, with the price of rice in Tokyo doubling between 1877 and 1880 (Smith 1955: 96). Not only did domestic inflation worsen Japan's overseas trade and financial position, but it also substantially reduced the real value of the government's revenue from the fixed-money-value land tax. There was fierce debate between factions within the government over whether or not to take out a large-scale foreign loan to tide them over the crisis, but eventually this course was rejected and instead a package of measures of financial retrenchment and stabilisation was instituted and carried out by the Finance Minister, Matsukata Masayoshi, who has given his name to the deflationary period which followed.

Matsukata's package included the establishment of the Bank of Japan, which was to organise the gradual withdrawal of excess paper money and stabilise the note issue. This was followed by the setting up of other government financial institutions, including the Yokohama Specie Bank, which was to specialise in foreign exchange dealings, and local and national banks to make long-term loans to industry and agriculture. It also included measures to cut imports and promote exports and to reduce government expenditure, among which, as we shall see shortly, was the sale into private hands of a number of industrial enterprises previously set up with government funds.

The effects of the Matsukata deflation on smaller businesses and farms are generally held to have been severe, with bankruptcies arising and tenancy increasing.[2] However, as a result of Matsukata's measures, over the 1880s and 1890s financial stability was established and a much more orderly system of government budgeting set up, so that, by the time of the Sino–Japanese War in 1894–5, the government was able to meet extraordinary expenditures through an organised system of borrowing and national debt creation. The deflation might almost be seen as the forerunner of the series of short, sharp deflationary shocks which the post-World War II Japanese government was to administer with such success as a means of controlling inflationary forces in a rapidly growing economy.

Industrial policy

What, then, within this macroeconomic framework, did the Meiji government do in pursuit of the goal of industrialising Japan and catching up with the economic development of the Western nations? Its actions can be seen as operating on two levels, firstly in providing the administrative infrastructure, and, closely connected with this, the supply of educated and trained personnel through which the state could contribute to the development of industry, and, secondly, in specific acts of 'industrial policy' aimed at establishing new industries or introducing new technology.

Through several decades after 1868 the locus of political power was to remain within the group, composed mainly of former provincial samurai officials, who had led the Restoration movement. This group, which has come to be known as the Meiji oligarchy, had no clear claim to legitimacy as a ruling group, but as long as they, and one or two of their closest protégés, lived, they remained the most powerful and influential figures in the drive for modernisation. Immediately after the Restoration they formed an executive council whose members supervised the various departments of the central government they had taken over (Home Affairs, Foreign Affairs, Finance, and so on). This council was eventually reformed to constitute a European-style cabinet as a prelude to the promulgation of the new written Constitution of 1889 and the establishment of an elected parliament, the Diet, and the departments developed into ministries. Recruitment into the bureaucracy in the early stages was largely by means of patronage and personal connections, as influential officials sought to bring in those who would be loyal to the new government and to themselves, and unemployed former samurai struggled to find official posts. Thus the manipulation of personal cliques early on became a part of the administrative processes of ministries.

However, the Meiji leaders were well aware that knowledge and expertise as well as loyalty would be increasingly necessary qualifications for recruitment into a bureaucracy which aimed to modernise and industrialise the country. In the short term, there was little alternative but to import such knowledge in one form or another. Many Japanese, from the leading Meiji oligarchs themselves downwards, went abroad at government expense to study Western institutions and technology and subsequently joined other recruits, who had acquired such knowledge in other ways, as officials in the bureaucracy. A substantial number of foreigners was also hired by the government to go to Japan to teach. But in the long run the Japanese educational system itself had to be able to generate a supply of suitably trained recruits for the bureaucracy, as well as workers and managers for the private sector. Moves towards the establishment of a nation-wide system of compulsory education began in 1872; existing local schools were taken over, new ones were built and, by the mid-1880s, almost half of school-age children were attending school for at least the four-year period then laid down as compulsory. More and more middle and higher schools were set up, along with local and national colleges to provide technical training, and at the top of the educational pyramid stood Tokyo Imperial University, officially created in 1886 out of the amalgamation and reorganisation of earlier higher education establishments.

It was against this background that, during the 1880s, the practices of the bureaucracy began to be regularised. The powers and responsibilities of officials were laid down, the number of posts set out, and eventually recruitment procedures based on examinations and educational qualifications were instituted. Patronage and connections continued for some time to be important for those seeking to obtain government posts, but it was during the Meiji period that the foundations were laid for a state bureaucracy staffed by the elite of a highly competitive national educational system.

Although the Meiji leaders, when they took over the government, were for the most part clear that the introduction of modern industry was crucial to the maintenance of Japan's independence, they were by no means so clear as to how the bureaucracy they were creating was to go about achieving this. The goal of industrialisation appeared to them in concrete terms as the creation of the capacity to do and produce the things which Western economies could do and produce and it was subordinated to, or tied up with, policies to deal with more immediate problems and crises. The initial strategy of the Meiji leadership seems to have been based on the expectation that, given certain obvious institutional changes such as the abolition of the feudal class system and the introduction of the legal framework for modern institutions like the joint-stock company, existing private capitalists would supply the finance and enterprise to set up new businesses. In this the new government was to be disappointed. The largest accumulations of private capital which existed at the end of the Tokugawa period were those of the great merchant houses who had made their fortunes in trade, money-lending and other services to the feudal upper classes. There were many reasons why such merchants, rich as they might have seemed, would be unwilling and unable to risk funds in new kinds of enterprise outside their (still profitable) trading and financial activities. The scale of investment required to construct a railway or build a cotton mill was far greater than anything they had been used to. Furthermore, such investments were highly risky, involving as they did the use of imported equipment and technology with which few Japanese had any familiarity. Thus attempts to attract investors into, for example, railway companies formed and guaranteed by the government failed to raise anything like sufficient funds (Smith 1955: 36) and the government found itself, by default, providing the investment and management for the new projects it deemed essential. Given that the Meiji state had also inherited the assorted modern industrial enterprises begun by the former *han* and Tokugawa governments, including their mines, shipyards and iron-works, the bulk of early modern industry thus remained in state hands until the early 1880s.

The areas of industry in which the government was involved, and the forms that involvement took, were varied. All railway construction up till the late 1870s was financed and managed by the government, as was the substantial expansion of the telegraph system. Various government ministries established and operated plant in a number of industries, frequently importing the necessary equipment and hiring foreign instructors. Three modern silk-reeling plants were set up, including the largest and most famous at Tomioka, in the main silk-growing region of the country, built for the government by a French company under what would now be called a turn-key contract. The country's only modern cotton-spinning plant, built by the former Satsuma *han* and equipped with imported English machinery, was taken over by the Meiji government and used, like the Tomioka plant, as a model factory intended to demonstrate and provide training in modern textile technology. Import-substitution was also a motive for government investment and state-run brick, glass and cement factories were set up to reduce imports of Western-style building materials. Policies of regional development and employment creation can also be seen lying behind, for example, government involvement in brewing and sugar refining in the northern island of Hokkaidō and in cotton spinning in regions badly hit by foreign competition. The Meiji state inherited and developed the country's largest mines and the two most important shipyards. It constructed a further shipyard and expanded all three for naval purposes and as pioneering machine-building and engineering centres. In such ways, a substantial share of scarce revenue at a precarious and difficult time was allocated to expanding direct government involvement in industrial development.

As subsequent examples from the textile industries will suggest, there is evidence that the government factories were subject to poor management, confused objectives, inappropriate techniques, difficulties in recruiting and retaining workers and in dealing with foreign advisers, and many other problems familiar to those who have studied similar projects intended to act as vehicles for learning whole new technologies in present-day developing countries (see ch. 11, and see also McCallion 1989). However, it seems to have been rather more as a consequence of the heavy expenditures that they entailed that the government enterprises both contributed to the budgetary crisis which had emerged by 1880 and were required to play their part in the deflationary policies designed to remedy it. Hence, as part of these policies, the decision was taken to sell off most of the government-owned enterprises to the private sector. Various interpretations of this decision have been offered, including a gradual government conversion to the prevailing world gospel of *laisser-faire*, or a desire by members of the oligarchy to help their business friends to bargains. But it now seems generally accepted that the chief motive was to raise revenue and reduce costs. Most of the enterprises were running at a deficit and although, in a number of cases, their buyers were closely connected to members of the government and were eventually able to use the facilities they bought as the foundations of future business empires, nevertheless the low prices obtained for the plants were more probably a reflection of the difficulty experienced in finding buyers for enterprises which looked far from viable in the conditions of the time, than the result of a government/business conspiracy (Smith 1955: ch. 8).

Despite its probably short-term inspiration though, the sale of the government enterprises had important long-term consequences for the state's role in Japan's development. It meant, firstly, that the state had, in some cases, borne the risks and supplied the initial investment required to establish a number of new industries until such time as the private sector was able to operate them. The success of the government-owned Tokyo-Yokohama railway line, which generated a substantial return on the capital invested, encouraged private railway investment and, by 1890, rail mileage constructed by private joint-stock companies amounted to three times that of government-owned lines (Nakagawa 1976: 4). With time, and the expansion of domestic demand, the former government mines, cement works and shipbuilding yards began to generate profits for their new private owners, which fuelled further investment. Secondly, though, the change in policy meant that, from then on, the state could not influence the industrialisation process directly through its own enterprises but instead had to make it worthwhile for private entrepreneurs to bring about the goal of industrialisation. Tentative steps in this direction had been taken earlier, for example in the shipping industry (see pp. 47–50), but the sale of the government enterprises in the 1880s strengthened the informal links between the bureaucracy and the private entrepreneurs who were to develop major areas of industry. The creation in 1881 of the new Ministry of Agriculture and Commerce to co-ordinate state activities in the promotion of industry and agriculture provided the institutional vehicle through which these links could operate. Through this Ministry, out of which were to be born the architects of full-scale 'industrial policy', the pre-war Ministry of Commerce and Industry and the post-war Ministry of International Trade and Industry, early industrial entrepreneurs were able to obtain a range of *ad hoc* subsidies, loans, technical assistance and so on, in developing the areas of industry the state considered essential (Johnson 1982: 85–6).

Nevertheless, one should beware of overemphasising, with the benefit of hindsight, the extent to which the Meiji state led a concerted and successful industrialisation strategy. It has often been argued that, since the Tokugawa merchant class proved incapable of supplying the capital and enterprise for new industrial activities, the state, manned by samurai bureaucrats, was obliged to step in to lead the way, assisted by a limited number of well-known business leaders of similar samurai background and outlook, inspired less by the profit motive than by patriotism and the 'samurai spirit' of self-sacrifice and duty to the nation (for this argument see Hirschmeier and Yui 1975 and Morishima 1982). While this provides a convenient, 'uniquely Japanese' explanation of Japan's early success as an industrialiser, serious doubts have come to be raised as to how far it can be supported by microeconomic research results for individual industries and projects.

It is true that most bureaucrats were of samurai background, since the necessary qualifications of literacy, administrative experience and family connections were more likely to be found within the former samurai class. It is also the case that many ex-samurai invested their commutation bonds in banks and other industrial and agricultural enterprises, with varying degrees of success, although the proportion of banking capital, for example, held by former samurai was exceeded by that held by commoners in the 1880s (Yamamura 1974: 176–7). Those who succeeded in their new enterprises certainly expressed themselves in terms of patriotic duty and community responsibility, rather than the accumulation of private wealth – a phenomenon not unknown elsewhere, but consonant with Confucian traditions and a society still close to a feudal past.

However, against this, it remains the case that the growth of by far the most important of Japan's nineteenth-century industries, silk and cotton textiles, was the result of a large amount of small-scale investment, much of it coming from rural and urban trading, landowning and early industrial interests. The extent to which state policy contributed to this, and to the militarily more strategic shipping industry, will be considered in more detail in the next section. Certainly, though, many of the government factories, including, it would seem, the Tomioka silk-reeling plant, were far from being model enterprises and required considerable determination and adaptive skill on the part of those who bought them up to make them successful (Yamamura 1974). Bureaucrats made mistakes in the kinds of technology they sought to introduce (e.g. in agriculture) and in the individual businesses they chose to back. Patriotic motives on the part of the famous entrepreneurs of the Meiji period (the samurai credentials of a number of whom, incidentally, were not of very long standing since, in the fluid late Tokugawa period, it was not difficult to acquire samurai status through purchase or marriage) did not appear to conflict with the accumulation of personal wealth, and their biographies suggest that, in addition to their samurai virtues, they possessed many more mundane entrepreneurial qualities, such as determination, the ability to take risks and, not least, the skills required in a bureaucratic state to manipulate the system in the interests of their businesses.

EARLY INDUSTRIALISATION AND THE ROLE OF THE STATE: CASE STUDIES

We can now turn to examining the impact of the initial efforts of the Meiji state to promote its industrialisation goals on the growth and structure of the Japanese economy in the second half of the nineteenth century, and to consideration of two very different industries, textiles and shipping, which were central to the early development process. The relatively well-developed traditional industrial and commercial economy of the Tokugawa period, with its tiny pockets of modern industry, had suddenly been threatened, in the 1850s, by the arrival of the Western trading powers. Denied the possibility of substantial protection behind tariff barriers, Japanese industries nonetheless succeeded, in many cases, in maintaining their domestic markets and gradually expanding their activities to meet growing domestic and foreign demand through investment and the adoption of new technology. Gross National Product (GNP) was growing steadily, apart from a slight downswing around the turn of the century, at a rate of around 3.25 per cent per annum from the late 1880s through to the end of World War I and manufacturing output is estimated to have been growing at an annual average rate of 4.7 per cent over the 1874–1900 period and faster thereafter (at constant 1934–6 prices; Ohkawa and Shinohara 1979: 10, 108). Investment (gross domestic fixed capital formation) continued to account for around 13 per cent of GNP (18 per cent if military investment is included), a rate, incidentally, well below the levels achieved by many present-day developing countries, until the 1910s, and it is worth noting that the private sector was by far the largest source of this investment (78.6 per cent in 1887, 64 per cent in 1901; Ohkawa and Shinohara 1979: 19, 27). The value of exports and imports grew steadily, with exports representing 6–7 per cent of GNP in the 1880s, rising to 20 per cent by 1910 (Nakamura 1983: 35; Ohkawa and Shinohara 1979: 134–6).

As a result, although agricultural production continued to grow and agriculture and services remained the dominant areas of economic activity, the share of manufacturing output in GDP steadily rose (table 2.1). Throughout the period up to World War I, the major sources of this manufacturing growth lay in the light industrial sector and, in many cases, in industries closely connected with agriculture which made use of rurally-produced inputs of raw materials, labour and energy. The most important such industry was textile production:

textile output represented around a quarter of total manufacturing output in the late 1870s and early 1880s, rising to 40 per cent by the turn of the century (at current prices; Ohkawa and Shinohara 1979: 105) and table 2.2 illustrates the importance of textiles in the shifting structure of Japan's trading relations. While in the 1870s Japan was still an importer of manufactured goods, half of which were textiles, and an exporter of primary products, including raw silk, by the time of World War I she had become an importer of primary produce and non-textile manufactured goods and an exporter of manufactured goods of which a large proportion were textiles in the form of factory-produced cotton thread and cloth.

Against this background, then, we can look at the impact of the state strategies described above on, on the one hand, the textile industries, the prime movers in the early industrialisation process, and, on the

Table 2.1 Growth and structural change 1885–1920

	GDP total (million yen)*	Proportion (%) produced in: Agriculture	Manufacturing
1885	3774	42.1	7.0
1890	4639	39.8	7.9
1895	5375	37.0	8.9
1900	5966	34.7	11.2
1905	6214	31.6	12.6
1910	7424	30.9	15.6
1915	8753	30.7	19.4
1920	10937	27.3	18.6

* Measured at constant 1934–6 prices
Source: Ohkawa and Shinohara (1979): table A.12: 278–9

Table 2.2 The structure of Japanese trade 1874–1921: percentage shares of total imports and exports*

	Imports			Exports		
	Primary products	Manufactured goods	of which textiles	Primary products	Manufactured goods	of which textiles
1874–83	8.8	91.2	54.0	42.5	57.5	42.4
1892–1901	36.4	63.6	16.8	21.0	79.0	52.6
1912–21	52.6	47.4	3.3	9.0	91.0	56.4

* Derived from ten-year moving averages of values calculated in current prices.
Source: Ohkawa and Shinohara (1979): table 7.1: 135

other, the shipping industry, whose development facilitated and was in many ways intertwined with that of textiles, but which the hand of the state, or perhaps one should say the hands of bureaucrats, touched more deeply and directly.

Textiles

The spinning and weaving of silk and cotton, the materials for most traditional Japanese clothing and household textiles, were of course well established industries in the Tokugawa economy. Both depended on the production of the necessary raw materials by farm households: in the case of silk, cocoons spun by silkworms which had been fed on leaves collected from mulberry orchards; in the case of cotton, plants grown by increasingly specialised farm producers in areas such as the Kinai around Osaka. In both cases, the next stage of production (the reeling of silk thread from the cocoons to produce raw silk and the spinning of cotton into yarn) was generally undertaken by the women of farm households, either at home or in small local workshops, and the final weaving stage was also frequently performed on handlooms in rural homes, although specialist urban weavers also produced the higher-quality ranges of fabric.

The arrival of Western traders had contrasting effects on the two branches of the industry. For silk producers, the opening up of the country meant a sudden large increase in the demand for both silk-worm eggs and raw silk for export, coinciding as it did with an outbreak of disease which severely curtailed production in the European industry. Cotton producers, on the other hand, faced severe competition from imports of cheaper and higher-quality yarn and cloth from Britain and India. The story of the responses made to these differing market conditions is summarised in table 2.3 and can be briefly set out before we go on to consider the part played by the state in the development of the industry.

In silk production, the expansion of the export market encouraged rapidly increasing numbers of farm households to take up sericulture, aided by the development of new silkworm varieties capable of producing cocoon crops over the summer/autumn period, when farmers had more labour time to spare than in the spring when traditional varieties spun their cocoons. The expansion of cocoon output put pressure on the reeling stage of production, which came increasingly to be carried out by specialist workers but still for the most part in small-scale silk-reeling establishments (filatures) in rural areas. However, the application of water, and later steam,

Table 2.3 Silk and cotton

(a) Value of output (million yen)

	Raw silk	Cotton yarn	Finished fabrics
1874	6	1	18
1880	20	1	40
1890	34	23	57
1900	90	70	178
1910	164	145	286
1920	570	706	1440

(b) Value of exports (million yen)

	Raw silk	Cotton yarn	Finished fabrics
1880	9	0	0
1890	14	0	1
1900	45	21	25
1910	130	45	54
1920	382	152	501

(c) Scale of factories: textile industries, 1919

	Percentage of factories	Percentage of employees
5– 9 workers	38.2	47.4
10– 99 workers	54.4	45.8
100–499 workers	6.0	5.4
500 or more workers	1.4	1.4

Sources: (a) and (b) Minami (1987): table 8.1: 174; (c) Lockwood (1968): table
15: 202

power to the reeling process was, from a technical point of view,
a relatively simple matter, resulting in the speeding up of work and
the production of a better-quality thread, while continuing to employ
traditional skills and working methods (see Minami 1987: ch. 8). Once
the European silkworm disease had been checked after 1869 and
Japanese producers found themselves facing increased competition
in their export markets, mechanised silk reeling spread rapidly in the
effort to maintain the quality and competitive position of Japanese
silk. Although towards the end of the century some concentration into
larger-scale filatures did take place and companies owning a number
of separate facilities began to emerge, it was nevertheless small-scale
mechanised filatures, located in rural areas in order to make use of

local sources of labour and power, that continued to provide the bulk of raw silk output for export and home demand. Japanese silk producers remained unable to compete in quality terms with their French and Italian competitors but they adapted their product to meet the needs of American silk manufacturers for large quantities of standardised silk and thus maintained and expanded their export sales as market conditions changed (Sugiyama 1988: 216–9).

By contrast, in the cotton industry, coping with the opening-up to trade was much harder. Raw cotton grown in Japan was of poor quality, unlike Japanese silk, but even making use of better-quality raw material imported from India and China, Japanese cotton spinners using traditional technology were unable to compete in price or quality with imported yarn. Imports of cotton yarn and cotton fabric came to represent an increasingly large item on the deficit side of the balance of payments in the years following the opening of the economy. Mechanisation of the spinning process was the key to the achievement of competitive levels of costs and quality but, given the technological constraints involved (see ch. 11), this could only be carried out through investment in relatively large-scale mills employing imported factory technology. It was not until the 1880s that the problems of technological transfer and adaptation had been sufficiently overcome and market conditions were sufficiently favourable for such investments to begin to be made. From the late 1880s onwards, however, the capacity of Japan's mechanised cotton mills began to grow rapidly. Home-produced yarn began to replace imports, and exports to China and other parts of Asia began to grow, so that, by 1897, the value of cotton yarn exports exceeded that of imports (Takamura 1982: 277). From around the turn of the century, the major cotton-spinning firms also began to develop their weaving operations as an outlet for their yarn production, and the cotton-textile industry continued to dominate the factory sector of Japanese industry, as manufacturer and employer, well into the inter-war period.

By 1900, therefore, one branch of the textile industry, raw silk, had played a major role as an export-earner, expanding its output significantly and maintaining its competitive trading position through the widespread introduction of mechanised technology. Another, cotton spinning, having initially suffered severe competition from imports, had succeeded in passing through an import-substitution phase and had reached the point at which it was able to export on a considerable scale. The textile industry as a whole represented the single largest element in the manufacturing sector, from the point of view of output, exports, employment of factory workers, and spread of mechanised technology. Nonetheless, most enterprises in the industry were relatively small-scale operations (see table 2.3 (c)), relying on local private-sector entrepreneurship and capital. Most silk filatures remained small-scale rural businesses, maintaining close economic links with the surrounding farm population. Although larger-scale factories and companies began to emerge in the cotton industry, the bulk of cotton yarn output continued to come from relatively small mills set up by traders, wholesalers and local entrepreneur businessmen. This being so, what role might the state be said to have played in the development of this key early industry?

There is no doubt that the Meiji government was concerned to protect and develop Japan's textile industries for a number of reasons. As already suggested, cotton yarn and cloth imports represented a significant drain of foreign exchange resources and silk was far and away the most important source of export income; textile-related work, either in the production of raw materials or in home- or local-based spinning and weaving, provided an important source of employment and income for farm families in many areas and, more widely, textiles represented a vital area of industrial activity and technological development in both the developed countries of the time and their colonies. Although efforts were made to protect domestic cotton growers through import duties, until these were eventually abandoned in 1896 in the interests of, and under pressure from, the cotton spinners (Ranis and Saxonhouse 1985: 147), protection by means of tariffs was otherwise ruled out, before the achievement of tariff autonomy in 1899, by the trade treaties made with the Western powers. The pursuit of the state's goals in this area would therefore have to take different and more specifically targeted forms.

The major role usually attributed to the state in the development of Japan's textile industries involves the easing of the problems of technology transfer and adaptation. Most of the first modern silk-reeling and cotton-spinning projects were government enterprises, intended to be used as a means of introducing and demonstrating imported equipment. In silk, the most famous of these was the Tomioka silk-reeling mill, completed in June 1872 by a French company and embodying the most up-to-date technology, in which over 400 female silk reelers, many of them from samurai families, were trained by European technicians with the intention of creating a nucleus of workers for subsequent privately-owned mills. Two other silk-reeling mills, one using state-of-the-art Swiss equipment for reeling waste silk, were also set up by the government during the 1870s. In cotton spinning, one of the three modern mills in existence in 1880 belonged to the state, having been confiscated from the Satsuma *han* shortly after the Restoration and thereafter run as a model mill. However, this, like the two other, privately-owned, modern mills does not seem to have been regarded as a successful venture and was sold off in 1878 when it was clear that technical difficulties and small scale were preventing the modern mills from making any impact on the foreign competition (Smith 1955: 61–2). Thereafter, the government began a programme of purchasing British-made spinning machinery, some of which was installed in two new government-owned mills and some of which was sold on easy terms to newly-established private mills. At this stage (the mid-1880s), though, 90 per cent of the cotton yarn used in Japan was still imported (Smith 1955: 63) and modern mills represented only a tiny proportion of total domestic production capacity. From then on, however, through the 1880s and 1890s, the number and scale of mills equipped with modern machinery began to grow rapidly.

It is clearly tempting to argue from this that state activity in textiles played the role of demonstrating modern technology and overcoming its teething problems under Japanese conditions. However, this has yet to be fully demonstrated in detailed studies. Both Yamamura (1974: 178–83) and more recently McCallion (1989) produce evidence to suggest that the Tomioka plant was far from being a model enterprise. Visitors were generally discouraged from viewing it and the best way to get in to see the plant was apparently to contact the cook (Yamamura 1974: 178). The workers trained there either did not stay long enough to learn anything useful or stayed so long that, although they learnt to operate the technology to a high standard and even enabled the plant to make a profit, they contributed little to the rest of the industry. As McCallion points out, the goals of the project were never made clear and the government seemed unprepared to allow the mill to run at a loss in order to fulfil its educational objectives.

The cotton-spinning mills set up in the early 1880s either directly by the state or with government subsidy also failed to act as technological models as a result of similar lack of clarity about, and conflict between, the objectives set by the government. They were required to use water power to economise on scarce and costly coal, and to work with domestically-grown cotton, the producers of which the state wished to protect. The mills were thus too small and produced too poor a product to be able to compete with imports and it was the much larger-scale, private-sector Osaka Spinning Mill which was to serve as the technological model to the industry (Minami 1987: ch. 9). In both silk and cotton, it was private-sector inventors and entrepreneurs who put in the hard work of adapting imported silk and cotton spining technology to Japanese conditions and it can be argued that the most important role in disseminating new cotton-spinning technology was played by the producers' own industrial association, and through this by Platt Brothers, the dominant supplier of equipment (see ch. 11 and Saxonhouse 1976: 115ff). Furthermore, a number of other factors can be adduced to explain the growth of the mechanised cotton-spinning industry from the late 1880s. These include generally rising prices stimulating private investment; the impact of the Sino-Japanese War, which opened up the Korean market to Japanese firms, and of an epidemic in Bombay in 1896 which cut off Indian exports to China; the inauguration in 1893 of the first Japanese shipping line to Bombay, which provided supplies of high-quality raw cotton to Japanese spinners at discount freight rates (see pp. 50–1 and Wray 1984: 295–6), and so on. Hence the case for a major state role in the introduction of imported technology is at best not proven.

It is also difficult to argue for any significant role for the state as a provider of capital for textile-industry expansion. Silk filatures were for the most part small-scale ventures making use of local sources of capital. Modern cotton-spinning firms were generally organised as joint-stock enterprises, raising share capital from private sources. In many cases, traders and wholesalers in the textile business raised the funds to establish silk filatures and, later, cotton mills, using loans from local private commercial banks. Behind this, it could be argued, lay the relatively sound financial system centring on specialised governmental financial institutions such as the Bank of Japan and the Yokohama Specie Bank, and the Bank of Japan did indeed give positive support to the provision of working capital to cotton-textile firms.[3] Nonetheless, the initiative in the raising of capital and the establishment of enterprises clearly lay in sections of the private sector which had little directly to do with the state bureaucracy.

In other less obvious or spectacular ways, though, it is possible to see, even in the early textile industry, the bureaucracy, in conjunction with associations of private businessmen, edging towards the kind of regulatory bureaucratic role through which the developmental state seeks to protect and promote national industry. For example, prefectural governments established systems for licensing silkworm egg producers and inspecting their products in an effort to maintain quality as output rose (Smethurst 1986: 204–5); the Japanese Consul in Shanghai sent back to Japan any interesting new silkworm varieties that he spotted (Smethurst 1986: 203), and numerous rules and regulations were issued throughout the 1870s in a not very successful effort to control and maintain the quality of silk exports (Sugiyama 1988: 113–4). In small-scale regulatory ways such as these, or in broader indirect ways ranging through to the provision of education for engineering and managerial personnel and the diplomatic and military support for the interests of Japanese overseas traders, for whom textiles represented the most important products, the government put into practice its commitment to industrialisation goals, but detailed assessments of the impact of these activities on the decisions and successes of textile-industry firms are largely still to be carried out.

Shipping

Transport and communications are areas of activity which all governments tend to regard as being of great economic and strategic importance. State involvement in the development of railways, roads, postal services, telecommunications, and shipping is commonly observed throughout the developed and developing worlds and Japan's case proves to be no exception. It was the government which carried out most of Japan's early railway investment and set up the postal and telegraph system, and similarly government agencies were indeed heavily involved in efforts to establish domestic and overseas shipping services. The particular significance of shipping to the state stems also, however, from its interconnections with other areas of national policy. The importance of the merchant marine in times of military activity proved to be a crucial factor in promoting state aid to Japanese shipping. The supply and price of the carriage of freight influences the development of trade and the balance of payments. Demand for shipping services can work back as a stimulant to the ship-building industry, which is again of strategic military importance. Ships carry mail, facilitate the movement of people and goods (especially in an island nation such as Japan), and generally promote national integration. Members of the Meiji elite were well aware of these linkages[4] and the history of shipping policy during the second half of the nineteenth century can be seen as tracing their efforts to find the right institutional framework within which to protect and promote the industry. On the other hand, though, shipping industry history also tells a story of entrepreneurship, managerial development, risk-taking, conflict, and political manipulation on the side of the businessmen, great and small, who profited (for the most part) from the transformation of a situation, at the time of the Restoration, in which all Japan's foreign trade and a growing proportion of coastal traffic were in foreign hands, into one in which, by the end of the century, Japanese shippers were able to hold their own, not only in Japanese waters, but also increasingly on the great international shipping routes.

As is well known, the Tokugawa government prohibited Japanese citizens from travelling abroad and forebade the construction of ships large enough to leave coastal waters. Ships exceeding these limits were certainly built, however, and coastal shipping routes were well established by the eighteenth century. Freight was transported either through the shipping organisations established by two quite large-scale unions of trade and industrial associations, or by smaller-scale independent shipowners who bought cargoes to sell at a profit at their destinations. All the vessels involved were Japanese-style wooden sailing ships, tiny by comparison with the Western steamships which began to appear off the Japanese coast in the nineteenth century, but in some respects well suited to the freight they carried and the waters they sailed.[5]

With the opening up of the country and the rescinding of the Tokugawa shipping restrictions in the 1850s, some domains and the Shogunal government itself began to purchase Western ships. However, these were no match for the foreign steamships now free to enter Japanese waters: not only did foreign shipping companies take control of all of Japan's growing overseas trade, but Western steamship operators also began to compete with Japanese shipping on major coastal routes. Even as late as the 1890s no more than around 10 per cent of Japan's overseas trade was carried in Japanese vessels[6] and import-substitution in overseas shipping was out of the question for the time being. Hence the most pressing threats were seen to be those to coastal shipping (for an example see Wray 1986: 258), the balance of payments and Japanese naval potential, and what brought the problem to a head was the military dimension. In 1874 a decision was taken to launch a naval expedition to try to strengthen Japan's claims to sovereignty over Taiwan. Although the navy had 3,700 men at its disposal, no transport facilities existed in Japan for moving them overseas. Furthermore, of the seventy four licensed mariners then operating in Japan, only four were Japanese (Wray 1984: 43). This revelation of the weakness of the merchant marine was to prove the turning-point in government policy towards shipping and in the fortunes of the company which was to dominate the nineteenth-century development of the industry.

In the years immediately following the Restoration, attempts had been made by the new government to set up an institutional framework within which to organise the shipping services which the nation and the state required, in particular the transportation of mail and of the tax-rice still being paid. This took the form of various versions of a joint government/private sector agency managed by officials from the relevant government bureaux and representatives of the traditional transport and shipping organisations. The first version of this agency operated with thirteen ships chartered from the government and the domains, but its management lacked appropriate experience and proved cumbersome and inefficient (Wray 1984: 31). Hence, when the government officially acquired the ships of the former *han*, on the abolition of the domains in 1871, and established a new Department of Ships within the Bureau of Posts and Communications, the opportunity was taken to create a new, larger-scale version of the agency. This new agency was heavily dominated by representatives of the Mitsui Company, the most important and successful of the surviving Tokugawa-period merchant houses, which had considerable influence in the government at the time. Officials from other transport organisations and relevant sections of the bureaucracy were also involved in the agency's management, however, and although it received subsidies to help develop its services, it again proved an unwieldy and largely ineffectual means of modernising the industry.

Meanwhile, on the one hand, foreign shipping companies, such as the American Pacific Mail Company and the British Peninsular and Oriental (P & O), were beginning to compete with Japanese shipping in coastal waters and, on the other hand, a private-sector rival to the government-sponsored agency was beginning to emerge in the form of the Mitsubishi Company, led by one of late nineteenth-century Japan's most formidable entrepreneurial figures, Iwasaki Yatarō.[7] Iwasaki, who came from a rural, ex-samurai family (he later bought back his samurai status), carved out a niche for himself in the administration of his domain, Tosa, as manager of the organisation it had set up to run its various industrial and trading interests, including its ships. When the Tosa domain was abolished in 1871, the agency's various assets ended up in Iwasaki's hands and he continued to manage them, no longer as a domain official but now as a private businessman, embodying in himself, as it were, the continuity between the activities of the more enterprising and radical domain governments, of which Tosa's had been one, and the post-Restoration development of new forms of industry and commerce. He set about developing his new business, renamed Mitsubishi, and bringing together a new management team with a more modern educational background (including, for example, his brother, who had been studying in the United States). Shipping proved to be the most profitable line of activity and although Iwasaki's ships were smaller and older than those of the rival government-sponsored company, Mitsubishi's management was much tighter and more effective. The company was regarded as promising enough for Iwasaki to be able to raise from foreign sources the credit he needed to buy new steam-powered vessels. Alongside these moves towards a more modern business and management structure, though, he was also pursuing another line of activity crucial to success in a developmental state and on the basis of his ties with Tosa, a domain which had taken an active part in the establishment of the Meiji government, continued to build up his connections within the bureaucratic and political worlds.

Meanwhile, the government-sponsored company, having enjoyed the benefits of its reliance on state patronage and subsidy, eventually suffered the costs when its leading supporters resigned from the government in 1873 and its financial position became increasingly shaky. Hence, when asked to assist in the provision of transport for the military expedition to Taiwan, it refused, basically, Wray argues (1984), out of fear of losing its home market position to Mitsubishi, thus demonstrating some distinctly unpatriotic entrepreneurial motives. With Mitsubishi supporters now occupying important posts in the government, the solution to the troop transport problem was eventually found in the expedient of contracting Mitsubishi to operate ships which the government would hastily buy abroad for the purpose. As a result of Mitsubishi's effective management of the transport ships during the military expedition, and Iwasaki's important political contacts, a gradual shift in the government's position took place over the course of 1873 and 1874, towards acceptance of a private company (Mitsubishi) as the best vehicle for promoting national interests in shipping. Consequently, in 1875, on the conclusion of the Taiwan expedition, the decision was taken to transfer ownership of the thirteen new ships which had been purchased (not all of which in fact arrived in time to take part in the expedition) to Mitsubishi, along with a substantial annual subsidy, in return for commitments on the part of the company to develop new lines, including its first overseas venture, the Yokohama/Shanghai line.

This decision marked a turning-point, both in the fortunes of Mitsubishi as a major shipping company and in the development of state support for the industry, which thereafter continued to follow the pattern of providing subsidies in return for the opening of new overseas lines and for co-operation in the pursuit of national objectives, for example in wartime. On the basis of its newly-acquired ships, Mitsubishi was able to absorb the by now more-or-less defunct government-sponsored company and to fight and win battles with first Pacific Mail and then P & O on the Yokohama/Shanghai line. It came to dominate coastal shipping in the 1880s and to start to expand its activities further afield, and it used the profits so generated to begin to diversify its industrial interests. But the need to retain political support remained and the company's vulnerability was demonstrated when the anti-Mitsubishi group within the government, supported by the company's great economic rival, Mitsui, set up a new government-sponsored company to challenge Mitsubishi's monopoly and Iwasaki's 'arrogance'. There ensued a ferocious price- and quality-cutting battle, which resulted in an increasing number of accidents and threatened bankruptcy to both companies. It ended, in 1885, with the merger (generally judged a Mitsubishi victory) of the two sides' shipping interests to form the Nippon Yūsen Kaisha (NYK), Japan's major shipping company ever since. The episode demonstrates the extent to which the Meiji state was not a monolithic organisation devoted to straightforwardly accepted national goals, but rather one within which internecine conflict could lead to fierce, and possibly 'wasteful', battles detracting from the pursuit of those goals.[8]

After the formation of NYK, the new company resumed the path of development towards becoming a major international shipping organisation, continuing to receive government subsidies for the opening of new transoceanic routes which were probably higher than those paid to the shipping lines of rival nations (Yui and Nakagawa 1985: 314), particularly after the passage of legislation, during the 1890s, expanding the scope for state aid to shipping services. Nevertheless, in order to establish long-distance international lines, NYK had to break into the system of shipping conferences, the cartel arrangements among European shipping companies which maintained freight rates and limited entry on major routes. NYK's first success in this, following a battle with a P & O-dominated shipping conference, resulted in the establishment of its first transoceanic line, between Bombay and Kōbe, in 1893, and reflected the emerging alliance of interests between Japanese shipping and Japanese manufacturing industry. NYK saw the battle through on the basis of an agreement with the Cotton Spinners' Association, under which the Association's members guaranteed NYK specific volumes of raw cotton shipments in return for rebates on freight rates. This cut the cost of imported Indian cotton (also newly freed from import duties into Japan) to Japanese spinning companies and enabled NYK eventually to force P & O to come to a deal recognising the NYK line. This was followed, with the assistance of substantially increased subsidies and profits resulting from merchant marine activity during the Sino-Japanese War, by the inauguration of the company's European line in 1896. Furthermore, as NYK continued to extend its subsidised routes throughout the world, it began to buy an increasing number of its ocean-going ships from its progentitor, the now land-based Mitsubishi Company, under legislation which also provided subsidies for the purchase of domestically-produced ships. Thus shipping and shipbuilding together were receiving around 75 per cent of all government subsidy payments in the 1897–1913 period (Wray 1984: 291, Blumenthal 1976: 36).

Clearly, then, state support, in the form of subsidies and other kinds of assistance in kind, played an important part in establishing NYK as a major international shipping line and, through its linkages with other industries and with naval activity, in the achievement of other economic and military goals. Nevertheless, two provisos need to be added. Firstly, the story of the development of Japanese shipping in the nineteenth century is not one of the pursuit of a clear and predetermined state policy or of the dominant role of state leadership. It is rather one of a series of *ad hoc* steps through which the state and private business accommodated to one another in the pursuit of what were seen as national ends, but not without considerable conflict and vicissitude. The skills of political manipulation, which enabled national goals and private profit-seeking to be pursued in conformity with one another, were vital weapons in the armoury of the Meiji entrepreneur, alongside the ability to take successful risks, lead and manage effectively, judge the market and the competition, and, perhaps, utilise some of the 'samurai' virtues of hard work, diligence and loyalty.

The second proviso is one against ignoring the continued growth, alongside the emergence of NYK, of other successful companies, larger and smaller, which operated without state assistance to anything like the same extent. The Osaka Shōsen Kaisha (OSK), established in 1884 through the amalgamation of a large number of Osaka shipowners, became Japan's second major shipping company, specialising in coastal and shorter-range Asian lines, and did receive subsidies for some of its routes, but not on the scale of those received by NYK. Equally, though, many much smaller shipping companies survived and prospered without subsidy in coastal and short-haul Asian traffic and for them the role of the general trading companies (see ch. 13) in chartering ships from smaller companies and organising their movements as freight carriers, is argued to have been particularly important. Towards the end of the century, smaller companies, many dating back to the independent Tokugawa shipowners, switched to steamships (sometimes bought second-hand from bigger companies) and continued to provide strong competition both to the government-aided Japanese companies and foreign shipping lines (Wray 1986: 270). Thus, although state support and subsidy were important in enabling NYK to pass through its import-substitution phase and become an international company, at a lower level it was possible to challenge foreign competition without government aid, though increasingly within the structure of symbiotic relationships between larger and smaller companies which later chapters will analyse.

3 The state and the growth of the modern industrial sector

The period of World War I and its immediate aftermath (1914–20) saw something of a transformation in the Japanese economy and its relations with the world economy. The growth in industrial output and employment which the wartime boom brought about signalled Japan's transition from a predominantly agricultural/light industrial economy to one in which urban factory industry represented the most significant form of economic activity, and the statistical outlines of this process are summarised in table 3.1. The growth in trade which constituted a necessary part of this transformation resulted in a new and much higher degree of involvement in and dependence on the world economy. The impact of this first made itself felt in the post-war collapse, which heralded a decade of depressed conditions culminating in the World Depression of 1929–31. Furthermore, the glimpse of total warfare which the conflict gave combined with the evidence of Japan's growing dependence on external economic forces to emphasise the nation's vulnerability to influences outside its political and military control. The demands of economic security, in the form of markets and raw material supplies within Japanese jurisdiction, in some ways came to conflict with the trading needs of the industrialised economy Japan was becoming, and this conflict, which, it might be argued, continues to bedevil Japanese economic policy and diplomacy, underlay the disaster which brought to an end the inter-war phase of state involvement in the development of the economy. Nevertheless, the pressure to develop the strategic heavy industries made essential by the demands of military security also helped to mould the forms of state involvement in ways which were to influence its future course to a high degree.

Table 3.1 Growth and structural change 1900–38

(a) Growth rates (% per annum) (A)

	GDP	Agricultural production	Manufacturing production	Exports	Imports	Investment
1904–19	3.74	1.81	6.80	7.42	5.23	7.03
1919–30	2.43	0.56	4.58	4.97	5.64	1.23
1930–38	4.86	1.30	8.88	8.05	5.34	10.95

(b) Structure of production (%)

	Manufacturing (B)	Agriculture (B)		Factory (C) production as proportion of manufacturing output
1904	17.4	37.8	1909	46.2
1911	20.3	35.5	1914	52.6
1919	26.2	29.9	1925	65.2
1930	25.8	20.0	1937	74.2
1938	35.3	18.5		

(A) Based on seven-year moving averages
(B) Proportion of Net Domestic Product, current prices
(C) Factory = establishment with more than five workers

Sources: (a) Ohkawa and Shinohara (1979): tables 2.6, 1.6: 38, 20
(b) Ohkawa and Shinohara (1979): tables 2.1, 2.4: 35, 37

WORLD WAR I AND THE DRIVE FOR INDUSTRIALISATION AND SECURITY

The involvement of the major industrial powers in World War I created a vacuum in the world economy which Japanese industry found itself well placed to fill. The textile industries, on which the earlier stages of Japanese industrialisation had been based, found British competition in the export markets of India and China suddenly removed and were able to step up their production to meet the consequent expansion in demand for their products. With the mercantile marines of the beligerent powers out of action, demand for Japanese shipping services also rose markedly and shipbuilding output grew in response. With imports from developed countries cut off, backward linkages into the fledgling domestic heavy industries were also strongly felt, and although their output remained still a relatively small proportion of total industrial production, substantial growth took place in such industries as iron and steel, chemicals, and machinery (see table 3.2). The period also saw rapid growth in domestic electricity generating capacity and the spread of electrification to many sectors of industry, large and small. Thus the war in effect created the conditions for import-substituting industrialisation which it had previously been impossible to establish.

The effects of this industrial growth were quite dramatic. Although agricultural output grew at record rates, it could not match the rate of growth of industrial output, and by 1920 industry's share of GDP had overtaken agriculture's.[1] This entailed a rapid expansion in the industrial labour force: while employment in primary industry gradually declined from 16.4 m in 1910 to 14.3 m in 1920, secondary-industry employment rose over the same period from 4.1 m to 6.3 m, with employment in the metals, machinery and chemical industries doubling (Nakamura 1983: 148). Around 50 per cent of the workforce still earned the major part of its living from agricultural or other primary-sector work, but nonetheless a marked shift had occurred in the structure of industry and employment. Internationally, the rapid growth in exports, unmatched by a corresponding flow of imports,

Table 3.2 Growth and structure of the manufacturing sector during industrialisation

(a) Growth rates of real manufacturing output (A)

	1878–1900	*1901–20*	*1921–38*
Textiles	6.93	5.88	5.59
Metals	3.98	14.82	10.23
Machinery	11.36	14.01	9.40
Chemicals	3.98	5.39	10.31

(b) Percentage shares of real manufacturing output

	1877	*1900*	*1920*	*1938*
Textiles	10.1	25.5	27.8	23.6
Metals	1.4	1.4	7.8	14.4
Machinery	1.1	2.9	13.7	20.4
Chemicals	11.1	9.0	8.9	16.6
Light industries (B)	68.6	72.7	58.4	38.1
Heavy industries (C)	13.6	13.3	30.4	51.4

(A) Percentage per annum based on seven-year moving averages, 1934–6 prices
(B) Textiles and food products
(C) Metals, machinery and chemicals
Source: Minami (1986): tables 5.13, 5.15: 131, 133

resulted in substantial balance of payments surpluses over the course of the war years, which were largely held in the form of gold reserves overseas. Rising demand, fuelled by expansion in the supply of money issued by the Bank of Japan, generated rising prices and increasing pressure on real wages.

The impact of rising prices on the ever more urbanised labour force gave rise to the first indication of the major changes the wartime boom had created in the Japanese economy. This took the form of rioting among urban workers and housewives protesting against the high prices of rice and other consumer goods, which spread widely through major urban centres in the summer of 1918. Although high food prices benefited farmers, they harmed the growing and increasingly important urban industrial workforce and brought into focus the familiar conflict of interest between agricultural producers and the rising industrial and business classes.

Not long after the riots had been brought under control, however, came the end of World War I, and as the developed countries sought to resume their economic and trading activity in Asia, the boom period for Japanese industry came to an end. Prices, particularly for major exports like silk, collapsed and import competition resumed. Nevertheless, although bankruptcies, lay-offs and the closing of excess capacity were widespread in the immediate post-war slump, and the problems facing the economy were intensified by the effects of the Great Tokyo Earthquake of 1923, the foundations of new industrial capacity had been laid, and in many cases new businesses succeeded in consolidating and weathering the crisis. The foothold which Japanese firms had gained in world markets was not lost and the resulting much greater involvement in the international economy meant that the World Depression, triggered by the Wall Street Crash of 1929, severely affected the demand and price conditions faced by Japanese exporters. However, by this stage the commanding heights of the economy were sufficiently strong once again to weather the storm, and it was small-scale producers, notably farmers in silk-producing areas and in more backward and less diversified parts of the country, who took the brunt of it. Recovery was relatively swift, though, as the 1930s progressed and industry and agriculture sought to meet the growing demands of military and territorial expansion.

From the point of view of the role of the state, the developments of the World War I and inter-war periods, generally regarded as transitional, fluctuating and confusing by economic and political historians, can be seen as profoundly influencing both the constraints operating on, and the goals of, economic policy-makers. As Japan became an industrial economy, the limitations of her raw-materials base became ever more significant and her reliance on international trade, both for the resources industry increasingly consumed and for the foreign exchange to pay for them, ever more crucial. Supplies of resources, most notably of oil, depended on trade relations with developed countries and on access to markets which they dominated. On the other hand, World War I had made clear that military success in the world of the Great Powers no longer depended solely on the ability to mount an efficient campaign in the field; it also demanded the capacity to mobilise the entire economy and nation over a protracted period. This lesson was not lost on certain sections of the military establishment, who came to believe that 'future wars would be fought not only with guns but with the entire resources of nations, from engineers to doctors, from cotton to iron ore' (Barnhart 1987: 18).

The search for economic security involved, on the one hand, control over the overseas territory which could supply Japan's needs for resources and markets, and, on the other, the techniques of bureaucratic management whereby domestic industry could be moulded into the forms required to sustain the military capacity upon which the acquisition and protection of that territory depended. However, given the economic and political positions of the Great Powers in Asia and the Pacific at the time, and perhaps, it has been argued, their failure to appreciate Japan's interests and security needs in the area (see Crowley 1970), pursuit of the goal of economic security would bring Japan into conflict with those very nations whose co-operation was essential to her overall trading needs. The tragic results of this conflict do not need repeating, but examination of the operation of state economic institutions in this period is important, not only in order to assess its immediate impact on the growth and development of Japanese industry and the emerging international economic and military conflict, but also for the experience it provided for those who would go on to administer the state's economic and industrial policies in the post-war period.

THE AIMS AND INSTITUTIONS OF ECONOMIC POLICY IN THE INTER-WAR PERIOD

In the period between World War I and Pearl Harbour, the Japanese economy faced a series of crises, largely the result of events beyond the control of economic policy-makers. The immediate aim of many of the policy measures taken in the economic field was therefore to mitigate and control the effects of these events. Hence, mention must be made of the macroeconomic steps taken to try to combat the depressions and balance of payments problems resulting from fluctuations in the world economy and to secure the level of government expenditure which military needs required. These involved initial acceptance and then abandonment of an industrialisation strategy working within the prevailing structure of international trade. While institutions such as the Ministry of Finance and the Bank of Japan were occupied with the relevant macroeconomic mechanisms, other arms of the state increasingly came to pursue the aim of establishing for Japan economic and military security based on independence from the international economic and political system. In the course of this, bureaucrats began to play a more active role in trying to develop efficient modern industries which could serve the overall needs of the state, building on the experience accrued in the effort to establish industry since 1868, but experimenting with new forms of institutional relationship between private industry and the representatives of the government. Meanwhile, the military arm of the state pursued the goal of economic security through expansion overseas, widening the economic net within which officials, civilian and military, had to operate, and creating ever greater demands on the capacities of the empire's industry and agriculture.

Macroeconomic policy

The World War I boom period came to a dramatic end with the financial panic of 1920. Wholesale prices fell by 40 per cent over the year of the panic, as they did in other industrial countries, but prices for silk and cotton fell even more sharply (Nakamura 1983: 153). Moreover, in Japan, this was followed by a series of financial crises and recessions, brought on by bank collapses, the results of the Great Earthquake, and the government's efforts to return Japan to the Gold Standard at the pre-war rate of exchange. On top of this there came the World Depression of 1929–31, which brought about a further drastic fall in the prices of Japanese export goods. Under a new Finance Minister, the attempt to revert to the Gold Standard was abandoned and a reflationary policy was put into effect which set Japan on the road to recovery earlier than other countries as government spending, initially for relief measures but increasingly for the military, expanded.

It is possible to view Japanese macroeconomic policy during the 1920s as a not very successful attempt, in the face of the still relatively underdeveloped domestic financial system, to keep Japan in line with the rules of the *laisser-faire* game currently in favour with the great trading powers. Largely as a result of the views developed by the Japanese representatives at the peace negotiations ending World War I (Iriye 1974), government leaders were in general converted to the prevailing orthodoxy of free trade, international co-operation and economic growth through peaceful competition. Japan's interests would be furthered by her increasing integration into the world economy, as her businesses developed their trading activities and invested in overseas projects, and as Japanese settlers emigrated to newly opening parts of the world.

This strategy of development through international co-operation and free trade was largely unsuccessful for many reasons, both domestic and foreign. Japanese industry, which had been able to expand rapidly through the re-investment of profits during the generally inflationary pre-war and wartime period, and for which the war itself had provided protection against imports and guaranteed export markets, now faced a much changed climate. Firms, and their financial backers, who had overextended themselves during the wartime boom collapsed and government relief to business and banking was required. Balance of payments deficits appeared as international competition resumed, worsened by such factors as the import of equipment after the Earthquake. The return to the Gold Standard, seen as a central plank in the policy of integrating into the world economy, was thus delayed and eventually carried out at the worst possible time during the world-wide 1929–31 depression. The Japanese also proved somewhat reluctant emigrants and the flow of permanent settlers to those countries which would accept Japanese immigrants remained fairly small. Thus the policy was pursued at a time when the Japanese economy as a whole was not in a condition to be able to take advantage of it.

Nevertheless, it can also be argued that Japanese policy-makers were somewhat naive in their belief in international commitment to peaceful economic competition. Protectionism, through the imposition of tariffs, was in fact rife; China, a key area from Japan's point of view, was a battleground of informal imperialism and rising nationalism and far from the free market envisaged, and while it is possible that the policy might have stood a better chance of success in an expanding world economy, growth everywhere was in fact substantially slower than it had been before the war.

Equally, though, the Japanese government itself did not whole-heartedly pursue a policy of economic non-intervention and fiscal austerity and to this might in part be attributed the fact that growth, although slower than it had been before and during the war, continued in Japan at a rate faster than that of the developed European and American economies. As we shall see, bureaucratic activity designed to assist major industries was developing, and at the macro level the decline in private industrial capital formation was offset by growth in construction and infrastructure investment, much of it government-funded. Thus, in part as a result of earthquake reconstruction, but also in response to the urbanisation of industry and employment during the earlier boom, local government authorities borrowed to invest quite heavily in public utilities and communications, offsetting declines in military expenditure, as disarmament took place, and in central government investment. Continued investment in electrification, railway construction and so on also helped to maintain the level of aggregate demand (Nakamura 1983: 157–73).

Nonetheless, the overall policy of international co-operation and disarmament was increasingly to come under attack within sections of the military and the bureaucracy. This was partly in response to its distributional effects, as big business appeared better able to cope with trade fluctuations than small firms and farmers, and partly of course on military and strategic grounds, as nationalism in China and the spread of Soviet interests in Asia began to be seen as threatening Japan's security. The impact of the World Depression, particularly on farmers and smaller businesses producing for export, compounded by the ill-timed attempt to return to the Gold Standard, proved the last straw and, as the Japanese army in Manchuria took matters into its own hands, macroeconomic policy in Tokyo was turned round. From the beginning of 1932, a new Finance Minister, Takahashi Korekiyo, pursued policies often seen as an early form of Keynesianism, under which the Gold Standard was abandoned and the yen substantially devalued, while government expenditure, financed by widespread public borrowing, increased sharply. Japanese firms, streamlined and technically improved as a result of their experience through the 1920s, took advantage of the devaluation to expand exports, and government spending, at first especially on relief measures for rural areas but increasingly for military purposes, stimulated rising levels of economic activity and faster growth. Policies designed to protect and stimulate strategic industries, and to develop in the growing empire the supplies of raw materials required, became increasingly important, and state planning and intervention in the economy grew more and more dominant as the 1930s progressed. What was therefore to endure out of the inter-war period, as far as the strategy of state involvement in the economy is concerned, was on the one hand the abandonment of the belief in international co-operation and economic expansion through free competition, and on the other a substantial body of experience of the policies and methods of state assistance, planning and protection in the development of crucial sectors of the economy.

Industrial policy

As described in chapter 2, the Meiji period witnessed the massive reform programme necessitated by acceptance of the goal of establishing modern industrial and military capacities and maintaining Japan's independence. This programme was initiated from above, but required considerable interaction between private business interests on the one hand and, on the other, civil servants unencumbered by Western liberal notions about the neutral role of the state, who were heirs to a Tokugawa tradition of government responsibility for the welfare of the people. This interaction had taken place through largely informal links between individual entrepreneurs and bureaucrats who had obtained their posts for the most part as a result of influence and connections. Before the turn of the century, however, formal structures determining the recruitment and career patterns of bureaucrats were beginning to be instituted and new mechanisms were starting to emerge whereby civil servants working within such structures sought to achieve the goal of industrial development. Against the background of overall economic policy already described, this section will look at the changing institutions and methods employed in the implementation of what was later to be called 'industrial policy'. The subsequent section will attempt to assess the impact of this policy on the development of particular pre-war industries.

In 1897 a law passed the Diet limiting civil service employment to those who had succeeded in an entrance examination. The acquisition of the necessary knowledge and educational experience, rather than the use of influence or connections, was thereafter to be the road to a government post. In practice, for the higher levels of the civil service, this meant obtaining a university degree. Although the provision of higher education facilities was steadily expanding, the first university to be established after 1868, Tokyo Imperial University, remained the most prestigious and, prior to World War II as also after it, the upper echelons of the civil service were dominated by its graduates, especially those of its Law Department. There, future bureaucrats obtained a general education in legal, administrative, political and economic matters, and, perhaps more importantly, a common ethos and background binding together each year-group of graduates.

With the institution of recruitment by examination came the establishment of formal procedures for promotion, security of employment and pension provision. Entry into the civil service could thus be seen as the start of a long-term career, with promotion dependent on the acquisition through experience of the knowledge and skills required. However, this tended to limit a bureaucrat's career to one ministry and, since the number of posts available necessarily declined with the seniority of the grade, internal pressures would build up for those who reached the top to retire relatively quickly in order to make way for those coming up. Hence, despite its elite status and relatively secure conditions, a bureaucratic career could not be relied on to provide employment throughout a complete working life and senior civil servants were thus obliged to cultivate the outside contacts through which to obtain second careers, for example in politics or business, to follow their relatively early retirements from their ministries. The creation of these contacts promoted and in turn was fostered by the institutional structures and working methods which began to develop as bureaucrats experimented with new ways of achieving the state's industrialisation goals, and gradually the close interconnections between the political, business and bureaucratic elites, so prominent a feature of the post-World War II government/business relationship, began to emerge in the inter-war period as civil service procedures became formalised (Silberman 1974).

The 1880s and 1890s had seen the establishment of the various independent ministries required to deal with the individual areas of the state's activities, and in each the formalised structure described above began to emerge. Senior ministries, such as Finance, as well as semi-governmental institutions such as the Bank of Japan, implemented the government's overall economic policies as regards the business, financial and trading environment. The development of individual industries, however, remained the responsibility of the Ministry of Agriculture and Commerce until 1925. In that year, as a reflection of the changing composition of economic activity in the country, the industrial and agricultural sides of the Ministry's work were separated and responsibility for industrial matters passed to the newly-formed Ministry of Commerce and Industry (MCI). Although bureaucrats in other ministries must at times have operated in similar ways and been able to exert influence in industrial matters, it was MCI officials who were most active in developing methods of promoting and protecting Japanese industries and in creating the experience and rationale of industrial policy which a number of them lived to recreate in new forms after the defeat in World War II.

At its formation, the new MCI took over those leading officials from the old Agriculture Ministry who had tended to believe, somewhat in opposition to the interests of landlords and farmers generally dominant in the old Ministry, in the promotion and protection of new industries (Johnson 1982: 93). The new Ministry was born into the midst of the depressed and crisis-ridden 1920s and the balance-of-payments difficulties caused by declining exports, and the problem which the new MCI officials saw themselves as facing was that of how the government could best help Japanese industry in this situation. Temporary subsidies and relief to help bail out failing financial institutions were being given but officials in the new Ministry began to experiment with more positive forms of assistance to businesses in their production and overseas trading activities. Their general diagnosis of the problem was that in many industries, as a result of the World War I boom, there were too many producers engaged in cut-throat competition, giving rise to low profits and export sales at prices which did not cover costs. They thus began their continuing search for the legislative and institutional means to bring firms together in co-operation so as to rationalise capacity and regulate the volume and quality of exports.

The need for these moves, and the emergence of the business environment within which they could be carried out, were intensified by the financial panic which occurred in 1927 and then by the Great Depression itself. These drove numbers of smaller firms into bankruptcy and strengthened the position of the big firms which dominated major industries as leading members of the emerging conglomerate groups of companies known as *zaibatsu*.[2] Against this background, the Ministry's Commerce and Industry Deliberation Council, established in 1927 to act as a sort of 'think-tank', began to develop the idea of 'industrial rationalisation' which was to emerge as the slogan of inter-war industrial policy (Johnson 1982: 102). This was a vague term, covering efforts to increase efficiency both through improved management and technology and through agreements to rationalise capacity within an industry. In 1930, the Temporary Industrial Rationality Bureau was created and this group drafted the major piece of legislation on which industrial rationalisation policy was based, the Important Industries Control Law of 1931. This law gave the MCI the power to authorise cartel agreements drawn up with the consent of two-thirds of the enterprises in a particular industry.

The cartels would enable the participating firms to regulate production and restore their profitability, but obliged them to report frequently to the Ministry for approval on matters such as investment plans.

Whatever the original intentions behind the law, it is clear that its major impact was to reduce competition by strengthening the position of the major *zaibatsu* firms. Twenty six cartels were organised in a range of industries and many mergers followed, creating such large-scale enterprises as Japan Steel, Mitsubishi Heavy Industries and Sumitomo Metals, and strengthening *zaibatsu* control over the modern industrial sector. As a result, the effort to achieve industrial rationalisation through 'self-control' by the firms within an industry, in co-operation with MCI bureaucrats, came increasingly into question as criticism of *zaibatsu* activity intensified, particularly among radical groups within the military and their supporters outside. As the demands of the military for the industrial base their activities required grew in the wake of the seizure of Manchuria, so MCI officials increasingly sought to replace 'self-control' with 'state control' of individual industries.

The aim of the military on the economic front was to create the institutional framework within which they could plan the production and allocate the output of particular strategic industries. In this they had support from within the MCI, which contained a substantial number of so-called 'reform bureaucrats', to whom the idea of greater state control of the economy in the interests of the nation as a whole, to counteract the power of the, as they saw it, corrupt and decadent capitalist *zaibatsu*, was not unappealing. The support from the military which this gave to the MCI helped it to increase in influence relative to other ministries, such as Finance, which presented greater resistance to the military's ideas. The training ground for many of the MCI reform bureaucrats was the newly-created Japanese puppet state of Manchūkuo (Manchuria), to which a number were seconded to assist in the development of resource supplies and heavy industrial projects. There, however, they learnt, through the problems encountered when the military sought to manage such projects themselves, that private-sector investment and assistance could not be avoided if their policies were to be successful. Hence, the legislation drafted in order to increase the state's role in the development of key industries, beginning with the Petroleum Industry Law of 1934 and proceeding through similar legislation for automobiles, steel, machine tools, aircraft, shipbuilding and so on, maintained private ownership in the hands of a limited number of major firms who would follow government guidance in return for the assistance, in the form of tax relief, capital provision and so on, which the government was empowered to give.

After the start of the war with China in 1937, the degree to which the economy was mobilised to meet military needs steadily increased. The Cabinet Planning Board, which was in overall control of the economic mobilisation, began to operate an almost Soviet-style material-balances planning system, under which available supplies, from domestic production and imports, of key materials were calculated and then allocated according to a system of priorities. The allocation of, initially, foreign exchange and, later, marine transport was the mechanism for controlling the system. However, in deference to the power and influence of *zaibatsu* business interests, the majority of production facilities remained in private hands and the Planning Board required the MCI to reorganise into vertical, industry-specific bureaux to co-ordinate with the private firms in each industry in administering the plans. So MCI officials were allocated, under the General Affairs Bureau, to one of the Minerals Bureau, the Machinery Bureau, the Textiles Bureau, the Iron and Steel Bureau or the Chemicals Bureau, a structure which in essence remained until 1973 (Johnson 1982: appendix B).

It is these two elements of pre-war and wartime planning, the co-operation with selected major private firms in each industry and the structure of industry-specific bureaux within the Ministry, which represent, according to Johnson, the most important legacy bequeathed by the MCI to its post-war re-incarnation, the Ministry of International Trade and Industry (MITI). Despite the disaster of the war and the massive reforms of the Occupation, the leading architects of the MCI's efforts to develop pre-war industry survived to apply their experience in the much more favourable environment of the 1950s and '60s. Once the power of the *zaibatsu* and the military had been broken by the war and Occupation, Johnson argues (1982), the methods of government/business co-operation in the development and protection of major industries, which the MCI had pioneered before the war, came into their own in the much more hospitable climate of a rapidly-growing world economy and a domestic political consensus in favour of economic growth. However, by no means all commentators would agree with Johnson's strong argument for the significance of MITI's role in bringing about the post-war economic miracle and it is in the light of this controversy that the following section will attempt to assess the role of the industrial policy of MITI's predecessor in developing Japan's substantial pre-war industrial capacity, by looking at case studies of various major industries.

THE ROLE OF THE STATE IN TWENTIETH-CENTURY INDUSTRIALISATION: CASE STUDIES

Although the period between the Meiji Resoration and the turn of the century saw transformations in many aspects of the social, economic and political life of Japan, nevertheless the economy in 1900 was still one in which agriculture and light industry predominated, in which factory workers represented only a relatively small proportion of the labour force and machine-powered modern technology was the exception rather than the rule. By the time that Japan became embroiled in war in China in the late 1930s, although almost 50 per cent of the labour force was still employed in primary industry, the share of net domestic product produced in that sector had declined to less than 20 per cent, while that produced in the secondary sector had risen from just over 20 per cent in 1900 to 36 per cent in 1935 and was to reach 50 per cent by 1940 (Nakamura 1983: 22–3). Furthermore, as table 3.2 showed, in the period between the World Wars especially, the composition of manufacturing sector output shifted significantly in the direction of heavy industry, so that, although the textile industries remained the most important manufacturing producers and employers, the structure of the economy was moving towards the pattern observed in the advanced countries of the time. The striking feature of the inter-war period was thus the rise of industries such as iron and steel, chemicals, shipbuilding and machine building, which constituted the heavy industrial base both for self-sustaining growth and for the economic and military capacity to pursue a long war.

The following sections examine the development, over the first half of this century, of two industries each producing goods which have come to be seen as having both real and symbolic importance in present-day developing countries. The significance of the iron and steel industry lies in the enormous range of applications for which its products are vital inputs, particularly in construction and machine-building in an industrialising economy. Automobile production involves a different kind of technology (assembling of parts as opposed to processing of raw materials), but is distinguished, like iron and steel, by its dependence on complex linkages with other industrial sectors. As a result of both its large-scale, capital-intensive technology and its economic and strategic significance, the iron and steel industry tends to be one which relies on state support in most economies, and Japan's has been no exception. Automobiles also have their military uses, as we shall see, and examples abound of state involvement, for an assortment of reasons, in national car industries throughout the world, but this case study presents the opportunity to assess the government's role in the early development of a less obviously state-dependent industry, whose products have come to symbolise for many in the West Japan's post-war emergence as an economic giant.

Iron and steel

For an industrialising economy, iron and steel represent the most vital common inputs required in the production of a whole range of modern products, 'the rice of industry' for Japanese writers, 'the key link' for Chinese planners, and the establishment of a national steel industry has become a symbolic step on the path to development. On the other hand, though, the technology of iron and steel production bears almost all the characteristics required to qualify it as inappropriate in the context of a developing country: it is capital-intensive and exhibits strong economies of scale; it requires a relatively small but skilled labour force to operate equipment embodying advanced, imported science and technology; it is fuelled by inputs of coal, iron ore, water and electricity which can only be supplied through a reliable and well-developed infrastructure, and it produces output the quality and range of varieties of which can make or mar the products of other industries. These characteristics also make it a line of production in which private investment is unlikely to appear initially very profitable, but in which tendencies towards oligopoly are strong, and hence it is an industry in which state involvement is widespread in both developed and developing countries.

The situation facing early twentieth-century Japan as regards iron and steel production could in essential respects be described in the same way. Although the best-practice iron and steel technology of the time was nowhere near as large-scale and capital-intensive as that facing, for example, contemporary China or South Korea, the construction of an up-to-date integrated plant, including blast furnaces to produce pig-iron, Bessemer converters or open-hearth furnaces to turn iron into steel, and rolling mills to produce the various kinds of finished steel, still represented a very major investment in a difficult technology. Japan had had a long history of metal-working and iron was traditionally produced from iron-sand using charcoal furnaces. In the late Tokugawa period, some domain rulers had constructed small-scale blast furnaces and steel converters, embodying modern Western technology copied from Dutch books, in order to produce iron and steel for weapons manufacture. But the relevance of the skills and knowledge thus acquired for the operation of Western technology on a large scale was not great. Furthermore, the raw materials (coal and iron ore) available in Japan were both limited in supply and of compositions and quality unsuited to the blast-furnace and converter technology developed in Europe. Hence, once economic growth began to speed up in the second half of the nineteenth century, reliance on imported iron and steel became heavy. By 1896, imports supplied 60 per cent of Japan's consumption of pig-iron and almost all that of steel (Allen 1962: 80).

It thus seemed clear that, if Japan was to have a modern iron-and-steel industry of her own and avoid dependence on imports for a key economic and military resource, state initiative would be necessary. The early Meiji government did indeed attempt to set up two iron-works employing imported modern blast furnaces, but neither was successful in government hands and both were closed down and eventually sold off to private investors in 1885. One of them was never successfully operated, but the other, the Kamaishi Works (now part of Japan Steel), was reopened by its purchaser who, after a number of years of experiment and adaptation, succeeded in refiring the large-scale English blast furnace he had acquired (Ono 1985: 238, 240). By the end of the century, however, the case for a second attempt to establish full-scale integrated iron-and-steel production in Japan had grown much stronger: after the Sino–Japanese War, imports of suitable-quality iron ore from China had become much more readily available and the demand for steel products for military production and shipbuilding was continuing to intensify. Hence a bill was put before the Diet proposing government funding for the construction of a large-scale iron-and-steel works, to be owned and managed by the Ministry of Agriculture and Commerce and located at the village of Yahata on the North Kyūshū coast, convenient for access both to imports of iron ore and to the country's main coal field. The plant was duly constructed, using technology imported from Europe and German technical staff, and the blast furnaces were first fired in 1901.

The Yahata works was to dominate the Japanese iron-and-steel industry throughout the pre-World War II period and it remained officially government-run until 1934 and heavily government-influenced thereafter. Its output accounted for over half of domestic pig-iron and steel output from its inception through to the 1930s, despite the establishment of a number of private producers during the 1910s (Johnson 1982: 87, Lockwood 1968: 109n). Nonetheless, it experienced considerable difficulties in the operation of its imported equipment under Japanese conditions, the range of steel products it could produce was limited, and it could not generate a profit at prices competitive with imports. Hence, although domestic output was growing fast, it could not match demand, and on the eve of World War I half of the consumption of pig-iron and two-thirds of that of steel were still being met from imports (Lockwood 1968: 24).

As was the case for many Japanese industries, World War I ushered in a boom period for iron and steel. With supplies of imports severely limited and domestic demand expanding rapidly as other industries invested to take advantage of the boom, production capacity was increased, both through expansion at Yahata itself and through the establishment and growth of private firms, and finished steel output more than doubled between 1913 and 1918 (Allen 1962: 122). However, with the post-war collapse and the resumption of imports, many of these firms found themselves in difficulties. Bankruptcies and mergers were frequent and the government's initial response was to step in to bail out some of the failing private steel producers (Johnson 1982: 96). At the same time, pressure for protection against imports was growing.

It was out of this situation that the first steps were taken towards the kind of co-ordinated government/business industrial policy which was to remain the hallmark of state involvement in iron and steel and other key heavy industries. As the Ministry of Commerce and Industry was being born out of the old Ministry of Agriculture and Commerce, carrying with it as its chief inheritance control of the Yahata works, the various government/business committees set up to examine the problems of the economy in the late 1920s (e.g. the Commerce and Industry Deliberation Council and later the Industrial Rationalisation Deliberation Council) began to produce recommendations for the rationalisation of industry, and the goal of a co-ordinated national iron-and-steel industry began to take shape as part of this. With the steel section of the MCI to act as general staff, the means of achieving this goal through mergers of existing companies and planned expansion of capacity could be formulated.

Meanwhile, however, the iron and steel firms themselves were undertaking measures to increase their efficiency in the face of renewed foreign competition. By means of improvements in plant management, training and technical efficiency, costs at Yahata were reduced and labour productivity substantially increased (Udagawa and Nakamura 1980: 86). The major private firms such as Nihon Kōkan and Kamaishi similarly rationalised their production operations and doubled output per man over the course of the 1920s. At the same time, increasing protection was being sought through the establishment of cartel arrangements and demands for increases in tariffs on imports. The differing interests of the firms in the industry, particularly depending on whether they produced pig-iron or steel or both, were already beginning to create strains, however, and the resulting compromise was a steady increase in the tariff on imported steel products, combined with direct subsidies paid to pig-iron producers (Udagawa and Nakamura 1980: 87). As a result of this protection and rationalisation, the position of the industry improved through the 1920s. The volume of output of both pig-iron and steel produced by Japanese firms (including some based in Manchuria and elsewhere in China) more than doubled between 1923 and 1929 (Nakamura 1983: 197) and the steel self-sufficiency rate is put at about 80 per cent by the end of the decade (Udagawa and Nakamura 1980: 87), although imports of pig-iron, scrap and higher-grade steel products remained significant.

When the world depression struck Japan in 1930, iron and steel producers were again hard hit and went into the red as prices fell. It was at this point that the deliberations of the MCI and its consultative committees bore fruit in proposals for legislation to bring about rationalisation in a number of important industries, including a plan for the amalgamation of the major firms in the iron-and-steel industry into a single enterprise centring on the Yahata works. The aim would be to co-ordinate production under government control so as to achieve economies of scale and lower production costs, thereby seeking 'to promote our country's iron and steel industry so as to block the inflow of foreign iron and steel and to increase exports of its products' (translated and quoted in Udagawa and Nakamura 1980: 88). It took until 1933, however, for the scheme to be finalised and for support in the industry and the government to be consolidated, with the aid of a large increase in the tariff on pig-iron imports long sought by some of the firms involved. Thus eventually, at the beginning of 1934, under legislation passed the previous year and alongside the achievement of similar state-sponsored mergers in other heavy industries, Japan Steel (Nihon Seitetsu) was created (Johnson 1982: 111).

Most of the firms in the industry had been keen to join in the merger plan in the dark days of 1930, but by 1934 their situations had changed somewhat and although the newly-created enterprise controlled almost all of the country's pig-iron production, its share of steel output was only around 50 per cent because a number of major firms, including Nihon Kōkan, the biggest private steel producer, refused to join. This was partly because of what they regarded as the unfavourable merger terms offered to specialist steel-producers (as compared with pig-iron and integrated iron-and-steel firms) and partly because economic prospects were improving sufficiently to justify remaining independent (Udagawa and Nakamura 1980: 90). The MCI used the weapons at its disposal to try to force the 'outsider' firms to join Japan Steel, for example by having Japan Steel sabotage cartel arrangements and refusing outsiders' applications to construct new plants, but the independent producers held out (Udagawa and Nakamura 1980: 91).[3] Hence the scope for co-ordinating and rationalising the complete industry remained restricted.

Meanwhile, moreover, the goal posts were moving. As the 1930s progressed and the economic and political influence of the military grew, the objective of the MCI steel section bureaucrats began to shift away from that of the achievement of international competitiveness and towards that of developing the industry to produce what the military needed. With the passage of the 1937 Steel Industry Law, iron-and-steel producers both inside and outside Japan Steel were given every encouragement to expand their production capacity in return for submitting to the increased control required in preparation for war, and gradually the industry was absorbed into the system of planning under which the war economy was managed (Johnson 1982: 133).

In tracing the history of state involvement in iron and steel, it still remains difficult to specify precise links between the first steps towards industrial policy taken by the MCI in the 1920s and '30s and the growth of the industry. The Ministry was not able to impose its will over the whole industry until war-economy conditions prevailed, and much that occurred was the result of the strategies and responses of the firms themselves. It is undeniable, however, that what the state did provide was the barrier of protection and subsidy behind which Japanese firms built up their production capacity and technical experience. Nonetheless, it is unlikely that, by the time of the Pacific War, they had reached a stage of being competitive with advanced-country producers and the Japanese firms which emerged from the war were cert ' operating at higher costs and lower labour productivity t' American counterparts (Lynn 1982: 46). Pre-war state i the industry did leave an important legacy, howev association between MCI (later MITI) burea' management and in the collaborative experience of the major steel firms. The government/business relationship, although not confined to the former government-owned company, was strongest in the case of those who had been involved with Yahata, which became a separate private company when Japan Steel was broken up during the post-war Occupation but which subsequently remerged with Fuji Steel (formed from much of the capacity contributed by private firms to the old Japan Steel) to form New Japan Steel. There are many examples of steel section bureaucrats who entered the MCI before World War II 'descending from heaven', on their retirement from senior posts in the Ministry, to join the boards of major steel companies, and post-war MITI bureaucrats made frequent use of this network of connections in their efforts to plan and protect the industry (see e.g. Johnson 1982: 245–6).

During the period of the post-war economic miracle, Japan's steel output rose at a phenomenal rate, as a result of rapid investment in new, large-scale integrated plants embodying the latest technology, and the Japanese industry grew to be one of the largest and technically most advanced in the world. Given that this growth occurred within an industry which carried the legacy of one of the highest levels of pre-war state involvement and in which, in the post-war period, a great deal of government/business and intra-industry discussion and planning continued to take place, it is again tempting to see a connection, operating through the encouragement to investment and technological improvement which resulted from the state's fostering of a key heavy industry. On the other hand, the technology of steel production naturally encourages oligopolistic cartel-forming and price-fixing arrangements, which are not exclusive to the Japanese industry, and a case can be made for arguing that planning and collusion resulted in overinvestment and excess capacity, together with higher but less stable prices than would have prevailed in a freer environment (Imai 1980). The individual steel firms continued to pursue their best interests within the framework of MITI's planning and cartel arrangements, and MITI's schemes were frequently frustrated by the steel firms' strategies in this situation. Leonard Lynn's fascinating comparative study of the adoption of the basic oxygen furnace, a major post-war technical innovation, in Japan and the United States examines why Japanese firms were quicker to in the new method and concludes that MITI's steel section did in securing a good deal on the purchase of the licence to the (by preventing competition among Japanese firms) making it widely available, but that many other factors were also involved, including, for example, the competitive atmosphere between Japan Steel and Nihon Kōkan.[4]

A balanced assessment of the effects of the pre-war legacy of state involvement in iron and steel would thus have to conclude that it bequeathed both costs and benefits to an industry which would almost certainly have grown anyway, as steel industries do in fast-growing economies, but in which the activities of bureaucrats did at times provide security and promote technical advance. It will be interesting to assess how well bureaucrats working within this same tradition have been able to turn their skills and experience to the task of easing the running-down of the industry, in the face of competition from those newly-industrialising rivals who are now themselves discovering the keys to successful promotion of their steel industries.

Automobiles

As is only too apparent to those of us who take our cars for granted until the failure of some seemingly insignificant component leaves us stranded, an automobile is a highly complex piece of machinery composed of thousands of parts, each of which must be carefully designed, engineered and manufactured from suitable material so as to fulfil its function in the greater whole. Automobile production is thus essentially an assembly operation, but depends on supplies of a wide range of specialised components produced through the application of machine tools to particular metals and other materials. Complete production of vehicles from scratch is therefore something which can only be achieved within a well-developed industrial sector, adequately provided with a high level of engineering skills and technical knowledge, and costs can only be kept down by mass production. On the other hand, although vehicles are desirable and even essential in many applications, they remain expensive items for which developing countries by definition cannot initially offer mass markets to potential local producers. Hence early purchases tend to come from abroad and are liable to represent a significant drain on foreign exchange resources, generating pressures for production, or at least assembly, at home. The classic strategy for developing countries with potential mass markets for automobiles has therefore been to encourage developed-country mass producers to set up, behind protective tariff barriers, subsidiary assembly plants putting together so-called 'knock-down' sets of imported components. The challenge has then been to find the means to oblige the foreign-based company, whose interests lie in maximising the proportion of components it supplies itself, to transfer technological knowledge and expand its local procurement of parts.

In a world in which so many people and things are transported in Nissans, Toyotas and Hondas, it requires a certain mental leap to recreate the situation in which automobile production first began in Japan and to see it as conditioned by many of the same economic and technical forces as have faced the car industries of present-day developing countries. Nevertheless, the early history of Japanese vehicle manufacture involved the same interplay between multi-national mass producers (Ford and General Motors), infant domestic parts and assembly firms led by the pioneering enthusiasts and entrepreneurs who created businesses which are now household names, and the state, with an added military dimension. Foreign companies supplied almost all of the vehicles on the road in Japan until the 1930s, but by the time of the outbreak of the Pacific War, vehicle imports had ceased, foreign subsidiaries had closed down, and the Japanese army was transported through World War II in vehicles made by Japanese companies. When trade opened up again after the war, however, American and British cars flooded in, and although the foundations for the domestic industry's economic and technical capacity had been laid before and during hostilities, it was only when the lessons learned from protective pre-war industrial policies were applied in the 1950s that Japan's major producers secured for themselves their competitive shares of the fast-growing home market and, eventually, their enormous success as exporters.[5]

Cars first began to be imported into Japan in 1899 and thereafter a few Japanese enthusiasts also began to build one-off vehicles to order and to experiment with parts production and assembly. The number of vehicles in operation nonetheless remained small – there were 3,856 registered motor vehicles in 1917 (Lockwood 1968: 107) – and the scope for their use must have been very limited. Ships and railways, horse-drawn vehicles and rickshaws dominated freight and passenger traffic, and the development of the road network has lagged behind the growth of the economy well into the post-World War II period. World War I, however, provided the army with a glimpse of the value of trucks and lorries and encouraged it to sponsor a law providing for subsidies to authorised Japanese companies to produce them. The three licensed companies had got no further than manufacturing some experimental vehicles, though, by the time of the Great Tokyo Earthquake of 1923, after which, as an emergency measure to offset earthquake damage to the rail and tram network, the Tokyo Municipal Government, encouraged by a reduction in the tariff on automobiles first imposed after World War I, set about importing several thousand Ford Model T trucks. This sudden expansion in demand alerted Ford to the possibilities of the Japanese market and by 1925 it had set up a Japanese subsidiary with a plant in Yokohama to assemble cars from knock-down sets. General Motors soon followed suit, establishing its assembly plant in Osaka in 1927. Sales of the products of these plants generated a sharp increase in vehicle registrations, but the few fledgling Japanese manufacturers were unable to produce anything to compete with the results of the American firms' mass-production design and engineering. Only the three licensed firms survived, relying on their subsidised production of military trucks, and the major *zaibatsu* companies remained unwilling to risk investment in producing a product for which they envisaged neither a large market in Japan, nor the possibility of competing with imports.

The MCI and the military, on the other hand, were less sceptical and more concerned about the strategic and balance-of-payments implications of dependence on the foreign companies' vehicles, and one of the Ministry's advisory bodies proposed the setting-up of a joint business/government committee to consider the establishment of a domestic motor industry. This committee drew up a plan for the design and subsidised production of a passenger car and recommended the merger of the three Japanese vehicle manufacturers in order to produce it. A modified version of the merger eventually took place, but the new state-sponsored firm, subsequently called Isuzu, concentrated on the production of vans and lorries which did not compete with Ford and General Motors passenger cars. After the seizure of Manchuria in 1931, though, the military need for lorries which could operate reliably in difficult conditions grew and the army became increasingly concerned at its reliance on American vehicles, against which its few Isuzus compared very unfavourably.[6]

Meanwhile, however, there were others outside the world of the big business/bureaucratic establishment who were beginning to develop an interest in vehicle production. The first of these was Aikawa (sometimes read as Ayukawa) Yoshisuke, an up-and-coming businessman in the process of creating one of the so-called 'new *zaibatsu*', which, with its interests in metals, chemicals and machinery and its key role in the development of industry in Manchuria, was to come, by the time of the Pacific War, to rival the longer-standing and more traditional old *zaibatsu*. Aikawa's business career began with the establishment of a firm (later to become Hitachi) to produce cast-iron.

This company benefited from the World War I boom and the shortage of imported cast-iron and its profits enabled Aikawa to widen his interests through the creation of a holding company to acquire assets in other industries. Aikawa had visited the United States on several occasions, including a spell working there not long after his graduation from the mechanical engineering department of Tokyo University, and this had generated an interest in the possibilities of manufacturing cars in Japan (Cusumano 1985: 30). His original casting firm made motors for boats and farm machinery and eventually moved into the production of parts for Ford and General Motors, but Aikawa initially failed to persuade his shareholders to back a move into full-scale automobile manufacturing. In 1931, however, he acquired shares in a company called DAT Motors, which had been one of the licensed firms producing subsidised trucks for the army in the 1920s but which was also experimenting with designs for a small passenger car, the Datsun. In 1933, DAT Motors entered the merger which was to create Isuzu and, since it expected thereafter to concentrate on truck production, it gave Aikawa the Osaka factory producing the Datsun in return for his shares in the company. In 1934, Aikawa merged his new car factory with the auto-parts section of his original company to form a new subsidiary, the Nissan Motor Company.

The second 'outsider' to be developing an interest in automobile production was Toyoda Kiichirō, the son of one of the heroes of Japan's early industrialisation who had invented and set up production of the Toyoda automatic loom. In 1930, the elder Toyoda sold the patent of his loom to Platt Brothers and gave the proceeds to his son to use to develop car production. Kiichirō, obliged to follow his father's wishes, soon used up this initial sum in setting up a car department within the Toyoda Loom Co., and relied on subsequent grants, somewhat grudgingly given by the other members of his family who ran the main company after the death of the elder Toyoda. Kiichirō, like Aikawa a mechanical engineering graduate of Tokyo University, had acquired experience in machine technology in the family business and had also spent some time in Britain, where he had taken the opportunity to visit car plants in pursuit of his father's dream. His strategy was not to try to acquire car production technology directly from a foreign producer, but rather to learn everything he could about what was available and put together a Japanese-designed automobile model, incorporating the best from elsewhere. By 1936, under the influence of changes in government policy to be examined shortly, the rest of the family became convinced that there could be a market for Japanese-made vehicles. They thus agreed to the construction of an automobile plant and the separation of the loom and motor production sides of the business, resulting in 1937 in the creation of an independent car company to be called Toyota.

As part III of this book will relate in more detail, the strategies adopted by Nissan and Toyota for acquiring the technological capacity to produce automobiles differed. Toyoda continued to seek to develop Toyota's own R & D ability and to recruit the best Japanese engineers available to work on the elements of their own design of vehicle (Cusumano 1985: 59). Nissan, on the other hand, actively sought a tie-up with General Motors, employed American engineers to design and direct production operations, and even purchased an entire American plant to re-assemble in Japan. The MCI, whose initial goal was the development of a domestic industry capable of competing with imports, continued to encourage Isuzu and did not oppose Nissan's links with General Motors, fearing also that a hostile stance towards the American companies could provoke retaliatory action from the United States (Cusumano 1985: 17; Udagawa and Nakamura 1980: 97). The military, on the other hand, were concerned about the strategic implications of reliance on foreign firms and maintained pressure on the Ministry to propose legislation which would put Ford and General Motors out of business in Japan and would result in the establishment of a protected and controlled domestic industry. As the 1930s progressed, the political influence of the military grew, strengthening the position within the MCI of the 'reform bureaucrats' who supported the army's strategy, and in 1935 the cabinet agreed to proposals for legislative measures to protect and develop an independent domestic car industry. In May 1936, these passed the Diet as the Automobile Manufacturing Industry Law.

This law embodied the classic industrial-policy framework which was to be employed less formally, and without such detailed legislative backing, by the MCI's successor in the post-war period. It made production of more than 3,000 vehicles per annum subject to the acquisition of a licence from the MCI and only firms with majority Japanese ownership were eligible to apply. Licensed firms were entitled to various tax-breaks, including exemption from duty on imported equipment, and assistance in raising capital, but in return had to submit their investment plans for Ministry approval and agree to requirements for the production of military vehicles. Given the refusal of the major *zaibatsu* companies to enter automobile production, it was Nissan and Toyota who were granted licences and who thus emerged, alongside Isuzu, as the favoured bearers of the Ministry's and the military's hopes for a Japanese car industry.[7]

The 1936 law did not explicitly expel Ford and General Motors from Japan but, when combined with a subsequent increase in import duties on both complete vehicles and knock-down sets and components, and with moves to restrict the access of the subsidiaries of overseas companies to foreign exchange, it made life increasingly difficult for them. Attempts to merge with Nissan and Toyota failed and both companies eventually gave up their Japanese operations. Thus vehicle imports, subsidiary assembly production and foreign investment were all effectively eliminated and the domestic market was left in the hands of Nissan, Toyota and, to a lesser extent, Isuzu, with the MCI empowered to assist these firms as best it could. With the onset of war, it was the military market which the licensed firms came to serve and they each abandoned their passenger car operations in favour of the production of military vehicles. Nevertheless, apart from a period of direct government control during the wartime and immediate post-war periods, the running of the industry remained in the hands of company managers, and MCI bureaucrats thus continued to invent and try out the tools of indirect influence and protection which they were to resurrect and perfect, under much more favourable conditions for the passenger car industry, after the war and the Occupation.

The automobile industry represented a relatively small element in the Japanese economy before World War II and although the famous company names of post-war car production were born during the economically and politically difficult times of the '20s and '30s, domestic vehicle manufacturers remained minor actors on the economic stage compared with the zaibatsu-controlled companies which played the leading roles. The significance of their story for our purposes lies rather in the parallels and contrasts to be drawn with the experience of present-day developing countries attempting to establish mass production, assembly-line industries in fields dominated by multinational enterprises, and in the stages which it illustrates in the development of the methods of bureaucratic industrial policy. Despite the MCI's early efforts to rationalise and support the domestic industry, the infant Japanese car companies of the '20s and '30s appeared to be no match for the competition of foreign subsidiaries and could look forward to a future as profitable independent producers only after a substantial period of technological learning as suppliers to the developed-country firms. It was only the much more drastic and strategically-motivated protectionist moves promoted by the military that enabled them to dominate the domestic supply of vehicles (mainly for military uses) in the later 1930s, and their continuing weakness in competition with large-scale Western producers was demonstrated once imports resumed after the war. Nonetheless, the MCI's post-war reincarnation continued to target automobiles as an industry to be promoted, even in the face of opposition from other sections of the bureaucracy, and to find ways of channelling investment funds, tax privileges and protection against imports and foreign investment in the direction of favoured car producers.[8]

By no means all MITI's schemes for the industry were realised (e.g. the major car firms successfully resisted efforts to bring about mergers and reduce the degree of competition between them) and Cusumano, in his massive study of the industry (Cusumano 1985), concludes that straightforward protection from imports in the rapidly-growing post-war domestic market was the key benefit derived from MITI's support. Yet there are numerous and varied examples of the ways in which the economically and technically dynamic Japanese car firms, dominated by Nissan and Toyota but including other post-war entrants into the industry, did gain in other, less obvious ways from the supportive attitude of MITI bureaucrats. To take one example: although post-war Japanese car producers, with the exception of Toyota, acquired up-to-date technology through licensing agreements with foreign firms, MITI retained strict powers of control over such agreements and used this to prevent any long-term use of knock-down sets and to ensure a rapid switch to domestic suppliers of parts (Magaziner and Hout 1980: 56–7). By such means, MITI bureaucrats, freed from the pressures of military needs and sustained by the expansionary domestic and international economic climate following the Korean War boom, continued to operate and improve their industrial policy methods within the framework bequeathed by pre-war experience.

4 Conclusion

Japan in the mid-nineteenth century was an 'underdeveloped', or at least non-industrial, country, abruptly brought into contact with an international economy dominated by the industrial might of the developed Western world. In this respect, therefore, her situation resembled that faced by many post-war developing nations, and the problems encountered and solutions sought can be described in very much the same terms as might be used in the analysis of development strategies in today's Third World. Thus Japan faced, for example, an influx of imported consumer goods threatening domestic industries and bringing about balance-of-payments problems; a technological gap, necessitating dependence on advanced countries for capital goods and a whole range of more sophisticated products, and the internal social and political problems generated by contact with people, things and ideas originating in the powerful and seemingly dominant cultures of the West. In other important respects, of course, the historical situation in which she found herself was vastly different from that faced by developing countries a century later: the gaps between the developed and the developing worlds in industrial technology, in the range and sophistication of consumer goods, and in military and political power were not of the same orders of magnitude, and Japan emerged on to the world stage without the experience of colonisation which conditioned the economic structures of many later-developing countries. But nevertheless, inasfar as she represented a state under threat of economic, not to say political and military, domination by advanced nations, against which a strategy of conscious industrialisation seemed the only weapon, her experience can be considered within the framework for analysing the role of the state in present-day developing countries set out at the beginning of this Part.

This framework sought to locate the strategies adopted by developing-country governments along two parallel but generally correlated scales, representing degrees of, on the one hand, state intervention in the economy and, on the other, involvement in and acceptance of world market forces. The first scale stretches from the fully-planned, Soviet-style economy, in which the state owns a substantial proportion of the means of production, through to economies experiencing minimal state intervention, in which capitalist enterprises compete for profit in freely operating markets. The other scale covers the range of possible strategies for interaction with the world economy, reaching from concerted import-substitution, seeking to produce as wide a range of products as possible within national boundaries guarded by trade barriers, through to *laissez-faire* trade policies, offering no protection to domestic enterprises in their competition with foreign producers and leaving the determination of the structure of the economy dependent on world market forces.

In the period between the mid-nineteenth century and World War II, the Japanese economy was transformed from one bearing the key characteristics of a developing country, such as the dominance of agriculture in production and employment, substantial commercial and handicraft activity but only tiny enclaves of modern industrial technology, and limited trading relations with the outside world, into at least a semi-industrialised one, capable of producing a wide range of modern consumer and capital goods and of sustaining a prolonged period of war, enmeshed in the world economy and in economic ties with her own empire, and dependent on industrial activity for the largest proportion of income and employment. In the preceding sections we have looked in some detail at the activities of the state and of private-sector businesses as this transformation took place. The concluding task is to consider how we might characterise and categorise the path followed by the Japanese economy, and the role of the state within it, in terms of the overall framework of state involvement and trade strategy outlined above.

The dominant view in much of the literature on Japanese economic development ascribes a highly significant, sometimes overriding, role to the state.[1] Industrialisation is commonly described as having been initiated 'from above' and the story of the development process is frequently set out in terms of the actions of the government, starting from the Meiji Restoration and the commitment to modernisation on the part of the new leadership. The underlying economic model often used is that developed by Alexander Gerschenkron in *Economic Backwardness in Historical Perspective* (1962). This rests on the hypothesis that the later a nation starts on the road to economic development, the greater will be the part played by the state as it seeks to substitute for the 'missing prerequisites' which enabled earlier developers to industrialise. Of course, the Meiji state was not equipped with the resources, the political control or the ideological underpinning necessary for the full-scale planning of the economy practised by Gerschenkron's archetypal late-developer, the Soviet Union. Nevertheless, it initiated, it is argued, the important first moves towards industrialisation, including the reform of the institutional structure of government and economy, the creation of a modern infrastructure and educational system, and the introduction of advanced technology.

Furthermore, an element can be added to this picture which makes it possible to argue that full-scale state control was unnecessary in the Japanese case. This is the apparent acceptance on the part of private-sector business leaders of the same national goals as held by the government. Meiji bureaucrats and business leaders alike had their origins, it is argued, in the samurai governments of the more progressive pre-Meiji *han*, for whom the promotion of industrial activity was simply part of the overall interest and responsibility of the ruling class. Hence, after 1868, they continued to pursue the now clearly-stated goals of industrialisation and modernisation, whether as civil servants or businessmen. Thus the 'community-centred entrepreneur', with his Confucian samurai code leading him to perceive no distinction between his private interests and those of the Japanese nation, opened up those areas of the economy essential to the fulfilment of national objectives into which ordinarily-motivated entrepreneurs would fear to tread, rendering the model of intervention in the economic domain by a discrete and separate state an inappropriate one.

It would be possible to follow this line of argument through to the later stages of industrialisation by suggesting that the government/business relationship through which bureaucrats sought to guide the growth of strategic industries in the inter-war and even post-World War II periods represents the institutionalisation, in an age of more formal bureaucratic structures, of this same commonality of interest in national economic development between the state and the leadership of private industry.[2] Hence could be constructed a model of the complete process of industrialisation as initiated and directed from above through the medium of the acceptance by both private- and public-sector decision-makers of the same national goals.

Although not generally explicitly stated as such, the development strategy implied by this model is one involving state protection or promotion for areas of economic activity which would not have existed under free-market conditions. Given the treaties imposed on Japan at the time of her opening up to the West, protection behind import barriers was not feasible until their abrogation at the turn of the century, but after that, as several of our case studies have shown, straightforward protection of infant industries was frequently used. Under the constraints of the treaties, other forms of protection and promotion had been devised, however, and these were also further employed and improved even when import-substitution through trade barriers became possible.[3]

In general, those who ascribe a key role to the state in Japan's development would accept the model set out above only implicitly, if at all, and many would certainly also wish to emphasise the areas of the economy in which the country's comparative advantages were exploited in world markets by a dynamic entrepreneurial class. Equally, others who describe a strong state see it as the oppressive agent of the ruling capitalist/militarist class, seeking to promote the interests of the big-business/heavy-industrial sector of the economy but neglecting those of the small-business, farming and working classes. Such distributional aspects of Japan's industrialisation will be the subject of later chapters, but the major point for present purposes is to stress that the commonly-held picture of Japan's pre-war development places the position of the state firmly, if somewhat eccentrically, at the interventionist and protectionist ends of the scales of possible strategies.

This model of the active and positive role of the 'samurai' or later 'bureaucratic' state in promoting and guiding Japan's development has been challenged from various different angles. We might label these the macroeconomic, microeconomic and world economy angles and each will be considered separately below, although all could be seen as interconnected parts of an overall critique which argues that state action, if not actually irrelevant, has been substantially overplayed as an explanation of Japanese economic development since the mid-nineteenth century.

The arguments that I am labelling the macroeconomic critique form in a sense the pre-World War II instantiation of what Chalmers Johnson calls the 'no miracle occurred' school of thought on post-World War II economic growth (1982). This refers to explanations of the growth of the economy in terms of standard economic theories which see output growth as the result of predictable responses to prevailing economic conditions and macroeconomic forces. Thus, for example, the very high rate of investment which underlay the post-war economic miracle can be explained as the result of rational decisions by profit-seeking businesses in the particular market conditions of supply and demand for labour, capital and output which prevailed through the 1950s and '60s. Despite the valiant efforts of Professor Ohkawa and his colleagues to build up a macroeconomic statistical picture of the forces making for pre-World War II growth, the application of macroeconomic theories and models to historical data remains a risky enterprise. The macroeconomic approach, as applied to earlier periods of economic history, thus relies less on the testing of macro models and more on the evidence of continuity in the development process and the demonstration of consistent patterns of response to broader domestic and international economic forces, explaining growth without recourse to any *deus ex machina* such as the actions of newly-formed governments or indeed the samurai spirit and other emanations of Japanese culture.

Important examples of such analysis are provided by efforts to demonstrate the essential continuities between pre-1868 and post-1868 economic change. Saitō, for instance, brings together a variety of sorts of evidence, economic and demographic, in support of the idea that the expansion of the economy up to at least the inter-war period was part of a general upswing in economic activity going back to the 1820s and 1830s (Saitō 1986(a)). The crux of this argument lies in the characterisation of this whole phase of expansion as based on the growth and spread of small-scale industry and agriculture, paralleling the phases of 'proto-industrialisation' observed in pre-industrial Europe. Thus, as we have already begun to see and will observe in greater detail in later chapters, Japanese economic growth well into the inter-war period was dominated by industries, such as textiles, in which the majority of output was produced in small-scale rural workshops or factories, and these, it might be argued, had more in common with, for example, the rural putting-out industries developed in areas such as the Kinai in the first half of the nineteenth century than with modern heavy industry. All the evidence which has been accumulating over many years of gradual economic change during the later stages of the Tokugawa period supports this line of argument and downplays the significance of the Meiji Restoration as a watershed and hence of the Meiji government as initiator of economic development.[4]

The microeconomic critique of the model of the state's role is exemplified by work on the private-sector side of government/business relations and seeks to re-emphasise the significance of the activity of profit-seeking entrepreneurs, whether of samurai, merchant or farming origins, in the growth of industry. This approach is related to the previous macroeconomic analysis inasfar as the characteristic industrial growth of the long expansionary phase relied on the decisions of small-scale entrepreneurs responding to prevailing economic forces and little affected by government planning or guidance. Equally, though, our case studies of the development of modern-sector businesses have provided many examples of the ways in which the decisions of private profit-seeking businessmen influenced the speed and character of industrial change, the early history of shipping being perhaps the clearest. Moving on to later stages in industrialisation too, we have observed private businesses resisting and subverting bureaucratic efforts to direct their decisions towards what were seen as national goals. Furthermore, the case studies of individual industries have shown that, contrary to the implied assumption of the standard model, economic development was by no means the only goal which the state was pursuing and many of the actions of the bureaucracy in the economic field were dictated by, for example, strategic and military considerations or political shifts within the government. Hence the state emerges as, at best, one of a number of actors on the economic stage, reacting to and in turn influencing the pattern of economic activity, in pursuit of different, and not necessarily consistent, goals in each individual case, rather than as the monolithic hand directing movements towards consensus-based national ends.

All the discussion so far has been, as it were, Japan-centred, but clearly the state's freedom of manoeuvre and the choice of trade strategy are conditioned by the nation's relationship, past and present, with other economies and with world economic forces. Although the appearance of foreign ships in Japanese waters and the forced opening-up to trade without the protection of import barriers certainly created an immediate economic and political crisis, nonetheless it could be argued that, compared with other areas at the time (e.g. China) and with present-day developing countries, the impact of foreign economic interests on Japan was relatively limited. International competition was detrimental to some areas of traditional economic activity (e.g. cotton growing, traditional shipping), but was positively beneficial to others (e.g. sericulture). Foreign capital played little part in Japan's development and foreign businesses, as opposed to foreign experts, made few incursions into the domestic economy except as suppliers of capital goods, some essential industrial inputs and a limited number of consumer goods, as and when required. Hence, for the most part, import substitution and export promotion were left to proceed on their own terms, according to a development strategy determined by Japanese economic forces and/or the independent Japanese state. It was only after World War I, by which time crucial Japanese industries such as cotton textiles and shipping had passed the infant phase and the state was strong enough to provide protection for others which had not, that the developed countries' interest in Japan reached the point of perceiving her industrial growth as a threat, but by this stage Japan was a sufficiently well-developed and internationally recognised nation for conflicts of interest to surface as trade (and ultimately military) 'frictions', rather than as catalysts leading developed states to incorporate a developing one.

The relevance of this for the present discussion lies in the argument, most forcefully presented by Frances Moulder, that Japan represents the exception proving that dependency theory rules (Moulder 1977). By means of a comparison with the concurrent experience of China, Moulder argues that Japan's success at industrialisation before World War I essentially resulted not from any particular strategy adopted by her government or any particular characteristics of her pre-industrial economy or society, but rather from the lack of interest of the Western powers in incorporating Japan, as a dependent economy, into the structure of world trading relations which they dominated. Her market potential was seen as unpromising, the resources she had to offer were few, and anyway the Western powers were too distracted by the far greater attractions offered by China. A less extreme version of this argument would stress the generally favourable world market conditions (e.g. for relatively labour-intensive manufactured goods) facing nineteenth-century Japan, as compared with present-day developing countries, and the strokes of good fortune represented by, for example, the occurrence of the European silk-worm epidemic just when Japan needed a ready export market and wars (notably World War I) which created the conditions for import subsitution and export growth without international competition. At any rate, such considerations do serve to emphasise the point that discussion of the impact of particular strategies is meaningless without reference to the international environment in which they operate.

In the light of the evidence and arguments presented by the proponents of the above critiques, the strong case for the state as initiator and director of Japan's development looks untenable. Nonetheless, it is difficult to avoid the impression that the role played by the Japanese state, through its bureaucracy, though not perhaps as dominant and successful as once thought, was still in important respects different from that played by states elsewhere. The formal and informal relationships built up between bureaucrats and private-sector businessmen, and the uses made of them in the pursuit of national ends, do constitute a system of economic policy-making and implementation not utilised to anything like the same extent, or so consciously towards developmental goals, either in the 'free-market' economies of the Western liberal tradition, or in the once fully-planned Soviet-style economies. The combination of bureaucratic economic intervention with private ownership of the means of production, which had its origins, if not in pre-Meiji local government industrial policies, then certainly in the emerging relations between civil servants and businessmen centring on the sale of the government enterprises in the 1880s, is therefore hard to place on the scale of degrees of state intervention. Equally, though, the occurrence in other developing states, not necessarily all in 'Confucian' East Asia, of similar kinds of industrial-policy activity, whereby a well-trained and high-status bureaucracy seeks to induce private-sector enterprises to pursue national economic goals, suggests that what we are observing is not a unique Japanese phenomenon, but rather the earliest historical example of the challenge to prevailing models and formulations represented by what has come to be known as the developmental state.

Similarly, just as the pattern of state intervention in Japan's early economic development is hard to fit into standard systems of classification, so are her pre-war trade relations hard to locate along the scale of possible trade strategies. Elements of import substitution, export promotion and unprotected interaction with the world economy can all be found at various times and in various industries. Pre-war Japanese bureaucrats could therefore be seen as feeling their way, not always safely, through the minefield of conflicting domestic and international forces and interests, towards the kind of pragmatic, *ad hoc* but goal-oriented industrial and trade strategy, generally credited with such success both in post-war Japan and in newly-industrialising Third World countries, under which those areas of economic activity which can effectively compete under free world-market conditions are allowed to do so, while those which cannot receive specific government protection in return for contributing towards national economic targets. Thus some industries, such as iron and steel, automobiles and shipping, were protected in quite straightforward ways not uncommon elsewhere at the time or since, but others, such as textiles, coped with, adapted to, and eventually profited from world market conditions, for a variety of reasons, including their pre-Meiji inheritance, economically-explicable entrepreneurial activity, the role (or lack of it) of foreign businesses, and luck, but with only marginal or background support from the state.

Throughout our discussion of the role of the state in Japan's development it has generally been taken for granted that Japanese industrialisation in the pre-World War II period represents a success story, as indeed, when compared with the experiences of other developing countries then and since, it probably does. Consideration of problems such as the emergence of inequalities between the traditional and modern sectors or the use of inappropriate technology, which have frequently been laid at the door of the development strategies pursued by post-war developing countries, have therefore been reserved for later sections, but will need to be borne in mind in any overall assessment of Japanese development strategy. Finally, it should also not be forgotten that, although in many respects the kind of combined import-substitution and export-promotion strategy pursued by pre-war Japanese governments could be regarded as relatively successful in the prevailing conditions of the late nineteenth and early twentieth centuries, the strategic targeting and protecting of key industries in pursuit of national goals, which the method involved, was already bringing Japan into economic conflict with the rest of the world in the much more protectionist environment of the 1930s, alongside the emerging political and military confrontation between Japanese and Western interests in Asia and the Pacific. As the 'trade friction' results of developmental-state industrial policy have made themselves apparent in the 1980s, not just to Japan but also to the 'little Japans' of East Asia, the extent to which the mass of contemporary developing countries can employ similar methods may be called into doubt.

Part II
Agriculture and economic development

Part II

Agriculture and economic development

5 Introduction

Agriculture paramount importance for Survival

It is a commonplace of economic development textbooks that under-developed countries are, more or less by definition, predominantly agricultural ones. That is to say, a large proportion of the population, ranging from 80 per cent in the least developed nations to around 35–40 per cent in semi-industrialised ones, depend for their livelihoods on agricultural activity. The proportion of total GDP contributed by agricultural production is generally somewhat smaller, reflecting both the relatively low labour productivity of agricultural work, as compared with industrial work, and the fact that many rural dwellers employed in agriculture spend at least some of their time in other non-agricultural occupations, but nonetheless agriculture, when defined as the production of food and raw materials grown on the land, still represents, in the majority of developing countries, the most significant form of economic activity. Furthermore, when comparisons are made with the economic structures of developed nations, the relative weight of the agricultural sector emerges as the most significant and consistent difference between rich and poor countries and it is obvious that a richer society is one which is able to produce and provide a wide range of industrially-manufactured goods over and above the basic necessities which agriculture generates. It follows from this that the process of economic development can very broadly be seen as one involving the proportional shift of resources out of agriculture and into the manufacturing and service sectors which dominate advanced economies.

The basic reason for this clearly lies in the nature of the products agriculture produces. The human being's capacity to consume food has its limits and as incomes rise, it is increasingly other kinds of goods that are demanded (that is, agricultural products have low income elasticity of demand). But there are also supply-side constraints on the ability of agriculture to raise the productivity of the inputs it uses which are inherent in the nature of production from the land itself. It has proved possible to raise yields, through the application of ever-increasing quantities of labour and fertiliser, to a degree never envisaged by those early economists who prophesied that diminishing returns in agriculture (combined with Malthusian population growth) would bring an end to any period of economic growth. But nevertheless the supply of cultivable land is ultimately finite and the returns from investment of resources in agriculture must eventually fall below those obtainable from industrial activities dependent on more abundant, varied and easily accessible inputs. Moreover, and perhaps more importantly, the cultivation of crops depends on the seasons and, despite great advances in the techniques of multiple cropping, necessarily involves a sequence of operations, ruling out the possibility of the kind of division of labour and simultaneous specialised production of individual components which Adam Smith saw as the essence of industry's ability to raise the productivity of economic resources.

The dependence of agricultural production on the controlled use of land under the passage of the seasons also results in the most significant characteristic of its economic organisation, since it severely limits the scope for economies of scale and hence the size of production units. Even the largest Australian or American farms, equipped with planes and all manner of large-scale agricultural machinery, are tiny businesses, in terms of turnover, employment and so on, in comparison with most industrial undertakings in their economies. Attempts to organise agriculture within large-scale co-operative or socialist enterprises have encountered enormous difficulties; few farms, even in the richest agricultural nations, justify joint-stock, limited-liability company status or employ more than a handful of workers each, and it has more or less universally proved to be the case that relatively small-scale operations, frequently based on the family, have persisted as the most viable and successful organisational forms in settled cultivation.

These factors – the inevitable decline in the importance of agriculture as a nation grows more prosperous and the marked differences between agricultural and industrial production as economic activities – led early development theorists, right back to Ricardo, Mill and Marx, to view economic development as a process of interaction between two distinct sectors of the economy, labelled industry and agriculture, with industry growing on the basis of resources drawn from agriculture. Post-World War II theorists, mostly from advanced-country backgrounds but faced with the problems and potential of the newly-independent Third World, rediscovered the earlier 'classical' economists' work on the industrialisation process. They relabelled the agriculture/industry distinction rural/urban or traditional/modern, and it was this two-sector or dual-economy approach which dominated thinking about development in the 1950s and '60s, profoundly affecting, among other things, the understanding of Japan's industrialisation process.

The seminal model of this kind was W. A. Lewis' reworking of the 'classical' economists' two-sector approach to economic growth (Lewis 1954). This was followed by more sophisticated versions, such as the well-known Ranis/Fei model which made extensive use of the Japanese example (Ranis and Fei 1964), but all began from the basic assumptions that, in underdeveloped economies, 'agricultural' or 'traditional' households controlled the bulk of available capital and labour resources, which they could only utilise at low levels of productivity, and that development depended on the transfer of those resources to the 'modern' industrial sector. The models then specified the various mechanisms whereby this transfer of resources might be achieved.

As far as the transfer of capital or savings was concerned, industrial growth could occur if any surplus output or income generated in the traditional sector was used to invest in the creation of modern industrial capacity. This could be facilitated in a number of ways: farmers could simply be taxed to provide government revenue to invest in industrial projects; better-off farmers might invest their profits, rents or savings in the establishment of industrial enterprises, or cultivators could be induced to sell their produce at low prices, enabling it to be resold at higher prices in urban areas to yield profits for reinvestment (an indirect way of taxing farmers). Better still, farmers could be encouraged to grow export crops, which would generate both investible profits and the foreign exchange needed to import capital equipment for new industries. Industrialisation therefore required some institutional mechanism whereby 'surplus' agricultural production, presently being consumed within the agricultural sector for traditional uses or, as we shall see shortly, as the means of supporting unproductive workers, could be drawn off to create modern industrial production capacity.

The other side of the transfer involved the workers who would be needed to man the growing modern industries and these too would have to be drawn from agriculture. Here many, though not all, dual-economy models make use of a further, more specific assumption: that a significant proportion of the labour force occupied in the traditional agricultural sector contributed little, or at least less than they ate, to agricultural output and could therefore move to higher-productivity industrial work without any loss in overall farm production.[1] This depended on the dual-economy model's analysis of the way in which farm households operated as economic units. Thus it was assumed that the farm family would divide up its income among its members regardless of how much any individual was able to contribute, unlike the standard industrial enterprise which only employs those whose contribution to output (marginal product) equals or exceeds the wage they receive. Hence, 'surplus' workers, who consumed more than their marginal product, could leave agriculture for industry, where they could contribute much more to total production, without reducing the overall availability of farm output. The remaining farm households could market, or pay as taxes, the produce formerly consumed by their surplus relatives, and this could be used to feed the growing urban industrial labour force. As long as such 'surplus' workers existed in the agricultural sector, they could be recruited by industrial employers at constant wages little above the subsistence they had received in the traditional sector, thereby leaving investible profits in the hands of industrial entrepreneurs.[2]

These models provided a relatively optimistic development scenario, within which the 'agricultural surplus' was redirected towards the creation of employment in industry; output and incomes gradually rose, as a result of the superior productivity of industrial work, and the economy was steadily transformed. As we shall see, the Japanese case was used as one of the prime examples of this process, illustrating the way in which a dual-economy development sequence could successfully occur. Moreover, thinking along these lines fitted in with and reinforced the approach to agriculture generally prevalent among Third World governments and planners in the 1950s and '60s. The passive role of the traditional sector in the model, according to which agriculture simply gives up resources to the industrial sector and itself demands little or no new investment, appeared to provide a theoretical justification for the neglect of agriculture generally promoted by the prevailing mood of what Michael Lipton was to christen 'urban bias' (Lipton 1977). Development and industrialisation were assumed to be synonymous; the key to economic growth lay in the creation of new modern industries, most frequently protected behind tariff barriers, and investment in raising output or improving conditions in rural areas (which Western-educated and -inspired planners and politicians tended anyway to regard as uncouth backwaters from which they had successfully escaped) was unnecessary because the growth created by the transfer of the surplus to industry would eventually pull the agricultural sector up behind it as wages rose and markets grew.

The problems to which this approach to development gave rise are by now widely recognised. A number of developing countries employing dualist ISI strategies did achieve high rates of growth of their modern industrial sectors, but, given the capital-intensive nature of the technology required to match that of the developed nations, relatively little industrial employment was created. The farm sector proved largely unwilling or unable to yield up any surplus it might have been producing: the rural rich turned out to be unsurprisingly difficult to tax, and any surplus generated by the mass of smaller-scale cultivators was being eaten away by population growth substantially more rapid than that experienced during the course of the industrialisation of the presently developed countries (including Japan). Developing nations were thus forced to rely increasingly on imports, foreign aid and overseas borrowing to support their industrialisation programmes and at the same time food shortages and rising prices resulted in unrest among urban workers. Rural dwellers nonetheless continued to migrate to the cities, attracted by the hope of the urban jobs which would provide prospects and conditions far superior to anything agriculture could offer, even if this meant a long period of waiting in one of the shanty towns which sprang up around many Third World cities. In planned economies, attempts to force farmers into institutional organisations (e.g. collective farms) which would permit the transfer of the surplus to industry met with considerable resistance and proved generally ineffective in sustaining levels of output sufficient to match urban needs and population growth. The idea of the dual economy became less the basis for a model of economic development and more an expression of the growing divergence in output growth, living standards and general conditions of life between the rural areas of Third World nations and their modern industrial enclaves.

The emergence of these problems brought about a degree of rethinking among development theorists and planners. The extent to which rapid industrial growth had led to anything which might be called development for the mass of the Third World population was questioned and a new approach, laying stress less on growth rates and more on indicators of the provision of 'basic needs', was developed. This involved efforts to reverse the neglect of agriculture and it was against this background that there emerged, to reinforce these trends, the new technological potential in agriculture whose realisation came to be known as the Green Revolution. This potential was embodied in the package of new methods, centring on the use of high-yielding, fertiliser-responsive varieties of rice and wheat, which began to be diffused through parts of Asia and Central America from the late 1960s. Green Revolution seed varieties, initially developed by national and international agricultural research bodies (in the case of rice, on the basis of varieties bred in pre-war Japan), opened up the possibility that the investment of resources in agriculture, in, for example, irrigation improvements or the provision of credit and extension services to farmers, was not only necessary to halt the decline in rural living conditions and urban food supplies, but might also yield a high return for a relatively small outlay. Rural development thus began to receive a much higher priority, at least among aid agencies and development theorists.

This shift in macroeconomic approach and the emergence of new technological potential in agriculture also brought about a reconsideration of the microeconomic and institutional assumptions being made about the nature of the farm households whose responses would be crucial to the achievement of the new rural-development objectives. Dual-economy models had tended to regard farm households as passive suppliers of resources, operating according to traditional forms of organisation which would wither away into modern types of business enterprise as development proceeded. They did not therefore encourage much research into the ways in which farm household economies actually operated in developing countries. Some attempts had been made, however, to test the surplus labour hypothesis and these had, for the most part, failed to find unequivocal evidence that farm households were maintaining substantial numbers of workers whose labour contributed little or nothing to the family's income, at least when looked at over the agricultural year as a whole. Such findings led on to further empirical and theoretical study, along the borderlines between economics and anthropology, into the ways in which farm households in poor countries worked, and the spread of the Green Revolution provided much increased scope for research into the responses of farmers and rural communities to the availability of new technology.

The picture of the rural sector which began to emerge from this work, though varied, was in general rather different from the 'traditional', 'backward' and largely passive characterisation assumed in the dual-economy model. In many cases, Third World farm households were shown to be responsive to changes in prices, to be making as effective a use as possible of the resources available to them, and to possess a valuable understanding of the environment in which they operated. However, it also had to be acknowledged that this environment frequently imposed constraints on farm-household decisions different from those which applied to, for example, modern-sector industrial enterprises. For households operating close to subsistence level, the problem of risk, for instance, was of a different order from that facing the textbook firms of developed countries. More broadly, the constraints imposed by land tenure arrangements and the associated social and political structures of village communities also had to be taken into account in analysis of the overall rural economy. The responses of a share-cropping tenant would be different from those of an owner–cultivator or landlord, and each might have to take account of the reactions of the others within the wider context of village social and economic relations. The communal organisation of some areas of resource allocation, most notably the supply of irrigation water, also had to be recognised.

Such analysis came into its own as the impact of the Green Revolution became more widespread and the nature of agrarian change a more pressing and controversial issue. The emergence of the Green Revolution could be seen as an excellent illustration of the theory of 'induced technical change', which argued that new technology does not just appear as 'manna from heaven' but is consciously produced by research activity deliberately directed towards economising on those resources which are becoming scarcer, and hence relatively more expensive, within the particular economy concerned. Thus, technical change in agriculture in land-abundant but labour-scarce countries such as the United States moved in the direction of greater mechanisation, substituting land and capital for labour, and raising output per worker. In land-scarce but labour-abundant areas, such as pre-war Japan or many present-day developing countries, on the other hand, research would be directed towards discovering new techniques which would save on land by applying greater quantities of capital (fertiliser) and labour, resulting in higher yields per unit of land.[3] What is more, given that Green Revolution technology appeared to be of this latter kind, and assuming that it was suited to the environment of the particular region in question, there seemed, on the face of it, no obvious reason why all farmers, whether large-scale or small-scale, owner or tenant, should not be able to adopt it. Seed and fertiliser are infinitely divisible inputs, neutral to scale in economic terms, and the new methods and higher yields might be expected to raise the returns to the work of the family labour force, thus intensifying the widely observed tendency for higher yields on smaller family farms than on larger holdings.

However, although the numerous studies of the distributional impact of the spread of the Green Revolution produced sometimes conflicting results, it seemed generally to be the case that larger-scale farmers adopted the new methods earlier and more widely, and at times followed up their advantage by evicting tenants, disposing of hired workers and cultivating on a larger scale with the use of tractors and other machinery (see e.g. Griffin 1979: ch. 3). Such results could only be explained by taking into account the larger-scale landowner's superior access to information about the new technology (through greater literacy, clout with the extension services, etc.), to credit with which to purchase commercial inputs, to the reliable water supplies on which successful application of the technology depends, and to other such advantages arising from social and political power and influence. Where it made sense within the economic and environmental constraints under which they operated, smaller-scale farmers did adopt and apply Green Revolution techniques, and their livelihoods did improve, provided the income effects of rising yields were not offset by reductions in opportunities for employment outside the household. Nonetheless, there could be no doubt that the spread of new agricultural technology, which clearly raised output and helped to solve the food-shortage problems of a number of Third World countries, at the same time had profound effects on economic and social relations in the countryside and on the responses of rural dwellers to the growth of industry.

By this stage it will have become clear that the 'peasant' farm household can no longer be regarded as a mere passive supplier of the resources required for industrialisation. Its responses can condition the character and success of the development process and cannot be ignored or assumed away. In recent years, moreover, interest in peasant societies has broadened beyond the scope of strictly economic models in the direction of efforts to understand the operations of agricultural communities in terms of the ways in which rural households themselves envisage their situations. The seminal work in this field was *The Moral Economy of the Peasant*, in which James Scott sought to explain peasant rebellions in nineteenth-century Indo–China through analysis of the 'moral reactions' of peasant farmers (Scott 1976). Scott argued that social and economic relations within pre-capitalist village communities were governed by the imperative of ensuring subsistence and that small-scale cultivators accepted their dependent status in, for example, patron–client or landlord–sharecropper relationships as a means of sharing the burden of risk, as long as the superior household used its economic strength to lessen the threat to the survival of the weaker household. Attempts by the rural elite, under the influence of colonisation, to introduce market or capitalist relations which broke this underlying subsistence insurance relationship threatened the survival of small-scale farm households and provoked moral reactions on their part which in their extreme form gave rise to revolt and rebellion. Opponents of Scott (e.g. Popkin 1979) argued that he was romanticising the pre-capitalist village and that entry into market relations might not necessarily be deleterious to the livelihoods of poorer farm households. They might even in fact seek access to the market where they saw this as providing better opportunities than existed within dependent relations with richer households. The important point, however, is that both Scott and his critics make the common assumption that the actions of peasant farmers represent explicable responses to, and efforts to change, the situations they face, whether these are treated in more narrowly economic terms or more broadly in relation to the social, political and cultural structures of peasant communities. Furthermore, they illustrate how these reactions can profoundly influence the direction of economic and political change in developing and industrialising societies.

Thus, approaches to the part played by agriculture in economic development have moved far away from the initial dual-economy models to a point where the characteristics of agrarian society and agricultural technology are beginning to be viewed as crucial determinants of the whole pattern of industrialisation, and the active responses of farmers themselves are seen as forces which development planners ignore at their nations' perils. Acceptance of this approach furthermore implies that, since the underlying environmental and technical conditions of agricultural production in most present-day Third World countries differ markedly from those in the generally more land-abundant, temperate conditions of the now-developed Western nations, development models based on the experience of the presently advanced countries may not be the most appropriate ones to adopt in the effort to understand contemporary development and underdevelopment. For example, intensive rice cultivation exhibits a number of characteristics which differentiate the institutional and economic organisation of rice-growing societies from that of societies based on the cultivation of other grains. Intensive rice cultivation depends on the provision of a reliable supply of irrigation water, which in turn implies a degree of inter-household co-operation and mutual interdependence not necessitated by land-intensive arable farming; through the effective use of the fertilising properties of irrigation water, it can sustain highly intensive multiple cropping, meaning that large amounts of labour can be productively absorbed and contribute to output on a relatively limited land area, and this at the same time provides abundant sources of slack seasonal labour time, tied to the land but available for other forms of economic activity, so that rice cultivation is frequently combined with side-line employment of many kinds.[4] The impact of such characteristics on, for example, demographic trends, the location and technology of industry, or the pattern of migration and urbanisation might be expected to generate an industrialisation process with rather different features from that experienced in the now-developed West.

Japan was the first rice-cultivating nation to become highly industrialised. On the face of it, the pattern of her industrialisation had enough in common with those of the Western developed nations, for instance as regards the macroeconomic decline in the relative share of agriculture in employment and output, to encourage early analysts to see her as a highly successful example of the basic two-sector development model.[5] However, as the problems inherent in applying this approach to the present-day Third World have become more apparent, and indeed as economic historians studying European development have come to view industrialisation as a more gradual and rural-based process, playing down the idea of a dramatic 'take-off' based on a purely industrial revolution,[6] Japan's experience takes on a new significance. In what follows, therefore, we shall look not only at the macroeconomic contribution of agricultural change to Japan's development, but also at micro-level historical evidence from a number of sources, anthropological and sociological as well as economic, concerning the role of rural Japanese men and women, industrially or agriculturally employed, in shaping the features of industrialisation in a densely-populated rice-growing society.

6 The macroeconomic role of agriculture in Japan's development

Settled agriculture, based on the techniques of rice cultivation, was probably brought to the Japanese islands around the third century BC by the influx of migrants from the Asian mainland known as the Yayoi people. Over the centuries thereafter, cultivation systems developed to high levels of technical sophistication to suit the climatic and geographic conditions of the various parts of the country. Paddy rice, which was capable of being grown annually without fallow periods and thus of supporting a densely-packed population on a limited land area, was cultivated wherever conditions permitted, but depended on a reliable supply of irrigation water. In Japan, where the annual rainy season (*tsuyu*) is only a poor relation of a full-scale monsoon and where the rivers are for the most part too short and fast-flowing to produce the great floodplains characteristic of other parts of Asia, the construction of man-made facilities for the storage and controlled distribution of water was a precondition for rice growing. Hence the spread of cultivation generally had to be preceded by a heavy investment of labour and resources on the part of farmers, not only for land clearance but also for the construction of dams, reservoirs and feeder-channel systems. Dryland cultivation of other grains, as well as pulses, fruit, vegetables and industrial crops (e.g. cotton), was also practised, of course, both in regions where paddy rice could not be grown and elsewhere on cultivable higher ground which could not be irrigated. Livestock were a rarity, though, being unsuited to the mountainous and damp environment, and pulses, particularly the soya bean, remained the chief source of protein, in addition to fish, in the traditionally vegetarian Japanese diet.

The initial construction and subsequent maintenance of irrigation facilities normally required the co-operation of a number of families, sometimes under the direction of feudal rulers or merchant investors, but the land so prepared generally came to be cultivated on a day-to-day basis by individual households, living in villages built on higher ground and surrounded by the paddy fields. Cultivation was thus directed by individual family heads, using household labour, but mutual co-operation among village households was essential in matters such as the allocation of water and the supply of labour at peak times, and communal organisation, both of the village as a whole and of groups within it (e.g. based on kinship) remained strong. Such organisation depended on and reinforced hierarchical social relationships between households which acted to reduce risk and provide mutual security.

By the Tokugawa period, the limits to the geographical spread of cultivation had been reached in many parts of the country, especially in the most heavily populated regions of south-western Japan where climatic conditions were most favourable. Later chapters will describe the technical, social and economic changes which resulted from the increasing intensification of economic activity as the period progressed. From the administrative point of view, with the institutionalisation of the Tokugawa system, villages retained and strengthened their autonomy as groups of cultivating households, while the specialised warrior class, who had once been cultivators and landowners themselves, left the land to serve their lords in the castle towns. However, the taxation of agriculture was the source of the livelihood of the ruling class and samurai administrators continued regularly to descend on the villages of their domains to assess and collect tax payments in rice and to administer law and order. A lord's wealth and power depended on the size and productivity of the land he controlled and the *daimyō* were ranked according to the assessed yields, in terms of volume of rice, of their domains. As their expenses rose with the commercialisation and development of the economy, feudal administrators were driven to try to extract more from the agricultural areas under their control, both through higher tax rates and through the encouragement of output increases, while villages in their turn sought to evade such impositions and to diversify their agricultural and other activities outside the net of the lords' tax-gatherers.

This, then, in brief, was the agricultural basis on which the new Meiji government had to build its development programme. With the abolition of the taxation rights and other privileges of the samurai and *daimyō* class, the Land Tax Reform, begun in 1873, placed in the hands of the new Meiji state the agricultural revenue previously used to support the non-cultivating feudal upper class. Moreover, although the survey accompanying the Reform for the most part gave title to land to the cultivator, thus leaving the majority of the cultivable area in the hands of small-scale owner-farmers, the subsequent continued spread of market relations in the countryside, itself in part the result of the conversion of the former feudal taxes in kind into taxes payable in cash, intensified the trend, observable even during the Tokugawa period in more advanced areas, towards the growth of tenancy. Thus a discernible landlord class also began to emerge, in control of a portion of the 'agricultural surplus' and representing a further potential mechanism for the transfer of investable resources into industry.

Given these developments, and the significance frequently attached to the role of the Meiji state in initiating and supporting industrialisation (see ch. 2), it was natural to view the Restoration and the Land Tax Reform as the starting points for a two-sector development process along the lines described earlier, whereby an 'agricultural surplus', transferred as taxation and other kinds of savings flow, provided the funds for industrial investment and growth. Certainly, in the broadest sense, given the predominance of agriculture in the nineteenth-century Japanese economy, it has to be the case that the foundations of development lay in the countryside and the initial resources invested in the transformation of state, economy and society had to be derived from the rural sector. Moreover, the pattern of structural change in the economy followed the pattern described by the standard two-sector development model, with a steady decline in agriculture's share of GDP, from around 40 per cent in the 1880s to 27 per cent in 1920 and 14 per cent by 1940, and of the gainfully employed population, from over 70 per cent in the 1880s to around 50 per cent by 1920 and 40 per cent by 1940.[1] Nevertheless, as we shall see later in this and other sections, the process of structural transformation and resource transfer was a more complex, and less strictly uni-directional, one than that portrayed in this straightforward model.

THE 'JAPANESE MODEL' OF AGRICULTURE'S ROLE IN DEVELOPMENT

Our present understanding of the macroeconomic structure of Japan's development process is largely the result of the monumental efforts of Professor Ohkawa and his colleagues at Hitotsubashi University in Tokyo in establishing the statistical basis for the long-term analysis of their country's economic growth.[2] The long-standing practices of data collection by the Japanese bureaucracy have made possible the compilation of aggregate series for the major macroeconomic indicators, such as those just used above, which go back to the 1880s, and it was on the basis of such official government figures that Ohkawa and others first began to describe and model intersectoral relations between agriculture and industry during Japan's industrialisation. The analysis which emerged from this work made use of a number of the conceptual tools of two-sector, dual-economy development models and sought to show how a successful development process had been achieved through the transfer of resources from a developing and changing agricultural sector to a growing industrial one, without the prior condition of an 'agricultural revolution'. The picture I shall label the 'Japanese model' of agriculture's role in development is a composite of the work of a number of scholars but generally reflects what was, in many ways, a path-breaking approach to the analysis of Japan's economic history within a non-Marxist, internationally comparative, theoretical framework.

Ohkawa's initial work on the overall pattern of agricultural change during Japan's industrialisation was based on figures collected in the course of the tax-collecting activities of government officials. Indicators such as rice yields and agricultural output per person derived from these figures suggested that Japan began her industrialisation process in the mid-nineteenth century on an agricultural base no more favourable than that prevailing in a number of developing countries in the 1950s.[3] The pattern of growth in agricultural output and inputs thereafter, based on the Ohkawa group's (LTES) revision of the official statistics, is shown in table 6.1. In the period up to World War I, agricultural output appeared to grow at a steady rate, substantially above the growth of population and in general faster than that achieved in pre-Green Revolution Asia. The growth rate fell in the inter-war period, but began to pick up again in the later 1930s and accelerated further after World War II. Analysis of the trends in inputs of land, labour and capital suggested that the source of the relatively rapid growth of agricultural output lay in the spread of Green Revolution-type technical changes which appeared to require little capital investment but which resulted in a more productive use of existing land and labour. Meanwhile, the land tax was providing the major part of the government revenue used to stimulate industrialisation, food supplies to the growing urban population were being maintained and rural savings, labour and export earnings (from silk and tea) were all contributing to the concurrent expansion of industry.

Table 6.1 Growth in agriculture output and inputs 1880–1935 (% p.a.) (A)

	Total production	Rice output	Sericultural output	Labour input(B)	Land input (C)	Fertiliser input
1880–1900	1.5	0.9	3.9	0.1	0.5	1.6
1900–1920	1.8	1.7	4.7	−0.6	0.7	7.7
1920–1935	0.9	0.4	1.7	−0.1	0.1	3.4

(A) Based on five-year averages, 1934–6 prices
(B) Male and female workers gainfully employed in agriculture
(C) Arable land area
Source: Ohkawa and Shinohara (1979): tables 4.6, 4.2, 4.3; 86–8

The accepted picture of sectoral growth patterns in the course of industrialisation in the West involved an initial increase in agricultural output and productivity (an 'agricultural revolution') preceding the growth of urban industry and generating the surplus available for transfer to industrial investment. The Japanese case, as outlined above, seemed to offer a rather different, and more optimistic, form of dual-economy development, in that, although the Restoration had placed the pre-existing agricultural surplus in the hands of the modernising state, it appeared to be, more significantly, subsequent growth in agricultural output which generated agriculture's ability to provide resources for industrialisation. The transfer of labour, savings and other resources did not seem to have inhibited this growth, and the technical change on which it depended was such that it seemed to require little in the way of resource flows from industry to agriculture. The spread of previously-known techniques, based on higher-yielding varieties and making more intensive use of labour and of locally-supplied fertiliser, had raised the output of food and export crops but at the same time had enabled agriculture to give up surplus labour time to new industrial enterprises and release its savings for non-agricultural uses.

According to this picture, this relatively cost-free process of technical change, 'taking up the slack' in Gustav Ranis' description (Ranis 1969), which produced both a more productive use of existing inputs in the rural sector and the ability to release surplus resources to industry, proceeded through the late nineteenth and early twentieth centuries, to the accompaniment of gradually rising agricultural prices. Subsequently, the rapid rise in food prices which followed the World War I industrial boom, and triggered the urban Rice Riots of 1918, signalled the exhaustion of the potential represented by the 'slack' and marked the end of agriculture's model contribution to the development process. In the inter-war period, alongside the slow-down in output growth, farmers were hard hit by price declines during the depressions of the late '20s and early '30s, and the plight of the rural sector became a national issue. The relative decline in farm incomes and the distressed conditions in some rural areas (notably the north-east) during the 1929–31 depression are frequently cited as major causes of discontent among the junior army and navy officers pressing for new policies and a greater military role in government during the '30s. In addition, in response to the Rice Riots efforts had been made to develop the production of food crops for the Japanese market in Japan's newly-acquired colonies, and the results of this, in the form of rice imports supplying about 20 per cent of the home market in the inter-war period, helped to keep prices down and discouraged the investment of resources in staple food production at home (Hayami and Ruttan 1971: 219). But the underlying problem was the shift to a situation in which output growth could only be achieved through the development of more diversified, mechanised and capital-intensive techniques in agriculture. Progress along these lines was beginning to be made in more advanced areas in the late '30s, but came into its own alongside the rapid industrial growth and urbanisation of the economic miracle period, resulting in the emergence of the small-scale but mechanised part-time farm households who produce the 'rice mountains' sent to plague recent Japanese governments.

Nevertheless, despite the problems of the inter-war period, the macroeconomic performance of Japanese agriculture over the course of industrialisation could be seen, on the basis of the initially available data, to present a new and hopeful model to later developing countries. From a roughly equivalent starting point, that is, without a prior agricultural revolution, Japan's small-scale, family-based rice cultivators had increased and diversified their output, while simultaneously releasing resources for use in industry and making few demands on the urban industrial sector. Freed from the restrictions of the Tokugawa system, but without any other major institutional reform, they had utilised their own resources of labour, capital and technical knowledge to produce the surplus that industrial growth required. The value of studying the successful Japanese experience of industrialisation had been established, but, as we shall now go on to see, the model was not without its critics, and in the challenges they presented lay the seeds of an approach which, it might be argued, provides a basis for transcending the original dual-economy development idea.

MODIFYING THE MODEL

The 'Japanese model' of the role of agriculture in a two-sector development sequence, and the efforts to establish the macro-statistical basis on which it stood, represented a major advance both in understanding the process of industrialisation in Japan and in enabling it to be compared with experience elsewhere. Like other such advances, however, it also stimulated criticism and new research refining and remodelling it. Much of the resulting work, detailing the economic, technical and institutional changes which underlay the model, will be considered in later chapters and will be argued to create the potential, at least, for a more accurate picture of the industrialisation process in a rice-cultivating society. But first it will be useful to set out some of the more strictly macroeconomic criticisms and modifications of the original, path-breaking, 'Japanese model' approach, which paved the way for later, more detailed, microeconomic studies.

In many ways the most serious and, on the surface at least, critical and controversial challenge to the Japanese model was the attack on its statistical foundations made by James Nakamura (Nakamura 1966). Nakamura argued that the official statistics from which Ohkawa had derived his agricultural production series substantially underestimated the levels of output and yields achieved by Japanese farmers around the time of the Meiji Restoration and the Land Tax Reform. He showed that villages had continued to make use of long-standing practices designed to conceal sources of output and undervalue yields, so as to reduce their tax payments. The figures obtained by the officials who administered the early Meiji land tax do not therefore reflect the extent to which farmers were already reaping the benefits of improved cultivation practices, irrigation development and so on, before the Restoration.[4] Subsequently, however, tax collection procedures gradually became more efficient and, with falling tax rates, the incentive for farm households to make efforts to conceal their sources of agricultural income declined. Hence, through the latter part of the nineteenth century, previously concealed output emerged in the statistics, giving the appearance of production increase. The import of Nakamura's work was therefore that the 'concurrent growth' of agriculture and industry, which had distinguished Japanese experience from that assumed to have occurred in the West and had been such a hopeful aspect of the Japanese model, was a statistical illusion. Rather, Japanese industrialisation had taken place on the basis of a pre-existing increase in agricultural output and productivity, along the lines of the agricultural revolutions which were thought to have preceded Western industrial revolutions.

Nakamura made some estimates of his own as to the levels of yields and agricultural output per head at the start of Japanese industrialisation, which suggested that these were substantially higher than those achieved in post-war developing Asian countries. Table 6.2 compares the various available estimates with figures for rice yields in other Asian countries at a comparable stage in their development. Given that arable land area per person was lower in Japan than elsewhere, the official figures suggest that the agricultural basis on which Japanese industrialisation began was no more favourable than that of present-day developing countries, whereas Nakamura's estimates imply a significantly greater availability of agricultural goods. Nakamura's own estimates were not widely accepted in themselves but they sparked off considerable debate and a search for alternative indicators of output levels and growth (e.g. calorie intake), and they led to some revision of the official output series. These revised figures are the ones which appear in volume 9 of the LTES series (see p. 260, note 3) and are widely used, although it would be hard to say that the controversy was ever really resolved. Rather, as later sections will indicate, the focus of enquiry has tended to shift to a more detailed examination of the forces underlying nineteenth-century agricultural development in Japan.

Table 6.2 Estimates of pre-industrial rice yields in Japan and other Asian countries

	Paddy rice yield (ton/ha)
Japan 1878–82	
Official figures	2.36
LTES (revised official)	2.53
Nakamura's estimate	3.22
Elsewhere in Asia 1953–62 (FAO figures)	
India	1.36
Thailand	1.38
Indonesia	1.74
Malaya	2.24
Korea	2.75
Taiwan	2.93

Source: Hayami and Yamada (1969), table 1: 108

As regards the overall mechanism of the industrialisation process, however, Nakamura remained within the dual-economy tradition. His attack on the Japanese model approach essentially concerned the *origins* of the surplus which was transferred to create the modern industrial sector in the later nineteenth century. He argued that the transfer was a reallocation of a pre-existing surplus, away from support of the feudal upper classes and 'traditional' forms of expenditure and towards industrial investment, but he did not challenge the assumption that industrialisation depended on the inter-sectoral transfer of resources. Others, though, did begin to ask questions as to the scale and significance of agriculture's contribution to industrial growth. For example, the land tax was undoubtedly the largest source of government income in the early years of the Meiji state, but it had been eclipsed by other sources of revenue by the turn of the century (Minami 1986: 340). It is difficult to argue that full-scale urban industrialisation had begun by that point and anyway, as we saw in part I, serious doubts have been raised as to the direct significance of state expenditure for early industrialisation.

In recent years a number of attempts have been made to measure in a more sophisticated way the contribution to industrial investment of transfers from agriculture, whether forced, through taxation, or voluntary, through investments by agricultural households in industrial undertakings. Apart from the question of whether or not taxation of agriculture should in fact be included, numerous difficulties bedevil such calculations, since the categories within which statistical data exist are not always the appropriate ones, especially in the early stages of development. Hence a farm household might carry out investment by using its own resources to improve the irrigation and drainage of its fields, or transfer savings from agriculture to industry by constructing its own silk-weaving workshop, in statistically totally unrecorded operations. Ohkawa and Mundle (1979), who try as far as possible to overcome these problems, conclude that the significance of the transfer depends on the point of view. If taxation is included, it does appear that a significant proportion of the savings (excess of income over expenditure) generated in agricultural activity must have found its way, by one means or another, into the hands of the state or of non-agricultural investors. However, this accounted for only quite a small proportion of the value of the investment taking place outside agriculture. Hence, although the transfer of resources from agriculture did represent quite a heavy burden on the traditional sector, the bulk of industrial investment was still financed through resources generated within the industrial sector itself. Given the additional likelihood that a great many savings and investment transactions have gone unrecorded, unequivocal statements to the effect that agriculture provided the funds on which state and private industrial investment depended have therefore to be treated with a degree of caution. A better understanding of the savings and investment interactions between agriculture and industry, and of the terms on which, and forms through which, agricultural households gave up their surplus funds to industrial uses, awaits further microeconomic study.

Similar questions can also be raised as to the role of the transfer of labour from agriculture to industry during Japan's industrialisation. The early Japanese model approach saw agriculture as a reservoir of surplus labour available for transfer to industry in the manner suggested by dual-economy theories. Although the absolute size of the agricultural population and the total number of farm households changed little before World War II, migration based on population growth facilitated a relative increase in the size of the industrial labour force and it is clear that many early industrial workers had their roots in rural households. As we saw in chapter 5, however, what matters from the point of view of agriculture's contribution to growth within the dual-economy framework are the terms on which this labour transfer takes place. Thus, if significant numbers of Japanese workers could be seen as having been 'surplus' in agricultural production, they could have been recruited into industry at constant wage rates little above accepted subsistence levels, generating the profits for industrial entrepreneurs which funded investment in the expansion of the modern sector. Hence it was argued that early textile mills, for example, were able to tap the reservoir by recruiting rural girls at low wages because such labour was able to contribute little to the overall agricultural income of farm households. A number of efforts were made to show that the predicted constancy of industrial wage rates as industrial employment increased did in fact exist in pre-World War II Japan, although there was considerable debate as to when this state of affairs ceased to hold ('the turning point'). On the other hand, some have argued that Japanese industrial employers never faced a situation of 'unlimited supplies of labour' and there is considerable evidence that they experienced instead increasing difficulty and expense in recruiting and maintaining their labour forces.[5]

Looked at from the point of view of the farm household also, the intersectoral transfer of labour was not as clear-cut a process as the two-sector interpretation of Japan's experience might imply.

Many rural households carried on both agricultural and industrial activity, for example combining rice cultivation with sericulture and silk reeling or weaving in the home. Since households have generally been categorised, for statistical purposes, according to their 'main' occupation, a relatively minor change in the balance of types of work within the family could appear as a large-scale inter-sectoral labour transfer (Tussing 1969). Furthermore, when we come to consider, in chapter 7, the nature of the changes taking place in agricultural technology, we shall see how it was becoming possible to make fuller and more effective use of the farm family labour force over the course of the year, partly through the spread of double-cropping and more diversified crop rotations, but also through improvements in the ability of the family group to combine farm labour requirments with other paid employment, for example in sericulture, textile work in the home or within commuting distance, or seasonal migrant work. This, along with rising crop yields, expanded the range of possibilities open to rural workers, improving their bargaining power with potential employers and lessening the applicability of a model of straightforward inter-sectoral transfer of surplus labour.

Analysis of inter-sectoral relations at the macro level has thus come to call into question some of the basic assumptions on which two-sector development models, derived fundamentally from European experience of industrialisation, have been based. The clear-cut distinction between the 'traditional' agricultural household and the 'modern' industrial enterprise is increasingly difficult to make as more is known about the structure of industry/agriculture relations in Japan's pre-war economy. Agricultural and industrial activity were intimately connected over the course of Japan's development, but perhaps in much more mutually interdependent ways than the two-sector approach can encompass. Farm households came increasingly to rely on industrially-produced inputs, on outside markets and on income from non-agricultural sources, as industry relied on food and raw materials, as well as labour and investment funds, from agriculture. Farmers were responding to, and themselves affecting, changes in market conditions for labour and goods, in available technology, and in the institutional organisation of industry and commerce. However, we must now turn to the microeconomic level for the evidence of these forces.

7 Technical change in pre-war agriculture

The previous chapter has set out the available macroeconomic evidence concerning agriculture's part in Japan's development. There we saw that, although there has been considerable controversy as to the timing of increases in agricultural output and the scale and significance of the contribution of resources transferred from agriculture to the growing industrial sector, nonetheless it has generally been agreed that Japanese agriculture did develop and change in ways which, to say the least, did not hinder the process of industrialisation.[1] This does appear to represent something of a contrast to the experience of agricultural sectors in many present-day developing countries, the rural areas of which have frequently appeared as neglected backwaters unable to produce the goods required by growing populations and the rising demands of their modern industrial enclaves. The previous chapter concluded that the extent to which macroeconomic data and analysis could explain the contrasting experience of Japan has probably reached its limits and so, in this and the subsequent chapters of part II, we turn to a more detailed consideration of the nature and causes of the technical, economic and institutional changes which constituted agriculture's part in the development process.

Agriculture's successful role in Japan's development depended fundamentally on the ability of the farm sector to increase and diversify the production of agricultural goods to meet the demands of the wider commercialising and industrialising economy. The source of this ability lay not in the expansion of the cultivated area, but rather in technological changes which made possible a more productive use of existing land and labour resources, combined with greater use of fertiliser and other relatively easily produced 'current inputs'. Following Hayami and Ruttan's 'induced innovation' model (Hayami and Ruttan 1971), such a path of technical change could be argued to represent an appropriate response to the relative availability (hence prices) of resources in an environment in which cultivable land is in short supply, and it has features in common with Green Revolution technology in present-day developing countries. However, unlike the Green Revolution case, improvements to the technology of pre-war Japanese agriculture cannot, by and large, be seen as 'imported' or made available to farmers from sources (e.g. international research organisations or state extension services) outside the agricultural sector. Hence, as this section seeks to show, they have to be explained as responses from within the farm sector to the economic, institutional and environmental constraints and changes which farmers faced. Chapter 8 will set this process of technical change in its broader context by examining the wider responses of the farm household sector to the impact of the spread of commerce and industry. First, however, we shall look at the underlying constraints and constants conditioning the cultivation of rice and other crops in Japan, and then at the characteristics, origins and diffusion of the technical changes which lay behind agricultural growth.

TECHNOLOGY AND THE ORGANISATION OF CULTIVATION

The cycle of production

Japan is a country of heavily wooded mountain ranges and only around 14 per cent of her land area is flat enough to be cultivable. As the population has expanded, cultivation has been pushed to the limits through reclamation and drainage of coastal areas and marshes, terracing of hillsides and the use of every tiny corner of land on which something could be grown. This extremely intensive cultivation, combined with the absence of grazing land, leaves the Western visitor with the impression that there is no 'countryside' in Japan: what is not built up is either forested hillside or an area of the continuously cropped, garden-like plots which constitute the Japanese farmer's fields. The climate is classed as temperate, but the high temperatures which follow the May/June rainy season make for uncomfortable summer humidity, contrasting with the pleasant warmth of spring and autumn and the crispness of winter. The south approaches tropical conditions, and winters are warm enough to permit a second grain crop in most regions except the far north and the northern Japan Sea coast, which can lie under snow for several months. In return for this relatively equable general climate, however, the Japanese farmer through the ages has been subjected to typhoons, floods, landslides, earthquakes and assorted other natural disasters, when fate so decreed.

Throughout the era up to World War II and beyond, rice was the crop most favoured by Japanese farmers and consumers and approximately 50 per cent of the cultivated area which could be irrigated to the standard required was almost exclusively devoted to its cultivation. A typical household's holding would consist of one or more irrigated plots suitable for rice, scattered about the area fed by the village's irrigation source, together with unirrigated upland plots and access to woodland. The high yields obtainable from well-irrigated, carefully-cultivated paddy rice explain the very small average size of holdings, with farms of no more than a hectare typical and two or three hectares considered large.

Given the central place of rice in Japanese agriculture, the cycle of production operations through which it was grown constituted the basic framework into which all other activities had to fit, making it the obvious starting-point for consideration of the background against which technical change took place. Most of the rice grown in Japan is of the Japonica type (round-grained and sticky when cooked), which is better suited to cooler climates and more responsive to intensive fertiliser application and cultivation practices than the alternative Indica (long-grain) varieties. Successful cultivation requires carefully controlled conditions and meticulous work, however, and the intensive application of skilled and experienced labour, particularly at key points in the growing cycle, has characterised Japan's rice-growing technology even up to the present day.[2]

The yield of paddy rice (and the scope for double-cropping paddy fields) is substantially enhanced by the practice of bringing on seedlings in a seed-bed early in the growing season and subsequently transplanting them into the field. For the pre-war Japanese farmer, therefore, the production cycle began with the careful selection of seeds for planting into the prepared seed-beds in which they would grow in dense and intensely green profusion. Meanwhile, the preparation of the paddy field itself began with the tilling or ploughing of the land (following the harvest of any winter crop). This was widely carried out by means of manual labour, although the use of draft horses or oxen spread in the nineteenth century, and since World War II the small, mechanised power-tiller has been almost universally adopted. The initial flooding of the field at this stage made possible the preparation of a suitably muddy medium into which the seedlings were transplanted. The operation of transplanting itself was generally viewed as the crucial point, both symbolically and practically, in the agricultural cycle, requiring the mobilisation of all available labour to complete it in time to take advantage of weather and water-supply conditions. The transplanting teams, often organised on a group or exchange-labour basis, moved through the fields at the backbreaking task of setting each individual seedling in its place, encouraged by the promise of celebration at the fieldowner's expense on completion of the work.

After transplanting, the fields needed to be flooded to a greater depth, allowing the seedlings to grow in the standing water which provided nutrients and kept down weed growth, and the greater the control over the timing and level of water supplies, the higher the yields to be expected and the less the risk of crop loss.[3] Pests needed to be kept at bay and unpredictable weather conditions could still ruin the crop. All being well, though, as the heads of grain formed and ripened, the water level could be allowed to fall, in preparation for the autumn harvest. Once again, all available labour was required to cut the plants in the fields, and then thresh, hull and polish the grain ready for consumption, sale or storage.[4]

The operations of rice cultivation were undoubtedly the most important and demanding tasks of the farm year for the majority of households and created the two major peaks in farm labour demand at the times of transplanting and harvesting. Around them, however, could be fitted a range of other kinds of work, either ancillary to rice cultivation itself or involving the production of other crops or goods. The former kind would include the general maintenance of buildings, land and irrigation facilities, or the collection and aplication of various forms of fertiliser, such as compost or silt. The latter kind of work, involving the cultivation of non-rice crops and the processing and manufacture of products in the home, although subsidiary to rice cultivation, often represented a vital source of subsistence or money income for farm households. Increasingly, with improvements to the drainage of paddy fields and changes in rice varieties, the cultivation of second crops on paddy land spread in areas where winter temperatures were not too severe, and the planting, tending and harvesting of a crop such as wheat through the winter and spring months made quite heavy demands on the household's labour force. Most households also cultivated some upland fields, growing fruit, vegetables, pulses and fodder crops for home use or sale, or, where environmental and market conditions were right, industrial crops, most notably mulberry leaves to feed to silkworms. Many households used slack periods for the production of simple manufactured goods, such as items made from rice straw or local specialities, but with the growth of markets, opportunities for by-employment expanded to include not only the care of silkworms but also silk reeling and weaving and other kinds of textile operations and manufacturing work in the home.

Although rice remained far and away the single most significant crop for Japanese farmers and the one on which depended their ability to meet the demands placed on them for taxes, rents and input costs, as well as subsistence, most households operated relatively diversified routines, within which there was always something more-or-less productive for the diligent farmer and his family to be getting on with. Nonetheless, although the control of drought and flooding, pests and other dangers improved, nothing completely removed the substantial risk which every cultivator faced, and increasing involvement with the market, along with the switch to a fixed money tax in place of the more variable share of the rice crop paid to Tokugawa-period rulers, in some ways intensified this. Although the steady growth in production charted in the previous chapter undoubtedly did result in higher levels of consumption for many farm households, output and income remained subject to uncontrollable and unpredictable fluctuations which could render worthless the labours of even the most industrious of families.

The supply of inputs

The critical input which characterises agricultural production is clearly land. Any individual farm household's income depended, of course, on the distribution of landownership and cultivation rights and this will be considered in detail in chapter 8. Land as a general factor of production in agriculture is not, however, simply a god-given natural resource, but rather requires, especially in the case of land for paddy cultivation, extensive investment to make it a productive input. Fields need not only to be cleared, drained and levelled, but also, if rice is to be grown, to be sealed and enclosed, so as to hold water, and provided with access to irrigation supplies through channels and water-gates. In Japan, where natural rainfall or flooding could rarely be relied on to provide adequate irrigation, large-scale work was often required to construct the systems of reservoirs, dams and channels needed to collect and distribute river water. Initially, individual villages or groups of settlers could accomplish this investment, but as irrigation systems spread and became more complex and interconnected, large-scale inter-village organisation was necessary to construct and maintain the facilities. Furthermore, in addition to such fixed and visible infrastructure, individual paddy fields themselves improve, in texture and composition, with the years of flooding, so that the land stock of a Japanese village could represent a long-standing and mature investment on a substantial scale.

As has been pointed out already, given the Japanese environment, the spread of cultivation by and large depended on the construction of controlled irrigation facilities. Since the limits to this spread had been reached, by the late Tokugawa period, in all but climatically and geographically marginal areas, it follows that the bulk of the initial investment necessary to be able to provide a reasonably controlled supply of irrigation water had been made before modern industrialisation began in Japan. Although many important improvements and refinements were made to irrigation facilities after 1868, Sawada has shown that at least 70 per cent of the irrigation systems in existence in the 1960s were first constructed before the Restoration (Sawada 1972). As was later to be strongly illustrated by Green Revolution experience, the cultivation of high-yielding varieties itself, and the use of multiple-cropping rotations which it permits, depend crucially on the ability to control the timing and level of the flooding of fields. Japanese farmers faced the possibilities and potential of new rice varieties already blessed with the investments of generations in the construction of a vital precondition.[5]

In addition to this fixed investment in the land, agricultural production also requires a range of other non-labour inputs, some current (used up in this year's production) and some longer lasting. Seed and fertiliser are the major items of the former sort and although rice is an economical crop in its use of both, farm households still had to find the resources for them. Seed was commonly retained from the previous year's harvest, until the advent of varieties bred commercially or by experiment stations, and it paid to take great care in the selection of the best and most suitable types to plant. Natural organic fertilisers, in particular human excrement (night soil) and collections of leaves and compost, were widely applied to the land from early times, although animal manure was little used as a result of the absence of livestock. In later years, the use of commercially-supplied organic and chemical fertilisers increased substantially, both substituting for traditional sources and making possible the much heavier applications of fertiliser which high-yielding varieties could effectively absorb. Every household also needed access to a set of equipment. Many of the tools used, although sophisticated in design, could be produced and maintained at home, or at least within the village. Iron-based ploughs and other improved items of equipment began to spread in the second half of the nineteenth century, but powered machinery for pumping, threshing and hulling was only beginning to come into use by the inter-war period. Draft animals came to be more widely employed as ploughing techniques changed, but their relatively limited usefulness meant that they could be shared or hired, or dispensed with if needs be, and their purchase, housing and feeding was therefore less of a burden than is the case in more land-using agricultures.

Labour, on the other hand, is the input which rice-based cultivation demands in relatively greatest abundance. Since each plant can bear such a heavy head of grain, meticulous cultivation practices, looking after the individual plant so to speak, produce greater rewards than would be the case with other grain crops. In addition to the concentrated demands of transplanting and harvesting, therefore, careful weeding, pest control, fertiliser application and irrigation maintenance throughout the year can all pay dividends in the form of noticeably higher yields. Hence, as has been suggested, rice cultivation both demands and supports a heavy density of population.

Two important characteristics of the labour requirments demanded in this sort of situation should however be pointed out. First, given that many of the tasks involved depended for their effectiveness on care and precision in dealing with each relatively valuable but delicate plant, skills born of experience were important factors in determining how well they were carried out, and although the work was often physically demanding, it was not 'just' manual labour. Furthermore, as with any agriculture, on-the-spot knowledge and judgement in deciding on, for example, the timing of operations were essential for successful farm management. This, when combined with the nature of labour demands, means that paddy rice cultivation, in Japan and elsewhere, has never lent itself easily to large-scale operation, requiring, as this would, the supervision of a relatively large, non-family labour force.

Second, however, the large population which rice cultivation demanded and supported was employed, as with any form of agriculture, in varying amounts depending on the stage in the sequence of production. Hence there were times in the year when substantial numbers of people could do little in rice cultivation itself, but at the same time existed as a resource which, although ultimately tied to the land, could be utilised in a range of other, complementary ways. By-employments of many kinds are a common feature of rice-cultivating economies and we shall see later how agricultural technology and the economic organisation of both agriculture and industry were adapted, as the economy developed, to make use of this resource.

This basic structure of agricultural technology, revealing both characteristics common to many Asian rice-growing societies and particular adaptations to Japanese conditions, remained largely unchanged throughout the period of Japan's industrialisation. Dramatic changes, such as the widespread introduction of new crops, livestock or mechanised equipment, did not occur, either as a consequence of indigenous developments or through the impact of, for example, colonial agricultural exploitation. Nevertheless, output did grow as a result of technical changes made within this overall system of production, and it is to the origins and characteristics of these changes that we now turn.

Conclusion:

THE SPREAD OF NEW TECHNOLOGY

Here we make the assumption, now but not always previously accepted in economic theorising on the subject, that technical improvements rarely simply spring from the heads of mad inventors operating in an economic vacuum. Inventions are sought, not without cost, as the means of overcoming particular problems arising out of the operation of particular technologies in particular economic and institutional environments. They are adopted to the extent that they succeed in overcoming these problems within the context of that environment, but it is rarely the case that they yield the same benefits to all producers, each operating in their own different circumstances, in any given industry. Hence some adopt and gain when others do not, and the structure of the industry changes. In the case of family-based agriculture, this means nothing so neutral as a mere shift in the size distribution of producers in an industry, but rather changes in the distribution of income, land, political and social power, and even, on the margins of subsistence agriculture, life and death.

In the introduction to part II, we touched on the debate as to the distributional impact of the Green Revolution in contemporary Asia. As was suggested there and will be argued in more detail shortly, the general technical characteristics of the changes taking place in nineteenth- and early twentieth-century Japanese agriculture resembled those of the Green Revolution package, centring as they did on fertiliser-responsive, high-yielding seed varieties. However, whereas Green Revolution varieties were developed by international scientific research institutions, their Japanese forerunners (in some cases literally their ancestors) were bred by private individuals and practising farmers and it is therefore in the problems and opportunities to which such pioneers were responding that the determinants of the characteristics of their inventions and discoveries must be sought. From these characteristics in turn follow the pattern of adoption of the new techniques and its impact on the economic and social structure of rural life.

The characteristics of the new technology

The increases in rice output achieved by Japanese farmers during the nineteenth and early twentieth centuries were essentially the result of the spreading use of varieties of rice which, if provided with sufficient nutrients and cultivated under the right conditions, could produce more grain per plant than earlier varieties. However, the establishment of the right conditions and the achievement of the full potential which the new varieties opened up involved a great deal more than simply planting different seeds. So, just as the cultivation of modern high-yielding varieties forms part of a complementary set of new technical and economic practices, so the output-increasing technology of pre-war Japan constituted what would nowadays be called a 'package'. Japanese writers often refer to this package as the 'Meiji Nōhō' or 'Meiji Agricultural Methods' and although, as we shall see, many elements of it were developed and used well before the Meiji period, it is a convenient term to employ. It is useful to begin by setting out the elements of the package and the conditions for its successful adoption and operation, before going on to look at its development and spread.

(i) Higher-yielding rice varieties

Information about the seed varieties planted by farmers in nineteenth- and early twentieth-century Japan is bound to be limited and difficult to interpret, since the naming of varieties was not uniform or consistent. Nonetheless it has been reasonably well established that farmers in many areas were increasingly shifting to the cultivation of varieties which possessed higher-yielding characteristics, the most famous and widely grown of which was called Shinriki (power of the gods). Such varieties were characterised by the short stems and many heads of grain which enabled them to respond to heavier application of fertiliser by producing greater quantities of grain per plant (rather than say, taller stems or more leaves). They also tended to mature more quickly, opening up greater possibilities for double-cropping paddy land, although this characteristic also made them less flexible and less adaptable to particular local conditions of sunlight and water availability. They were sometimes believed, at least, to be more susceptible to pests and diseases than the tried and tested traditional local varieties, but in general, when grown in appropriate circumstances, they were capable of yielding substantially more rice per hectare than other varieties.

(ii) Fertiliser

It was the capacity of varieties like Shinriki to absorb and convert into grain larger quantities of nutrients that made them higher yielding. Hence, their use had to be accompanied by increased levels of fertiliser application. Traditional sources of fertiliser (grass, leaves, etc.) were generally inadequate for this, both because the supply of them was limited and because the labour required for their collection and preparation was simply not available in sufficient quantity at the right times. The use of commercially-acquired fertiliser was therefore essential. Up until about World War I, this typically took the form of waste fish or bean products, but thereafter the growing domestic chemical fertiliser industry began to meet more and more of the demand.

(iii) Ploughing and other cultivation practices

The use of seed varieties with higher-yielding characteristics and of larger amounts of fertiliser had implications for many other aspects of cultivation practice. The absorption of more fertiliser required the land to be ploughed more deeply and thoroughly than traditional methods could achieve, and this encouraged the use of differently designed ploughs pulled by draft animals. More thorough weeding and pest control became increasingly beneficial and were greatly facilitated by adoption of the practice of transplanting seedlings into the paddy in straight lines. This made possible the use of a rotary weeding tool and in other operations too, improved equipment helped to make the adoption of the package both more feasible and more productive. Given the stricter time limits within which tasks had to be performed, and the greater volume of crops involved, equipment which speeded up certain individual tasks by saving labour (e.g. improved threshers) also featured in the package.

(iv) Irrigation, drainage and double-cropping

The value of the Meiji Nōhō package to farmers lay not only in higher yields of rice but also in the increased scope which the quicker-maturing rice varieties offered for the cultivation of another crop on paddy land in the winter. This could not be realised, however, unless it was possible both to provide water to the rice crop exactly when it was required and subsequently to drain the paddy ready for the winter crop. The practice of keeping fields flooded during the winter as a means of conserving water supplies had to be abandoned and substantial investments were frequently required in order to adapt the irrigation system for winter drainage. This often meant group action on quite a wide scale, given the ways in which irrigation networks were constructed and the absence of the kinds of small-scale tubewells and pump-sets which enable present-day farmers elsewhere in Asia to control their irrigation supplies on an individual basis. Once suitable conditions had been established, however, the Meiji Nōhō package enabled Japanese farmers to grow a winter crop, such as wheat, utilising the slack-season labour of their families, and thereby to raise the overall yield of their holdings.

(v) Commercialisation

The Meiji Nōhō package depended on purchases of commercial inputs, in particular fertiliser, and, all being well, generated increased output in excess of subsistence needs, which could be sold in order to pay for inputs, taxes and, hopefully, a wider range of consumer goods. Its adoption was therefore only possible and only made sense for farmers who had access to commercial markets, that is to say to the organisational networks through which they could sell their products and purchase inputs and consumer goods. By the end of the Tokugawa period, farmers in many parts of the country were already involved in commercial transactions, but access to markets varied regionally and even within particular areas, depending on location and communications.

(vi) Outside knowledge

On the whole, the techniques of the Meiji Nōhō did not require skills (e.g. mechanical expertise) with which the majority of cultivators were unfamiliar and the new inputs and methods fitted relatively easily into the existing body of knowledge and practice. Nonetheless information about them had to be acquired and some new ideas and techniques learnt. Hence practising farmers did need access to channels of information, such as practical examples to copy or organisations through which knowledge could be transmitted.

Taken altogether, therefore, the Meiji Nōhō package represented the means whereby the total output of a given area of land could be increased and diversified through the application of greater amounts of fertiliser and the more productive use of existing resources of labour. Its successful adoption presumed the existence of certain preconditions, that is to say, on the one hand, access to commercial markets and sources of outside information and, on the other, adequate control of water supplies, but, given these, it presented few technical or economic difficulties even to small-scale cultivators. Indeed, since, taking the year as a whole, it probably demanded increased labour input on the part of workers more fully occupied in tasks necessitating higher levels of care and attention to detail, in many ways it put the smaller-scale cultivator, utilising his own family labour only, at a greater advantage than before, as long as institutional arrangements were such as to provide him with access to water supplies, markets and information sources. In turning now to the question of how a package with such characteristics came to be developed and widely diffused in the nineteenth-century countryside, we shall also see how the operation of the Japanese rural economy and society in fact made such provision possible.

The development and diffusion of new techniques

There is considerable evidence to suggest that almost all of the techniques which made up the Meiji Nōhō package were known and practised, in at least some parts of the country, in the Tokugawa period (Smith 1959: 92–9). The selective breeding of seeds, use of commercial fertilisers, and improved methods of transplanting, weeding and pest control are all described in the published agricultural treatises of the period as accepted parts of best-practice technology. Shinriki, the culminating element in the package for many farmers, was not developed until 1877, when it was bred by a practising farmer from the area around Osaka, but it came from a long line of higher-yielding varieties, possessing the characteristics necessary for fertiliser responsiveness, which were already in use in this commercialised and advanced region of the Tokugawa economy (Francks 1984: 61). The origins of other elements in the package are impossible to trace, but it can be deduced that they must have been the result of the same kind of trial-and-error experimentation as produced improved seed varieties. There are records of farmers who actively researched agricultural improvements, travelling about the country on the trail of new ideas, developing and adapting them for use in their own areas, and publishing their results in pamphlets and manuals of good practice.[6] As the old picture of Tokugawa society as a static order, within which communication and change were highly restricted, breaks down, so it becomes reasonable to assume that enterprising travellers, on the lookout for ways to respond to growing commercial opportunities as markets grew, took note of the best practices of other areas and attempted to adapt them for use at home. Thus improved varieties, and the sets of inputs and practices which complemented them, suitable for each particular environmental area would gradually have emerged.

Nevertheless it is true that the scope for communication between agricultural enthusiasts did increase with the breakdown of the Tokugawa system and the commitment to growth and change after 1868. Increasing numbers of agricultural discussion groups and so-called seed-exchange societies were formed on local or private initiative and it was through this network that the first efforts of the state to promote the diffusion of improved agricultural technology were made. The newly-established Ministry responsible for agriculture, reflecting the early enthusiasm of the Meiji state for all things Western, initially attempted to import Western farming technology in the form of cows, sheep, grapes, olives, American farm machinery, and such like. However, it realised relatively quickly that such exotic flora and fauna could not easily be adapted to the Japanese environment, and by the 1880s it was to indigenous techniques of the Meiji Nōhō type, emerging from the experiments and expertise of pre-Meiji enthusiasts, that it turned. Farmers with experience of such techniques were employed as itinerant lecturers to tour round the various local discussion groups, which were eventually organised into a national network of prefectural, county and village agricultural associations. It was only later that the experiment stations and agricultural colleges set up towards the end of the century began to apply Western scientific methods to Japanese agricultural practice, by which time the pattern of influences on the direction of technical change had already been firmly set by the spread of the locally-produced Meiji Nōhō.

It is to be expected that those farmers with the time, interest and educational background to engage in agricultural research or take part in agricultural societies would have come from the upper echelons of village society. What is known about individual pioneers and about the more general run of enthusiasts in the villages does indeed suggest that most were larger-scale landowners. However, a large holding in Japanese terms was rarely more than 2–3 hectares and, in the Meiji period at least, the majority of those who owned land on this scale cultivated at least some of it themselves, renting out whatever their household labour forces could not manage.[7] Hence, those who found out about new techniques and introduced them to their villages were typically members of the class of so-called 'cultivating landlords' (*tezukuri jinushi*), who had farming experience themselves but who also, while by no means particularly rich or powerful in wider regional or national terms, tended to occupy the leading positions in village social and political life (Dore 1960). This conforms with the more recent experience of other agricultural societies facing technical change, but what distinguishes the Japanese case is the degree to which new techniques successfully spread from larger-scale cultivators and landowners to other farmers, working against the emergence of the increases in inequality alleged to have accompanied the spread of the Green Revolution.

A number of reasons might be put forward to explain this. In part, of course, the ease with which smaller-scale cultivators can adopt a new technology depends on its technical characteristics. As we have seen, the Meiji Nōhō involved few economies of scale and even, in some respects, favoured the farm which could be operated with family labour alone. It did, though, require preconditions of adequate irrigation control and access to markets and information, and it is in these areas that larger-scale cultivators might have been favoured. As we shall see in the next section when we consider the wider involvement of rural areas in the development of the economy, the growth of commerce and the widening of production and employment opportunities during the Tokugawa period had already drawn more than just the rural elite into the market relationships which provided both the means and the incentive to adopt the new techniques. On the other hand, villages had long operated as relatively autonomous but internally interdependent groups so that, particularly as regards the improvements to irrigation networks which the Meiji Nōhō frequently required, it remained difficult for even the largest landowner to effect changes without the consent and involvement of other cultivators dependent on the same irrigation source. Hence the pre-exisitng development of the Tokugawa period provided relatively widespread access to the necessary preconditions for adoption in those parts of the country where the economic and physical environment was suitable.

In addition, however, it can be argued that the changing economic and social structure of Japanese villages forced the 'cultivating landlords' into the position of acting as the channels through which knowledge of the new technology passed to other cultivators. There are many examples of such landlords, whether out of missionary zeal, social responsibility or self-interest, exhorting and encouraging their tenants and other villagers to adopt new methods and indeed, given the close interrelations between village households, whereby cultivators helped one another out at transplanting and harvest, shared tools and animals and frequently met to organise co-operative tasks such as irrigation maintenance, it would not have been easy to keep knowledge and experience of new methods to oneself. Nevertheless, for significant numbers of larger landowning households, both social position and economic interest pointed towards the desirability of encouraging tenants and other villagers to adopt improved methods. Given the accepted practice of adjusting rents in the light of the state of the harvest, improvements which raised or stabilised yields benefited landlords as well as tenants, while at the same time reducing the dependence of smaller-scale cultivators on those larger landowning households with whom they had real or fictive kinship ties and to whom they looked for protection. Larger-scale cultivators experienced increasingly less need to be able to call on the labour and services of their poor relations as, under the impact of the industrialisation of the economy, they began to develop non-agricultural interests and to find that it yielded greater profits, and fewer troubles and responsibilities, if they hived off the cultivation of their land to the more independent tenant farmer who could operate the new technology most effectively with his family labour force.[8]

In the next chapter, we shall observe the impact of this process of technical diffusion on the distribution of income, land and political power in rural Japan as industrialisation proceeded, but the generally rising levels of output and yields observed during the nineteenth and early twentieth centuries testify to the existence and effectiveness of the kinds of diffusion mechanism suggested above. Other, more direct, indicators of the spread of the Meiji Nōhō are also available, however, and throw additional light on the wider economic and environmental factors which conditioned its development and diffusion. Such evidence includes prefectural and other local data on the use of improved varieties and on the extent of double cropping. This suggests that the use of higher-yielding varieties within a double-cropping rotation developed earliest in those south-western areas affected by the urbanising and commercialising impact of Osaka and other centres along the Inland Sea coast, as far as northern Kyūshū. Prefectures in these regions consistently achieved the highest average rice yields in the country in the late nineteenth and early twentieth centuries; double-cropping rates appear to have been substantially higher than in other places, and reached about 70 per cent of the paddy area in such regions by the turn of the century, and data on the spread of Shinriki and other high-yielding varieties show them as having been planted very widely in such areas, covering as much as 50 per cent or more of the paddy area in Osaka, northern Shikoku and northern Kyūshū by about 1910 (Francks 1984: 60–2; Hayami 1975: 125).

The reasons for these regional divergences in the spread of the Meiji Nōhō are partly environmental and partly economic and reflect the incentives and constraints determining adoption and diffusion. Since the package was essentially one designed for a double-cropping rotation, it was less effective in places where climate or irrigation facilities were unsuited to a winter crop. Hence it did not spread in the regions of the north-east where the winters are too long and cold for a second crop, nor in those scattered areas throughout the country where technical difficulties put the achievement of winter drainage beyond the reach of available investment resources. Equally, though, it depended on access to a commercial infrastructure and hence was less likely to be adopted in more remote and less market-oriented areas away from the main centres of population and industry. The slow-down in the rate of output growth in the inter-war period can in part be explained by the fact that, by about 1920, most farmers in those areas in which the package could be successfully and profitably adopted had done so, leaving only areas in which it could not be utilised without investment in large-scale irrigation improvements or technical adaptations to make it more suitable for colder climatic conditions. These developments depended on local or national government assistance, both in providing the scientific resources required for the cross-breeding of cold-resistant higher-yielding varieties and in organising and subsidising large-scale water-control projects. State expenditure in these directions increased steadily during the 1920s and '30s, providing capital for irrigation investment and funds for research work in the growing network of experiment stations, resulting, by World War II, in the development of the varieties which formed the basis for the rapid growth of agriculture in the north-east after the war.

The Meiji Nōhō was developed by practising farmers in regions undergoing the economic change and diversification of the early stages of industrialisation. Through the efforts of such landowners and cultivators, it was adapted to suit local conditions and enabled the majority of farmers, whatever the size of their holdings, to respond to the opportunities presented by growing involvement with the market. The characteristics of the technical change on which output growth depended, and the pattern of its diffusion, cannot therefore be considered in isolation from developments in the wider economy, to which farmers were responding and which they in their turn affected. Hence we must now turn to the broader interrelationships, of which technical change represents one aspect, between agricultural developments and commercial and industrial growth in the expanding Japanese economy.

8 Industrialisation and the farm household

Our story so far has largely concerned the growth of agricultural output and its nature and causes. At the same time, however, as we saw in part I, the rest of the economy was being transformed as economic development became the nation's goal, as new industries took root, and as Japanese business became increasingly involved in the world economy. The development and diffusion of new technology was only one aspect of the change occurring in the agricultural sector as demand and supply conditions for its products altered, as labour requirements in industrial production grew, as international economic forces penetrated the world of the farm household and as the state intervened in farmers' lives in new ways, imposing new taxes, creating new administrative structures, obliging children to go to school and young men to war. The underlying assumption of much of the literature on these wider aspects of agricultural life in pre-war Japan has been that change was the result of the impact of the onslaught from outside on farm households who were, for the most part, obliged to suffer a heavier share of the burden of industrialisation than most other sections of the population. Whilst it cannot be denied that the small holdings cultivated by a substantial proportion of rural dwellers were often unable to yield more than a bare living, after rent, taxes and other costs, from agricultural activity alone, and at times when harvests were bad or prices low were hardly able to do even that, nonetheless the tendency to disregard the more positive ways in which farm households adapted to, and in turn influenced, the wider changes going on around them denies recognition to a significant force determining the nature and pattern of Japan's industrialisation.

In this chapter we shall look at changes in the economic and social lives of Japanese farm households in the light of the kinds of analysis of the positive reactions and responses of 'peasant' farmers to economic development described in chapter 5 with the aim of illustrating the ways in which Japanese farmers succeeded in conditioning the characteristics of the first successful Asian industrialisation. We shall begin by looking at evidence of the ways in which rural economic and social structures changed as industrialisation proceeded, in particular at shifts in the distribution of land and economic power, and then consider some of the underlying forces behind these trends.

INDUSTRIALISATION AND THE DISTRIBUTION OF LAND: THEORIES AND INTERPRETATIONS

The dual-economy model, the dominant theoretical approach to agriculture's role in development which underlies much Western work on Japan, operates essentially on a macroeconomic level and has little to say concerning the relative gains and losses or conflicts of interest, hence structural or distributional changes, which industrialisation must involve. For information and interpretation relating to these questions, we have to turn initially to the work of Japanese economic and agricultural historians, many of whom have made use of Marxist theoretical frameworks which do provide tools of analysis for such problems. The Marxist model, like the dual-economy one, can be said to be based on Western historical experience and much effort has had to be expended in the attempt to apply its categories and concepts to the Japanese case. Out of this effort has emerged a picture of rural life in industrialising Japan which is still widely current and which provides both a basis of information and a convenient starting point for consideration of the question of who gained and who lost as farmers were drawn into the developing commercial economy.

Industrialisation, according to this model, takes place within the context of the historical process of conflict between the feudal ruling and landowning class, the capitalist bourgeoisie and the labouring proletariat, both rural and urban. As the industrial sector grows and capitalist forms of economic organisation develop, the agricultural sector is increasingly drawn into new economic relationships. Where agriculture was once organised along essentially feudal lines, with subsistence producers constrained to supply the surplus output which supported the ruling military class, the growing impact of the market on agricultural production leads to the emergence of capitalist landowners who cultivate by means of hired, landless workers. The growth of capitalism thus leads to the privatisation of landownership and its gradual concentration in the hands of larger landowners, while those unable to maintain their feudal cultivation rights are driven to become the rural proletariat which constitutes industry's reserve army of labour.

The effort to discern these forces at work in Japanese history produced much of the information on which our present knowledge of rural life in pre-war Japan is based and led to various conflicting modifications of the highly simplified model suggested above.[1] Nevertheless the underlying view remained that the spread of capitalism into the countryside, from the Tokugawa period onwards, produced differentiation among farm households such that the ownership of land and other means of production became increasingly concentrated in the hands of those able, for whatever reason, to operate most successfully in a world of market relationships. These landowners were driven to try to extract increasingly more, in the form of rents, interest on debts and so on, from the remaining mass of the agricultural population, whose only recourse was to revolt and rebellion in the Tokugawa period, group action against landlords (tenancy disputes) later, and population control through abortion and infanticide, or flight to the cities, throughout.[2]

Consistent representative data against which to test this picture are difficult to obtain since the compilation of official, national-level statistics on landownership and tenure did not begin until 1908. Although tenancy was in theory impossible under the Tokugawa system (since all land was deemed to belong to the Emperor and hence could not be privately owned or, therefore, rented out), the survey accompanying the Land Tax Reform, on the basis of which ownership of land was allocated to the former tax-payer, usually but not necessarily the cultivator, indicated that even then not all land was farmed by its owner. Thereafter, given the picture which emerges in the 1908 statistics, the proportion of the cultivated area under tenancy must have steadily increased and a growing number of farm households did come to rent rather than own all or part of the land they farmed.[3] This is taken as evidence of the increasing difficulties faced by small-scale cultivators in adapting to production for the market. The imposition of the new land tax, which had to be paid in cash not rice, forced inexperienced producers into market dealings; while agricultural prices were rising with the general inflation of the Restoration period, they eagerly embraced commercial production, only to be thrown into difficulties by the falling prices of the 1880s (the Matsukata deflation). As a result, many were driven to mortgage their land, or to sell off parcels of it, thus drifting increasingly into tenancy. Those who acquired the ownership of their land formed a landlord class with interests in money-lending, trading and rural business to supplement their income from rents. With the development of these interests, their involvement in village life lessened and they emerged, after the turn of the century especially, as a class of absentee or 'parasitic' landlords. Meanwhile, the tenant class, burdened by high rents and gradually losing control over their means of production, could be seen as identifying increasingly with the rest of the growing proletariat in the cities and reacting in the only way they could, through group action in tenancy disputes, to landlords' attempts to extract more from them.

This picture of agrarian differentiation over the course of industrialisation was very much the one predicted by the initial Marxist model but a number of problems have arisen in squaring it with certain of the data and analyses now available. Although it was certainly the case that tenancy increased as commercialisation proceeded during the nineteenth century, and examples of large-scale landowning families and absentee landlords who conformed to their role in the differentiation model could be found, nonetheless few Japanese landlords ever owned enough land to be able to live exclusively from rents or to support lifestyles substantially different from those of the solid owner or owner-tenant cultivating class (Dore 1960). Rents, generally assessed as fixed amounts of rice but adjusted downwards at times of bad harvests, failed to keep pace with output growth and diversification. The unit of cultivation obstinately remained the small-scale family farm and the institutional organisation of the agricultural economy failed to make the transformation into a structure of large-scale farms or landholdings worked by a landless hired labour force.

Furthermore, analysis of the statistics, available from 1908 onwards, on scale of cultivation, as opposed to landownership, showed that, although there might have been some tendency early on, and by extrapolation back into the nineteenth century, for the proportion of households cultivating very small holdings to increase alongside the concentration of landownership (bipolarisation), this trend had been replaced, certainly by the World War I period, by an increase in the proportion of cultivators in the middle of the distribution, farming holdings of around one hectare (see table 8.1). This was accompanied by a gradual rise in the proportion of households who both owned and rented in land for cultivation, rather than in that of pure tenant (landless) cultivators. At least after the turn of the century, therefore, the impact of industrialisation on agriculture seemed to be producing, not differentiation into large landholdings and landless cultivators, but rather a structure in which the family-based cultivator, owning some land and renting in more, increasingly predominated. Regional data also suggested that the more advanced and commercialised the area, the earlier this tendency had set in and the greater the predominance, therefore, of the medium-scale family cultivator, with the bipolarised structure increasingly relegated to less developed and more remote parts of the country (for data, see Francks 1984: 89–90).

It seemed, therefore, that the impact of industrialisation on the structure of rural society had not produced quite the predicted result and the problem of how to analyse and categorise the small-scale, commercialised, family farm which had emerged continues to exercise scholars of agrarian Japan. One approach has been to argue that Japan suffered an, as it were, incomplete bourgeois revolution, leaving the landowning class still tied to certain aspects of the role of their feudal forebears and preventing them from developing as business-like capitalist farm-operators. Alternatively, it might be argued that the rather more limited impact of the industrial sector, in the Japanese case, in transforming labour and product markets throughout the economy left the farm household with little alternative but to continue to cultivate and to seek its own survival through harder work ('self-exploitation') on increasingly unfavourable terms, paying

Table 8.1 Changes in the distribution of land among farm households 1908–37
(a) The distribution of farm households by tenure status (%)

	Owner-cultivators	Part owner/ part tenant	Tenants
1908	33.3	39.1	27.6
1917	31.0	40.9	28.1
1927	30.7	42.1	27.2
1937	30.5	42.3	27.2

(b) The distribution of farm households by area cultivated (% of households)

	Area in hectares					
	−0.5	0.5–1	1–2	2–3	3–5	5–
1908	37.3	32.6	19.5	6.4	3.0	1.2
1915	36.3	33.4	20.0	6.1	2.7	1.2
1925	34.8	33.9	21.5	5.9	2.5	1.4
1935	33.7	34.3	22.5	5.8	2.3	1.4

Source: Kayō (1958): 94, 135

high rents, receiving low prices for its output and having to send family members out to work for low wages at whatever employment was available on the fringes of modern industry. Tenancy disputes arose out of this struggle for survival, as cultivators tried to resist the drain which rental payments exacted or to hold on to their cultivation rights.

In many ways the phenomena which these scenarios describe, that is to say the increasing incidence of tenancy disputes, by-employment and part-time farming, the changing role of larger-scale landowning households in economic and social relations, and the relative inequality between agricultural and urban industrial incomes are not disputed. However, these same phenomena can be viewed in a somewhat different light, less as the negative results of the exploitation inflicted on the rural sector by increasingly powerful industrial and capitalist interests, and more as the results of the positive, and relatively rather successful, responses of farmers, individually or as groups, to changing commercial and technical opportunities. For example, this more favourable light can be given to events by pointing out that, although rural living standards did not keep pace with urban industrial ones, they nonetheless improved substantially over the course of Japan's pre-war industrialisation; that although tenancy survived and rents continued to have to be paid, landlords, particularly in technically and commercially more developed regions, appear to have been unable to maintain their share of growing and increasingly diversified farm household incomes and that, although the incidence of tenancy disputes increased, their regional and temporal distribution does not suggest that they were directly related to particularly high levels of rural poverty or landlord exploitation and other causes need to be sought.[4] The remaining sections of this chapter will attempt to analyse these phenomena in more detail by considering, first, the changing structure of the farm household economy and, second, the nature of tenancy disputes as indicators of economic and social change in rural areas. By applying to them some of the ideas derived from development experience elsewhere in the Third World, some progress can perhaps be made towards a better understanding of the role of the small-scale, rice-cultivating, farm household in a successful industrialisation process.

THE CHANGING ECONOMY OF THE FARM HOUSEHOLD

So far this chapter has led us to the conclusion that, contrary perhaps to expectations, the small-scale family farm survived the industrialisation process in Japan and indeed, some would argue, came through in quite good order, producing more output but also, generally speaking, with a higher, though not necessarily more secure, standard of living. The object of this section is to try to show how and why this might have been so. However, one important aspect of the explanation has already appeared in the previous chapter where we saw how the direction taken by technical change in agricultural production favoured the skills and resources of the small-to-medium-scale family farm, as opposed to those of the larger-scale cultivator. As we shall now see, the development and adoption of this new technology formed part of a wider process of change, social and political as well as economic, among farm households, as the market for agricultural products grew and as employment opportunities for farm family members expanded.

Part I of this book traced the origins of Japan's economic development back into the Tokugawa period, to the growth of towns and urban markets consequent upon the removal of the ruling samurai class from the land into the castle towns of their lords. Improvements in communications facilitated the nationwide movement of goods to the expanding urban centres, and while Edo (Tokyo) became established as the political and administrative capital of the country, Osaka developed as the commercial hub around which trade and finance were co-ordinated. Few villages could have remained totally cut off from developments in their local castle-towns, but those within the communications orbits of the larger cities were strongly drawn into the market networks created by the growth in urban demand.

Evidence of commercial production among Tokugawa farmers is well established (see e.g. Smith 1959: ch. 6; Hanley and Yamamura 1977: ch. 4; Crawcour 1965). Trade began in rice and other basic foodstuffs, but increasingly, especially in the regions around the main urban centres, villages began to specialise in the products to which their area was suited: silk, cotton, sugar, indigo, speciality fruits and vegetables, and so on. National markets developed for major crops such as rice, silk and cotton, and merchants travelled the villages buying up produce. But rural dwellers were also increasingly buying and selling ordinary consumer goods and agricultural inputs for day-to-day use, through local markets, travelling salesmen and even internal trading within the village, and the use of money became widespread. Hanley and Yamamura cite evidence of market purchases of ordinary consumer goods even in quite remote parts of northern Japan (Hanley and Yamamura 1977: ch. 6), although specialised production for the market was nowhere near as highly developed in such places as it became in regions like the Kinai around Osaka. Here it was even possible to find households reliant on the market for their own food, but in most places cultivation of crops for sale remained integrated within a production structure which also catered for most of the household's basic subsistence needs.

In the early Tokugawa period, such craft and manufacturing industry as existed was largely concentrated in the towns, where specialist weavers or metal-workers, for example, operated workshops producing for the predominantly samurai market. Such production was heavily regulated and, as far as possible, taxed by the local feudal authorities and by craft guilds. As demand grew, however, enterprising producers and merchants began to establish workshops or putting-out systems in rural areas, avoiding official control and making use of cheaper rural labour. Thus new opportunities opened up for rural workers, not just through migration to look for jobs in the various craft and service industries in towns and along commercial routes, but also through part-time or temporary employment in local workshops or in manufacturing at home. Textile merchants rented out looms and brought round yarn to be woven in farm households. The business which was one day to become the multinational Kikkoman soy sauce company began operations as a 'factory in the country', manned by temporary workers looking for a few weeks' employment in the off-seasons of the agricultural year (Fruin 1983). Developments such as these explain the stagnation and even decline in urban populations in the latter half of the Tokugawa period, as compared with the rapid growth observed earlier, as the focus of economic activity shifted into the countryside (Smith 1973).

The widening range of income-earning possibilities opening up for members of farm households competed to some extent with the demands of rice cultivation and subsistence farming and threatened the tax-base of the *daimyō*, who issued streams of edicts aimed at reversing the trend towards diversification. Furthermore, competition for labour time also began to make life increasingly difficult for those families who controlled and cultivated larger-scale holdings. Such cultivators had customarily met their labour requirements by adopting into their households, as long-term agricultural servants, poor relations or younger sons and daughters of other kinds of dependent family. Such workers were treated as (inferior) members of the household, provided with board and lodging and frequently, if they proved loyal and hard-working, rewarded after many years' service with a grant of land of their own to cultivate, although they and their families would still be expected to help out their patron household when required. However, as profitable opportunities for commercial production or for alternative forms of employment opened up, it became increasingly difficult to find men and women willing to enter the households of larger-scale cultivators as agricultural servants on a long-term basis. Periods of employment became shorter and wages higher and more clearly specified in relation to work to be done. Under these circumstances, therefore, households with more land than could be managed by the immediate family labour force found it increasingly more practical and profitable to reduce their scale of cultivation by setting up their younger sons and other poor relations on independent, though possibly rented, holdings of their own. The main household retained the largest and best holding, along with tools, draft animals, and so on, for itself, and maintained hierarchical kinship (or fictive kinship) relations with its new branch households which enabled it to call on their help from time to time, but relieved itself of the problem of finding extra labour and the burden of responsibility for junior members of the family.[5]

This process resulted in the establishment of precisely the kind of holding, of a size which could be operated by a family labour force of, say, a parent couple with their eldest son and his wife, best able both to adopt the emerging Meiji Nōhō technology and to take advantage of the income-earning potential of new employment opportunities. As we saw in the previous section, the new agricultural techniques were developed in and for regions experiencing the growth of markets and of new forms of industry and employment, and required the kind of intensive and careful work which was hard to achieve with the extended labour force of the traditional larger-scale holding. In addition it was the smaller-scale family-based household which could manage its operations so as to be able to fit in off-season migrant employment, textile putting-out work in the spare time of its women members, or the care of silk worms, with all such activities contributing to the household's overall income. Only the institution of the relatively close kin- (or pseudo kin-) group could provide both the incentive for cultivators to learn and apply the new technology and the ability to internalise within the household its members' earnings from other occupations.[6] The processes of technical, economic and institutional adaptation thus went hand in hand to generate, most typically in the economically more advanced south-western regions, the kind of family farm unit which could combine the complex operations of high-yielding rice cultivation with the other forms of manufacturing and agricultural activity demanded in the increasingly commercialised environment of the Tokugawa economy.

Households able to organise themselves in this way, operating within the favourable conditions of developing and commercialising regions and blessed with a reasonable amount of luck as regards harvests, prices and the health and competence of family members, were undoubtedly able to prosper during the latter half of the Tokugawa period. There are plenty of examples illustrating rising standards of living, the growing rural market for consumer goods, and the accumulations of capital which enabled rural businesses to grow, and, for the reasons set out above, the opportunity to follow such examples was open to the substantial proportion of village households cultivating average-sized holdings. How far such opportunities were translated into an overall rise in the standard of living, discernible at a national level and reaching down to the lower strata of village society, has, however, been a subject of controversy. Counter-examples of poverty and, indeed, of famine can be produced and there was plainly a good deal of regional variation in the level and stability of rural livelihoods. One factor frequently used as evidence of the prevalence of difficult conditions in rural areas is the acknowledged slow rate of population growth and much of the controversy has centred around explanations of this, which are also of considerable relevance to the question of the objectives and modes of operation of farm households in the early stages of Japan's development.

There seems little doubt that the rate of population growth in Tokugawa Japan was lower than that in European societies over comparable periods, and certainly lower than that observed in present-day developing countries. It was traditionally assumed that this reflected the poverty, disease and famine afflicting rural areas, which led to high mortality and to the economic necessity for the practices of abortion and infanticide known to have been widespread in the Tokugawa countryside. Alternatively, it has more recently been suggested that, since low birth rates rather than high death rates lay behind the slow growth, it can be explained in terms of the effects of malnutrition on fecundity (Mosk 1981). On the other hand, however, those who wish to argue that conditions improved for Tokugawa farm households interpret the slow rate of population growth as evidence of conscious family planning, using the traditional and accepted forms of abortion and infanticide, by households attempting to control the size and sex composition of their families so as to take advantage of the prospects for higher standards of living. Family planning is seen as a means of achieving the optimum balance between mouths to feed and household labour requirements, in relation to employment opportunities, and thus as another aspect of the strategy pursued by farm households in response to commercialisation and technical change (Smith 1977; Hanley and Yamamura 1977: ch. 9).

Clearly, as to be expected in a relatively underdeveloped economy, there were considerable regional differences in the economic prospects and overall living standards of the rural population and a general picture can only be pieced together from scattered local information. What the 'revisionism' in the interpretation of Tokugawa-period agricultural development and population change does give us, however, is a model of the decisions and actions of farm households which allows for positive and explicable responses to the economic forces unleashed by commercialisation and urbanisation and is thus much more in line with current approaches to the activity of 'peasant' farmers in developing economies. It suggests that, in the Tokugawa period, farm households who did experience the impact of the expanding commercial economy were already responding by adapting both their technology and the institutional organisation of their economic and social lives so as to form units capable of making the most of changing conditions. This process continued to underly developments in the rural economy during subsequent periods of much more rapid change, although, as the last section of this chapter will suggest, it does not follow that this did not at the same time generate conflict within the shifting structure of rural society.

The changing economic and political face of Japan in the mid-nineteenth century brought new forces to bear on the situation confronting rural households. The opening of the country to foreign trade in the 1850s produced the sudden expansion in the demand for silk for export which led many more farm households in environmentally suitable regions to begin to combine mulberry cultivation and silk-worm raising with their previous agricultural activities.[7] This laid farmers more open to the effects of uncontrollable fluctuations in market demand and prices, by which they were at times to be hard hit, particularly during the depression of the late 1920s and early 1930s, but at other times provided them with a significant additional source of income and employment, leading to steadily rising living standards in sericultural regions through the late nineteenth and early twentieth centuries. Saitō's careful analysis of the impact of different kinds of by-employment on farm household economies also reveals how participation in sericulture lessened the likelihood of members of the family (particularly women) seeking employment away from the farm (Saitō 1986(b)). Thus the most important form of diversification pursued by farm households under the impact of the opening-up to foreign trade appears to have resulted not in the creation of a labour force available for migration to industry, but rather in a strengthening of the economic advantages, for its members/workers, of the farm household able to achieve the optimum balance of activities.

Nonetheless, the development of the industrial sector in the later nineteenth century did lead to the expansion of new forms of employment for members of rural households, though not necessarily or predominantly, until at least the turn of the century, to full-scale migration to urban areas.[8] Rural women continued to make up the majority of the labour force employed in 'factories' and they, like many of the men who also sought periods of employment in rural or urban industry, maintained their ties with their farm families and continued to contribute labour to agricultural operations and income to agricultural households. An urban industrial labour force, divorced from the rural economy and dependent on the demands of industrial employers in urban labour markets, is largely a twentieth-century phenomenon in Japan, dating particularly from the time of the World-War-I boom and the subsequent growth in heavy industry. Even then, though, a great deal of small-scale industry, operating on the margins of the modern industrial sector with a fluctuating and mobile labour force, continued to survive into the post-World War II period, and the interconnections between agricultural and industrial labour use within the small-scale farm household are still to be observed in the lives of the part-time farmers who dominate Japanese agriculture today.

Alongside the effects of foreign trade and industrial growth, other forces generated by the modernising state also began to permeate rural society. Although prior to the Restoration formal schooling had largely been limited to the upper levels of society, it is thought that general educational levels in Tokugawa Japan were relatively high, as compared with other developing countries then or since, and village children frequently received some basic teaching at schools run by temples. However, after 1868, with the state takeover of existing schools, the establishment of many more, and the passage of legislation making periods of education compulsory, rural children came to receive increasing amounts of formal instruction through the state system, and by the turn of the century there would have been few in the younger age groups of village society who had not attended school for a number of years. The assumption of basic levels of literacy and numeracy underlay the increasing ability of farmers' groups, such as the network of agricultural associations and co-operatives, to organise themselves and to make use of written circulated material. By the turn of the century, many middle- and smaller-scale cultivators had acquired the educational skills and the confidence, as well as the economic interest, needed to take part in such groups and to make use of them to provide such things as credit, technical knowledge and marketing or storage facilities which the individual household could not supply for itself. Other forces which brought villages into increasing contact with the outside world, such as conscription, the widening of the franchise, the development of transport and communications, the establishment of the local government network, and the growing diffusion of bicycles, books and newspapers, labour-movement activists, teachers, policemen, and so on, all contributed towards the growth in the social and political, as well as economic, role of farmers below the level of the larger-scale landlord/cultivator who had previously tended to exert the greatest influence on village life.

As table 8.1 showed, once figures for the distribution of households according to the scale of cultivation become available after 1908, it is possible to demonstrate statistically the effects of the trends in farm household economies described here. Prior to that, only scattered village data exist, but the forces operating on households from the Tokugawa period onwards appear to have been resulting, in the advanced south-western regions at least, in a trend towards the concentration of holdings in the middle range of the size distribution. It is possible that the difficulties experienced by many farmers during the 1880s may have set in motion opposing forces causing more farmers to slip into the category of very small cultivators, but the later official figures show that by the 1910s and 1920s the superiority of the middle-sized holding had re-asserted itself sufficiently for the 'concentration in the centre' to be observable at the national level. With larger-scale cultivators continuing to break up their holdings and rent them out in parcels to those better able to take advantage of new technology and widening income-earning possibilities, the proportion of households farming large holdings steadily declined. At the other extreme, for those intitially cultivating very small holdings, opportunities to leave agriculture altogether for industrial employment, or to rent in more land, were increasing, so that the proportion of households farming very small areas also declined. The growing economic superiority of the family-sized farm is corroborated by other forms of evidence, showing, for example, the generally higher yields obtained by those in the 1–2 hectare range and the increasing influence of such households on the organisations through which new technology was diffused and the direction of research and development activity determined (e.g. Francks 1984: 237–45).

The greater involvement of rural areas with the market economy, and through that the world economy, with industrial development and with the state inevitably imposed new sources of instability on farm households, resulting in the nationwide agricultural depressions of the 1880s and the inter-war period and in fluctuations in the fortunes of particular localities and individual families. Moreover, the gap between rural and urban incomes remained and urban levels of amenities, education and culture were not achieved in most rural areas. Rural dwellers and their spokesmen therefore came to feel increasingly disadvantaged as urbanisation and industrialisation proceeded, and their discontent became a potent and emotive issue in the politics of the inter-war period. Nevertheless, as compared with their predecessors, though not perhaps their urban contemporaries, the lot of Japanese rural dwellers did improve over the course of pre-war industrialisation. By the late 1930s, famine, epidemic, malnutrition and illiteracy were considerably rarer occurrences; farm output and, more significantly, the average income of farm households had substantially increased; better diets, improved housing conditions, higher standards of education, health care and social welfare were generally available, and goods and services such as electric lighting, improved farm equipment and travel by train were within the reach of many households. A price was paid in terms of, for example, increasing state interference in day-to-day life, periodic unemployment or low prices and a growing discontent with the limitations of rural life. However, as compared with the experience of many of today's developing countries, it can be argued that the distribution of the benefits of Japan's economic development between the urban and rural sectors and among larger- and smaller-scale cultivators within the agricultural sector was relatively more equal. A further corollory of this was the way in which Japanese farm households made their mark upon the character of the industrialisation process, by obliging the industrial sector to come to terms with the economic and technical strength of the family-based, rice-cultivating but diversified farm household, and much of part III will be concerned with describing the effects of this process. However, it should not be assumed that the survival and growing strength of the small-scale cultivating household was achieved without generating a degree of social, political and economic conflict in rural areas, and it is to evidence of this, and analysis of its significance, that we now turn.

ECONOMIC CHANGE AND CONFLICT IN RURAL AREAS: THE ANALYSIS OF TENANCY DISPUTES

Terms such as 'modernisation' and 'development', which might well be used to describe the sequence of technical and economic change set out in the earlier chapters of part II, give an impression of smooth progress to what was, in fact, a process in which, inevitably, some gained relatively more than others and in which conflicts of interest were aroused. The manifestations of these conflicts – peasant revolts and uprisings in the Tokugawa period and tenancy disputes later – have long been a focus of attention for Japanese historians, and analysis of their causes and patterns can be used to reveal much about the nature of economic change in rural areas and its wider social and political ramifications. The initial interpretation of such conflicts was largely in terms of simple, so to speak instinctive, reactions on the part of the poor and oppressed to intensified exploitation at the hands of rulers and landowners, but more recent work suggests a more complex pattern of causation which can be related to approaches to the study of rural protest and the motives and strategies of peasant farmers, stimulated by the 'moral economy' idea (see ch. 5). Tenancy disputes in particular can be seen as manifestations of the social and political conflicts engendered by the same efforts to survive and benefit from the industrialisation of the economy as produced the technical and economic changes described in previous chapters.

The participants in the tenancy disputes which were to become a feature of agricultural life in early twentieth-century Japan were heirs to a long tradition of rural protest and revolt. Records of local peasant uprisings during the Tokugawa period abound and indicate that some protests developed into regional movements sufficiently serious as to involve the Shogunal government, although widespread violence was rare. The petitions presented by those taking part generally included reference to bad harvests and threats to farmers' survival and requested reductions in taxes and other impositions. It was natural to conclude from this that the uprisings occurred in response to particular hardship or particularly heavy exactions on the part of feudal authorities and to interpret them in terms of conflict between the feudal ruling class and the peasantry.

However, more detailed analysis of individual uprisings occurring at different points in the Tokugawa period suggests that the character of protests in fact changed over the course of time reflecting the changing structure of the economy.[9] Protests in the seventeenth century tended to take the form of appeals by villages to the benevolence of the feudal lord, requesting reductions in taxes at times of hardship, such as bad harvests, in order that cultivators could 'continue as farmers', that is, maintain their security over their holdings by providing for their own subsistence and meeting their tax obligations. Later in the Tokugawa period, however, not only did protests tend to become more frequent and violent, peaking in widespread peasant uprisings during the disturbed time leading up to the Meiji Restoration, but their nature also changed. With the commercialisation of the economy and the spread of market relations, the threat to the ordinary farmer's livelihood in difficult times, or the obstacles to a household's achievement of a higher or more secure standard of living, lay less in the exactions of the feudal authorities, which had in practice failed to keep pace with the growth and diversification of the rural economy, and more in market conditions, as embodied in the actions of those other members of village society who engaged in trading and industrial activity as well as landowning and cultivation. Protests came to change in form from petitions to the feudal authorities to riots and the destruction of the property of rural rice traders and merchants. The traditional techniques and rhetoric of protest were adapted to deal with threats to farmers' livelihoods resulting from fluctuations in a commercial economy rather than a subsistence one, utilising the idea of the cultivator's right to subsistence and the superior's obligation to ensure the inferior's survival but now within a market context. Conflict within village society had replaced conflict between the samurai ruling class and the peasant cultivating class, but group action was being adapted by smaller-scale cultivators as a weapon in their battle for survival and improvement in a market economy which, by and large, they accepted. Thus, according to Vlastos, peasant protests remained localised, with the overthrow of the system rarely taken as an objective, and rural uprisings played only an indirect role in the downfall of the Tokugawa government.[10]

As the agricultural economy adapted to the radical results of the Restoration period, including the growth in foreign trade and the effects of the Land Tax Reform, farm households became increasingly embedded in market relations and dependent on them for the sale of produce and the purchase of inputs. Land changed hands more easily and frequently and, as we have seen, when fortunes were bad, tenancy increased. There undoubtedly continued to be cases of resistance to those actions of both the state and the local landowning class which were seen to threaten the interests of smaller-scale cultivators and tenants,[11] but official records of instances of organised protest action were not collected at the national level until the World-War-I period. Moreover, during the second half of the nineteenth century a great many larger landowners still fell into the cultivating-landlord category, remaining resident in the villages where their land was located and farming some of it themselves, performing the social and administrative functions demanded of senior figures in the village's kinship and status hierarchies, and not pursuing lifestyles markedly different from those of many other village residents. Dore and Waswo have both argued that landlords of this type played a positive role in introducing innovations to their villages and mediating between smaller-scale cultivators and the outside world (see ch. 7 and Dore 1960; Waswo 1977). Hence it seems plausible that, in the period of, for the most part, rising prices and increasing output between the Restoration and the World-War-I boom, grievances remained localised and targets for wider protest action difficult to define.

By the late 1910s, however, concerted protest action by organised groups of farmers, usually tenants, had become sufficiently conspicuous to be regarded as a national issue and to warrant the collection of official statistics and reports. Hence we know that, from this time onwards, recorded instances of tenancy disputes increased sharply, from 85 in 1917 to annual totals of over 2000 in the 1920s, rising to a peak of 6800 in 1936 (Waswo 1977: 100). These disputes ranged from polite petitions to the local landlord through to concerted, and sometimes violent, action organised by tenants' associations covering a considerable number of villages, and consistency in the definition and coverage of disputes in the statistics cannot be assumed (Smethurst 1986: 316–37). Nonetheless, they clearly do indicate that organised collective action on the part of cultivators became a recognised and relatively widely-used weapon in cases of conflict during the 1920s and 1930s. Arbitration procedures were established to aid in the settlement of disputes between tenant unions and landlords acting singly or, increasingly, in their own associations, but some conflicts still reached the stage of legal procedures and police intervention.

In the pursuit of their objectives in disputes, tenants made use of the traditional rhetoric of the threat to their survival caused by bad harvests and demanded reductions in rents, so that an explanation of the observed increase in protest action in terms of the economic hardship of tenants obliged to pay high rents was a natural one, especially given the occurrence of the world depression, from which Japanese farmers undoubtedly suffered, in the midst of the rising trend. The higher educational levels and political awareness of smaller-scale cultivators by this time, and the links between national tenant-union leaders and the increasingly active urban labour movement, made possible the addition of a revolutionary dimension to the interpretation of the increase in disputes and the use of the observed trend as evidence of the kind of differentiation into a landowning class and a rural proletariat which Marxist models would predict. However, a number of problems with this interpretation have been raised by Japanese scholars and in English by Waswo (1977) and, more radically, Smethurst (1986), suggesting that disputes were not simply straightforward reactions to poverty and exploitation but rather an aspect of the more complex process whereby farmers adapted and strengthened their position in the industrialising economy.

The major problem with the poverty/differentiation interpretation of disputes lies in the pattern of their timing and regional distribution, since, at least in the period up to 1931, the majority of cases arose, not in the poorest parts of the countryside, but in the rural areas of the much more highly developed and industrialised south-west of the country. The typical disputes of the 1920s were initiated by tenants themselves in areas where levels of income and farming technology were generally higher, by-employments more widely available and tenancy conditions better than in the poorer and less developed north-east. Waswo argues that a major factor in explaining the upsurge in disputes is therefore the improved negotiating strength given to tenants by the range of alternative job opportunities offered in such areas and by the experience gained in finding industrial employment during the World-War-I boom. She goes on, however, to add a moral–economy strand to her explanation by arguing that it was in the industrially more developed areas of the country that landlords were more likely to acquire non-agricultural interests and to neglect the village responsibilities and functions that legitimised their position and their right to receive rent. Thus tenants complained not only of absentee landlords, but also of resident landlords who were more concerned with their business interests than with their traditional role of ensuring the security and welfare of their dependent households. Smethurst goes further and denies that disputes can be seen, even to this extent, as reactions by tenants in the face of landlords' actions. Rather, for him, disputes arose as part of the long-term process whereby small-scale cultivators achieved higher incomes and greater control over the conditions under which their farm businesses operated. Tenants entered into disputes, typically behind the leadership of the village's middle-scale, owner-tenant cultivators, as conscious moves to make use of their collective bargaining strength to reduce the landlord's share of the crop and improve the cultivator's ability to make the most of his holding.

Disputes in the early '30s were generally of a different character and occurred with greater frequency in the poorer north-eastern regions. Landlords in these parts of the country had fewer opportunities to develop outside interests and hence, when the Depression hit their incomes and savings, they saw little alternative but to try to remedy matters by seeking tenants who would pay higher rents or by taking land back into cultivation themselves. Tenants in these regions borrowed the tactics of their counterparts in more industrialised areas to try to resist such moves, typically in small-scale disputes aimed at maintaining tenure rather than reducing rents.[12] From the mid-1930s, however, the number of disputes began to decline as village organisations became absorbed into the wartime drive for unity and patriotism.

The typology and periodisation of disputes outlined here is by no means watertight and it is in fact difficult, as Smethurst shows, to produce a clear correlation between any one indicator of farmers' real or perceived economic position and the recorded incidence of disputes. Nonetheless, although the landlord system as such was not overthrown, at least until the post-war land reform which did, to all intents and purposes, abolish tenancy, and neither was the insecurity experienced by cultivators dependent on price movements and outside employment completely removed, as the depression years revealed, yet most disputes ended in some form of compromise, which meant, in effect, a reduction in rents. This contributed to the overall tendency for the value of rents to fail to keep pace with rises in yields, let alone farm incomes from all sources, so that landownership had become, by the 1930s, a less profitable investment as well as a less gratifying way of life. To an extent, as Waswo argues, Japanese landlords unwittingly brought about their own long-term undoing, by encouraging the spread of new cultivation techniques which ultimately gave their tenants the economic advantages they needed to enable them to dispense with the landlord's functions. Equally, through their investment and involvement in rural business and industry, they helped to create the employment opportunities which gave cultivators additional sources of income and alternatives to life as tenants. In doing this, however, they were themselves responding to the forces generated by the nature of rice cultivation itself, the past accumulations of commercial and economic experience, the interrelations between the Japanese and the world economies, and the characteristics of industrial technology at the time. Tenancy disputes can therefore be seen as an outcome of the direction of change in the technology of rice cultivation and the integration of industrial activity within the rural household, both of which favoured the family-sized holding, and the results of the overall tenancy-dispute movement appear in turn to have contributed to this trend.

All in all, the work of Waswo (as of the Japanese 'revisionist' scholars whose views she reflects) and, more radically, that of Smethurst represents a fundamental challenge to long-accepted views of the distributional effects of the spread of market/capitalist relations in the Japanese countryside and the scale of the burden which Japanese peasant farmers bore in the interests of industrialisation. The far-reaching implications of this challenge are reflected in the heated controversy which Smethurst's book has generated.[13] From the point of view of the understanding of development processes, however, the evolving reinterpretation of the nature of economic, political and social relationships in Japanese villages falls into line with the prevailing emphasis, both of writers of the moral–economy school and their opponents, on the significance of the attitudes and actions of farmers and their communities in determining the course of economic and political history. In much development literature, peasant farmers are no longer regarded as pawns to be manipulated by a merchant/landlord/capitalist class, an all-powerful state or even a subversively-organising Communist Party, but are now viewed as significantly attempting to impose their own interests and values on the course of change, whether through more or less concerted political revolt or through efforts to make the most of market opportunities. Just as the activity of the peasantry in the development processes of India, South-East Asia and China is being re-evaluated, so, gradually, is that of Japanese farmers, with potentially drastic results for the interpretation not just of Japan's economic past, but also of her political and social history.

9 Conclusion

For most scholars working within the Western tradition at least, the history of agriculture's part in Japan's pre-war development is a success story and, indeed, looking at that history in the light of the experience of post-war Third World countries, it is hard to deny this characterisation. Steady growth in agricultural output for much of the time provided food and raw materials for a growing urban population, keeping the need to import agricultural products to a minimum and even simultaneously generating export income; farmers submitted to taxation to support the industrialising state and transferred their savings and the labour of their sons and daughters to the modern factory sector, but rural areas continued to provide enough employment to prevent the large-scale drift to the towns with which present day developing countries struggle to cope; technical change in agriculture took an 'appropriate' form, making few demands on the nation's scarce capital resources and resulting in a more productive utilisation of existing resources of land and labour, while enabling smaller-scale cultivators to survive and, to a moderate degree at least, prosper, and all this was achieved without the kinds of massive, disruptive and divisive institutional reforms which have represented, to many developing countries, the only means of securing the 'agricultural surplus' for developmental ends.

Initial attempts to model and explain agriculture's role in Japan's development made use, as chapter 6 sets out, of the dual-economy development theories then widely prevalent in development economics. Although changes during the Tokugawa period had created favourable preconditions for agricultural growth, it was the institutional reforms initiated by the new Meiji state which were seen as the key to the utilisation of agriculture's potential to support and contribute to industrialisation. The establishment of the land tax enabled the state to tap a share of growing agricultural output for investment in industry, and the removal of the feudal government structure, as well as of restrictions on communications and trade and on economic choice, made possible the spread of the new technology which generated that growth. As industry grew, under the stimulus of the new policies of the state, it was able to draw on the supply of rural surplus labour, thus accumulating profits for re-investment, but without, given the character of technical change in agriculture, threatening the growth in farm output.

Agriculture's role in this model was essentially a passive or reactive one. Industrialisation was set in motion and, given the institutional changes brought about by the state, fed on resources of labour and capital drawn from the agricultural sector. Little consideration of the nature and determinants of agriculture's response to the growth of industry, or of changes and conflicts within the rural sector itself, was called for by this approach. However, by the late 1960s, the results for developing countries of the neglect of agriculture which the dual-economy model tended to foster were beginning to generate a new concern to understand how farm households operated and hence why they seemed unable to produce the kind of simultaneous output growth and resource transfer apparently observed in the Japanese case. This concern, fuelled by the emergence of the Green Revolution, led to many more detailed studies of the economic and social organisation of agriculture in the Third World and to a new appreciation of the objectives and strategies pursued by rural households and the constraints, such as the need to minimise risk or to participate in village groups and social hierarchies, within which they operated. In most cases, such studies sought to explain problems in rural development, such as failure to adopt new technology, growing poverty and inequality, or the inadequacies of research and extension services for farmers. The Japanese case, on the other hand, presents the opportunity to apply these new approaches to situations in which, for example, technical change did occur and was widely diffused, small- and medium-scale farmers did survive and rural living standards, at the level of 'basic needs' at least, were improved. Hence this chapter will endeavour to bring together the story told in part II in the light of these new approaches to the study of peasant economies and in an effort to determine what made the Japanese case different.

A key element in explaining both the growth in output that facilitated agriculture's contribution to industrial development and the relative absence of the trend towards increasing inequality observed in parts of the present-day Third World clearly lies in the characteristics of the technical changes diffused among Japanese farmers during the nineteenth and early twentieth centuries. These were initially the result of research and experimentation carried out by numerous practising farmers and, since there was no suitable technology readily available to import from the developed world, it was this package of indigenous techniques which formed the basis on which the official research and extension services worked when they began to come into existence towards the end of the nineteenth century. These techniques were therefore already tried and tested under many local environmental conditions and reflected the needs and capacities of the practising cultivators by and for whom they were designed. They made use of the resources most farmers possessed – local knowledge and careful and experienced labour – and did not demand either skills or capital investments beyond the reach of the majority of cultivators.

Given this pre-existing technological base and the need to rely on the knowledge and experience of the so-called 'veteran farmers' who had developed it, those who worked in the official research and extension system were bound to maintain relatively close links with the cultivators they served. Much of the early work of the state-funded experiment stations, the local government agriculture departments and the technical officers of the network of agricultural associations consisted in surveying, formulating and diffusing practices already in use in their areas or elsewhere, and research and extension were not treated as separate functions until after World War II. Some training in Western agricultural science increasingly became a necessary qualification for recruitment into the official agricultural services, and scientific techniques, such as laboratory cross-breeding of seeds, were utilised in the national and regional experiment stations set up around the turn of the century, but by this stage a pattern had been laid down which precluded the extension official from adopting the exclusive role of the outside expert and thereby helped to ensure the 'appropriateness' of the technology to local conditions (for a case study, see Francks 1984: chs. 5 and 7).

Moreover, when this picture is combined with the observed changes in the distribution of cultivated land and of power and influence in village society, and with a theoretical approach which assumes that the direction of technical change is induced, not only by changes in the relative supplies and prices of production inputs, but also by the particular problems arising out of the operation of particular techniques in particular conditions, it would follow that the kinds of technical development taking place would reflect the needs of the strengthening small-to-medium class of family-based farm households. Their strength had arisen in part from the results of the earlier efforts of the landlord class, which was not as clearly differentiated in the Japanese case, economically or socially, from the remainder of village residents as in some other developing rural economies, to introduce and diffuse technical improvements in the operation of which, in the long run, smaller-scale cultivators possessed the advantage. As the landlord class declined, therefore, and state and local-government organisations took its place as the source of new technology, it was the needs of the small-to-medium scale cultivator group which increasingly demanded to be met. Hence, for example, there was little interest in the mechanisation of field operations, such as ploughing, which could adequately be carried out by the average family labour force, and experiment-station research was concentrated on improvements to seed varieties and fertiliser application or, inasfar as mechanisation was considered, on methods of saving labour in such operations as threshing and hulling, which did represent bottlenecks for the family group wishing to plant a second crop.

In a sense, farmers thus reaped the benefits of Japan's early start as a 'late developer', as an outcome of which she was faced with no readily available technology to import as a means of 'modernising' agriculture and was hence forced to appreciate the results of a long-standing tradition of agricultural research and experimentation. It might be argued that this need was reinforced by, and in turn strengthened, prevailing approaches to the status and practical application of scientific knowledge in Japanese philosophic traditions, with results still to be seen in the technical practice and policy of modern industry. Whatever else, however, it did produce an appropriate and widely diffused high-yielding agricultural technology.

The problems experienced by smaller-scale farmers in adopting Green Revolution methods and inputs are not in fact, as a rule, the consequences of the characteristics of the techniques. Like the methods of the Meiji Nōhō, such techniques do not in themselves exhibit economies of scale, since seed and fertiliser are inputs infinitely divisible down to the scale of the smallest plot. Their adoption does, though, require the provision of some facilities to which it is frequently difficult for the small-scale cultivator on his own to gain access. These include, especially, adequate and controlled supplies of irrigation water, credit for the puchase of fertiliser inputs, and sources of information about, and training in the use of, the new methods. In the Japanese case, it has been suggested that, in the earlier stages of agricultural development, members of the cultivating landlord class tended to view the provision of these facilities to their tenants and other client-households as in their own interests and/or as part of their social and moral function in the village community. As landlords' interests changed, however, group activity among the increasingly less dependent small- and medium-scale cultivators began to fulfil these functions in their place, and it could be argued that the capacity of Japanese farm households to act together in co-operative groups represents another key factor in the successful and relatively equal diffusion of output-increasing technology.

The Japanese village has a long tradition of acting as a social, political and economic unit. As is well known, in Tokugawa times the village as a whole was responsible for its tax payments and the deficits of those unable to meet their share of the village's assessment had to be made up by others. Underlying this, however, lay the fundamental mutual ties resulting from reliance on the same interconnected irrigation system. This not only necessitated a high degree of communal organisation of the maintenance of the system and the allocation of water supplies, but also, especially given the fact that each household cultivated several plots scattered throughout the village's paddy area, made the economic fates of all to a considerable extent interdependent. Thus, if another village upstream took more than its customary share of scarce water supplies, it was vital to the interests of all within a downstream village to organise as a group to protest and, if needs be, fight (for an example, see Shimpo 1976); if one household failed to keep its feeder channels clear, then all others with plots below it in the system would suffer. In the provision of the preconditions for the adoption of the new technology, irrigation improvements, such as the conversion of permanently flooded fields into drainable ones, represented investments which villages as groups had to decide to undertake, and to those accustomed to organising village-based fire services, shrine maintenance, road repair, young men's societies, and so on, the establishment of agricultural co-operatives, village credit associations, group marketing and storage facilities and such like was a natural development.

It is of course but a short step from this point to the argument that 'group-based culture' lies behind Japan's agricultural, as well as her industrial, success. However, what I hope the detailed study of Japan's rural economic history shows is rather that the need and capacity to act in groups was the result of a complex combination of forces which would have to include the Tokugawa government system, the requirements of irrigation provision in the context of the

Japanese environment, and all the technical and economic factors which led to the decline of the larger-scale cultivating elite. Ishikawa's pioneering work on the development of economic models of group behaviour in agriculture, based not on 'culture', but on the constraints and requirements of risk minimisation and output growth in the Asian context, shows that, under plausible assumptions, communal action produces the best outcomes for all categories of farm household within the village (Ishikawa 1981: ch. 3). Japanese farmers, with experience of group activity by no means unique in the paddy-rice cultivating world at least, opted for communal action in those areas of their economic lives in which it offered the best solution. In other areas, they chose to act as independent operators in the market. This suggests that models which work exclusively in terms of either group culture or competitive market behaviour are inadequate tools of analysis in explaining the relatively successful response of Japanese farmers to industrialisation, and attempts to force the behaviour of peasant households in other developing areas into such limited models may prove equally unsatisfactory. Community activity and market relations can co-exist and interact, as the Japanese case at least shows, as a positive means of limiting risk, promoting agricultural development and reducing tendencies towards inequality.

One of the recurring themes of our discussion of agricultural development has been the continued capacity of the farm household to combine basic subsistence (rice) cultivation with other forms of agricultural and industrial activity. The prevalence of manufacturing activity within farm families and villages is a characteristic of pre-industrial, or proto-industrial, societies in general, but in the Japanese case by-employment among members of agricultural households did not die out, but flourished and developed as the market grew during the Tokugawa period and even, later, when factory production began to take root in the industrial sector. It made rural labour available for use in industrial production without necessitating migration to urban areas and was, as we have seen, a major factor in ensuring the survival of the small-scale family farm as an economic unit.

As Bray has shown, rice cultivation, with its ability to make productive use of large amounts of labour over the course of the agricultural year, naturally lends itself to combination with by-employments which take advantage of the seasonal slack periods of this ample labour force (Bray 1986: ch. 4). In the Japanese case, the restrictions imposed on manufacturing industry in urban areas during the Tokugawa period encouraged entrepreneurs to

develop the means of tapping this rural labour supply, in order
to meet the growing demand for manufactured goods. By the time
that the adoption of larger-scale factory organisation began to be
technologically necessary in industries such as textiles, therefore,
Japanese rural dwellers were well used to forms of organisation which
permitted them to earn income from industrial sources while at the
same time contributing to the economies of their family farms, and
the characteristics of Meiji Nōhō technology were such as to enable
them to continue to raise agricultural output without sacrificing these
alternative income-earning possibilities for members of the family.
Although, with time, increasing numbers of people, mostly younger
sons and daughters, did move permanently into industrial work in the
towns, employers did not find it easy, as chapter 12 will demonstrate,
to recruit and maintain permanent factory labour forces. Recruitment
practices, wages, and employment conditions had to be adapted in
varying ways so as to encourage rural dwellers to take up industrial
employment and to stay in the factory once they had been recruited,
and the results of the history of interaction between the demands of
modern factory technology and management and the strengths of the
farm households from which industrial workers came have left their
mark on the nature of Japanese industry.

In other respects too, the long experience of rural Japanese men
and women in combining industrial operations with their household's
agricultural activity conditioned their characteristics as industrial
employees when they did eventually become factory workers. It
is frequently suggested that Japanese girls proved adept at silk and
cotton textile work because of their prior experience of spinning and
weaving in their farm homes. More clearly demonstrated (in Smith
1986) is the unusual ability of Japanese factory workers to adapt to
factory standards of punctuality and timing, which Smith attributes
to their experience of the complex organisation and timetabling
of rice cultivation combined with other forms of work. Nothing
comparable to Emily Honig's study of the impact on factory life
of the experiences rural Chinese women brought with them to the
Shanghai textile mills (Honig 1986) has been carried out in the case
of their earlier Japanese counterparts, and the tendency, originating
perhaps in surplus labour-type models, to assume that the demands
of factory life are able to override the characteristics rural migrants
bring with them remains strong. However, a recognition of the
part played by the economic and technical structure of the farm
household in shaping the characteristics of Japanese industrialisation
might represent an unexpected result of the effort to give greater

weight to understanding the decisions and motivations of the peasant farmer.

The stress in all that has gone before has been on the significance of the technical and economic strategies pursued by Japanese farm households as they played their part in the nation's development. This resulted from the effort to redress the balance, in the light of contemporary thinking in development studies, away from the view of agriculture as a passive reservoir of labour and other resources for industrialisation and towards a picture of the farm household as a positive actor in the economic field. However, it is important to conclude by pointing out two broader factors which nonetheless did create particularly favourable conditions for the relative success of Japanese agriculture in the development process, as compared with the situation facing many present-day Third World agricultural sectors.

First, the long period of steady development and change, secluded from the forces of the outside world economy, which preceded the early stages of modern industrialisation, left Japanese farmers with an inheritance of capital, skills and economic experience which many Third World farmers, emerging from periods of, for example, colonial market domination, do not possess. Particularly important in this respect is the pre-existing development of irrigation facilities, which enabled nineteenth-century Japanese farmers to adopt high-yielding rice cultivation technology without the large-scale investment in irrigation projects many Third World governments have been obliged to provide. When industrialisation began, many Japanese farmers were already endowed with commercial experience, relatively high educational levels, an acceptance of the value of population control, access to a relatively well-developed communications network, and so on. Whether or not they were already by 1868, as James Nakamura suggested, achieving levels of output well in excess of those prevailing elsewhere in Asia in the 1950s, Japanese farmers faced the growth of modern industry with resources, experience and potential unavailable to many of their present-day counterparts.

Second, little has so far been said, in advance of part III, about the characteristics of the industrial sector with which Japanese agriculture interacted, but a further major factor affecting the conditions facing farm households was the scope and nature of the employment opportunities opened up to them by nineteenth- and early twentieth-century industrialisation, as compared with those resulting from the post-World War II industrialisation of present-day developing countries. Even without the labour-using adaptations to industrial technology made by Japanese producers, the world best-practice techniques of, say, 1900 required substantially more labour, per unit produced or sum invested, than their equivalents of, say, 1960. Altogether, therefore, the demand for labour resulting from Japan's pre-war industrialisation was considerably greater than that created by the enclaves of modern industry in the Third World today. Thus the impact on the labour and product markets through which agriculture and industry interacted was more marked and although, even so, the growth of industrial employment never did more than draw off the increase in the rural population, nonetheless, at times and in places at least, rising wages and labour shortages affected both industrial employers and farm households. In all sorts of wider respects also, including, for example, the spread of social, political and cultural change, the impact of the much more labour-intensive industrialisation of Japan on the lives of the farm population must have been greater than that experienced by many rural dwellers in the present-day Third World.

The comparative context implicitly assumed throughout the above has been that of those developing countries, such as India and a number of Latin American states, whose agricultural conditions have been extensively studied. The agricultural sectors of the success stories of post-war economic development, notably Taiwan and South Korea, have received less consideration and yet, interestingly, have a number of features in common with the agriculture of Japan. These include not only broadly comparable environmental conditions and the predominance of irrigated rice cultivation, but also more direct similarities resulting from their experience as Japanese colonies. Thus, both benefited from substantial pre-war investment in irrigation development and in the establishment of research and extension systems and agricultural associations modelled on Japanese examples, and both undertook land reforms, prior to their periods of rapid industrialisation, which consolidated the position of the family-sized farm, just as the slower process of technical and economic change had done in pre-war Japan. The lessons to be learnt from such comparisons, however, await acceptance of the importance of understanding the role of farm households in the development process which part II has sought to illustrate in the Japanese case.

Part III

Industrialisation: technology, labour and the industrial structure in Japan's development

10 Introduction

Despite all that was said in part II about the importance of recognising the role of the farm sector in developing countries, it remains nonetheless the case that industrialisation has always been the central phenomenon in the process of economic development. Although economic historians may not now regard nineteenth-century industrial revolutions as being quite as revolutionary as they once thought, nonetheless there is no doubt that it was the emergence and spread of new forms of industrial production that constituted the essential element in the development of the economic strength of the now-developed world. As we have seen in the Japanese case, 'pre-industrial' economies can produce a wide range of manufactured goods of many different types, qualities and degrees of sophistication. Hence industrialisation means, not the establishment of manufacturing as such, but a transformation in the scale on which, and methods by which, it is carried out, and in the characteristics of the goods produced to meet consumer demands. Industrial growth is an integrated process, with new forms of production being dependent on new types or qualities of raw materials and on the use by final consumers of different kinds of goods. Workers and managers need to acquire new skills and operate new kinds of equipment within new forms of institutional organisation. The growth of the automobile industry, for example, requires, on the one hand, the supply of specialised kinds of steel to be processed by workers brought together in large-scale and complex organisations, and, on the other hand, the existence of the roads, fuel supplies, maintenance facilities, and so on which enable its products to be utilised by, among others, workers making their way to car factories.

A number of developing countries have achieved considerable success in establishing new forms of industrial production within their borders, and the rate of growth of industrial output in the contemporary Third World is almost certainly greater than that achieved during the equivalent stages of the industrialisation of today's developed countries. Steel mills, chemical plants, car assembly and electrical appliance factories have been springing up throughout Asia and South America, alongside the textile mills and raw-material processing facilities more commonly associated with the early stages of industrialisation. Development-studies theorists and practitioners have naturally been much concerned with the analysis of this process and of the problems to which it has given rise, and it is in the light of this work that later chapters will consider the equivalent development of industrial production in pre-war Japan. Before that, however, it will be helpful briefly to compare the backgrounds to industrialisation in the Third World today and in Japan in the nineteenth and early-twentieth centuries, and then to consider development-studies approaches to three particular aspects of the process in which current development theories and experience seem to intersect most clearly with issues in the study of Japan's economic history.

For all later-developing countries, the prior existence of established forms of industrial production in the already-developed world creates the potential for a rapid process of industrialisation. The technology and production organisation required for the manufacture of the whole range of industrial goods are already known, tried and tested. Developing-country entrepreneurs and technologists do not need to reinvent the steam engine or rediscover the systems of division of labour that enable groups of workers to produce the quantities and qualities of complex goods on which developed-country consumers choose to expend their incomes. Rather, they need only engage in the less costly and less time-consuming process of discovering how things are already being done elsewhere and acquiring from abroad or creating at home the knowledge, skills and resources necessary to replicate what producers in industrialised countries already do.

The fact that catching-up must be, to an extent at least, quicker and cheaper than pioneering clearly lies behind the relatively rapid industrialisation achieved in the post-war Third World as compared with, for example, early European industrialisation. However, the simple picture described above has proved to be seriously misleading as a result of its implicit assumption that technology and industrial organisation can be regarded as neutral, transferable phenomena, capable of being abstracted from the environments which gave birth to them and conditioned their subsequent upbringing. The industrial technology and production systems available as models to later-developing nations are the results of long histories of adaptation to the conditions of the Western European and American societies in which they have predominantly been used. For example, and perhaps most importantly, the longer an economy has been growing and developing, the higher are wages and incomes likely to be and the greater the past accumulation of, and present capacity for, saving and investment. Faced with a situation in which labour is growing increasingly expensive while capital funds are becoming increasingly easily available, businessmen will be searching for the means to economise on labour by substituting for it the machinery and equipment which are becoming ever cheaper and technically more efficient. Scientists and engineers will spend their time devising such means, and the resulting methods of production will be increasingly capital-intensive and mechanically sophisticated. The organisation of production will reflect this direction of change, with businesses requiring fewer workers, relative to output and capital input, but demanding of them higher levels of skill and education. At the same time, other inputs will need to reflect the increasingly detailed and sophisticated requirements of mechanically and organisationally complex production processes, and consumers will become ever more used to the variety and quality of the goods produced in this way.

Entrepreneurs in developing countries can therefore skip the long and costly stages through which industrial production methods have developed only at the price of adopting technologies and institutional organisations adapted for conditions very different from those with which they are likely to be faced. In their economies, the wage rates of most workers, though not of the relatively few who possess the experience or education needed to operate developed-country technology, are low and capital funds are hard to come by. The immediate demands of the majority of consumers, mostly rural dwellers, are for basic food, clothing and shelter rather than for the complex, high-cost products which developed-country markets demand, and the infrastructure, input suppliers, educational facilities and so on needed to support the sophisticated industrial systems of the developed world are generally not yet well established. This means that the techniques and products of developed-country industry, while epitomising the goals of development, are frequently 'inappropriate' to the needs and conditions of developing countries. Nonetheless, as newly-independent Third World nations launched their development plans, few alternatives seemed to exist other than to seek to introduce the technology and organisation of industrial production then in use in the developed world.

The consequences of this gradually became apparent as industrialisation proceeded through the '50s and '60s in the Third World. Scarce investment resources were directed towards the limited number of capital-intensive, 'high-technology' projects which indigenous supplies of capital could fund, and foreign investment frequently had to be sought, from aid agencies or from Western or multinational companies, to supplement domestic sources. Such projects generated only a limited demand for labour, although, given the relatively high productivity of workers operating advanced equipment, high wages might be paid to those with the training, luck or connections needed to obtain employment. Given the lack of local supporting facilities, dependence on foreign suppliers for inputs and for technical skills remained, operating against the objective of industrialisation as a means of establishing independence and world market competitiveness. The tendency towards the creation of enclaves of capital-intensive technology, manned by a high-wage 'labour aristocracy' and dominated by foreign or multinational company interests, which we saw was fostered by the adoption of ISI strategies in many post-war developing countries, was thus intensified by the constraints on technical and economic choice facing investors and decision-makers at the micro level.

The international economic and technical environment in which Japan's pre-war industrialisation took place was in many respects very different from that facing post-war Third World countries. The speed of technical development and economic growth since World War II, and the consequent expansion in the scale and complexity of industrial plant and equipment, have far outpaced pre-war rates. Large firms and trading companies with international interests did operate in the pre-war economy, but the post-war development of rapid worldwide communications has made their present-day counterparts vastly different and more powerful phenomena. Nonetheless, in other ways the problems faced in establishing new industries and new technologies have not changed. For pre-war Japan too, the models of advanced technology and industrial organisation were to be found already in existence in the developed world and knowledge about them was to be acquired through imports of equipment and technical expertise. The operation of new production processes required skills with which Japanese workers were largely unacquainted, even though a substantial proportion of them did have experience of industrial work in more traditional forms. The infrastructure of communications and the capacity to provide suitable inputs and technical skills were only gradually built up as industrialisation proceeded, and dependence on foreign suppliers remained unavoidable. In part III we shall be considering three particular aspects of the experience of Japanese industry as modern technology and new forms of industrial organisation were adopted. It is in these areas – the import and assimilation of technology from abroad, the creation of an urban industrial labour force, and the relations between 'modern' large-scale businesses and the other parts of the industrial sector – that Japanese experience can most productively be brought to bear on the micro-level problems facing present-day industrialising countries, and the remainder of this chapter will therefore outline the relevant theoretical frameworks within which comparisons and contrasts can be made.

Technology can be defined in various ways but for present purposes it will be taken as a broad term covering knowledge of the techniques for the production of particular goods and services.[1] It is a marketable resource, usually the property of an individual or a company, and can be transferred between economic organisations by a variety of methods. These include, for example, spying, theft, or 'reverse engineering', but also, more legitimately, the sale or transfer of technical knowledge 'embodied' in plant, machinery and the services of technical experts, or 'disembodied' in the form of patents, licences and blueprints.

Within the developed world, where a fairly high degree of similarity can be assumed in economic conditions and in levels of technical and scientific knowledge, the transfer of technology through the straightforward sale of equipment or patents on production processes ought to involve few difficulties. However, this common background cannot be assumed when the transfer takes place from a developed to a developing country. In this case, the buyer is often forced to rely on the seller for more than just the knowledge of the technology, and the transfer frequently forms part of a wider deal under which the seller will set up the production process on site, provide the necessary training and see the plant over the initial stages of operation at least. Arrangements for the capital funds involved, and hence the ultimate ownership and control of the production facilities, may range from simple 'plant export' contracts, under which the developing-country side buys and owns the plant from the beginning, through varying degrees of 'joint venture' to complete ownership by the technology-seller. The transfer of technology is thus intimately connected with the issues of economic and political control to which direct foreign investment by developed-country and multinational firms have given rise.

However, much of the initial work on technology transfer to developing countries was concerned not so much with ownership and control over the process as with the 'appropriateness', especially as regards the degree of labour or capital intensity, of the technical choices made by those carrying out industrial projects. The assumption implied by existing economic theories on the subject was that decision-makers would be faced with a range of possible techniques for the production of any given good, offering infinitely varying degrees of capital or labour intensity. Wheat could be grown by a great many men using hoes, intensively working a small area of land, or by one man covering a wide area with tractors and combines, or by any combination of inputs in between. The appropriate techniques for developing countries clearly ought to have been those which utilised relatively large amounts of labour and economised on capital, and yet it appeared that those making technology choices in or for the Third World were not selecting such techniques but were opting for the same relatively capital-intensive, 'high technology' methods as prevailed in developed economies.

Many possible explanations and solutions were offered for this. In some cases, it was clear that the only labour-intensive options available were the obsolete ancestors of present-day methods, for which equipment and spare parts were no longer produced, so that 'appropriate' techniques which did not use more of all inputs to produce a unit of output in effect no longer existed. This was especially the case where 'advanced-country' product characteristics were specified, leaving little scope for adaptations which might have permitted more labour-intensive production of more 'appropriate' products. Furthermore, on a less strictly technological level, studies of the institutional arrangements for technology choice suggested that there might be many forces operating on decision-makers which pushed them in the direction of 'inappropriate' techniques. Multinational companies have obvious reasons for opting for the kinds of advanced technology with which they are familiar and in which they have interests, but aid agencies and local entrepreneurs have also reacted in similar ways as a result of, for example, preferences for small and more easily managed labour forces, or for methods regarded as superior from an engineering, rather than an economic, point of view, or simply because of the availability of aid tied to high-technology projects.

It therefore seemed that, given the forces operating against it, progress towards the development of more appropriate, labour-intensive techniques and products for developing countries was likely to be slow. Moreover, as time went on, success stories indicating that the adaptation and assimilation of modern industrial technologies might not prove so problematic began to emerge. The most notable of these related to the East Asian Newly Industrialising Countries, whose steel, ships and cars were beginning to follow their textiles and electronic goods on to world markets, but other cases were appearing in, for example, Brazil and India, and the growing intra-Third World trade in capital goods bore witness to the emergence in developing countries of the indigenous technological capacity required to utilise once-imported knowledge. Technology transfer has come to be viewed more as a learning process whereby developing-country buyers may select the most up-to-date, 'inappropriate' plant and equipment as a means of acquiring, in the long term, the skills and knowledge which are needed in an industrial economy. Attention has shifted towards the study of the mechanisms whereby this has been achieved, concentrating on, for example, the methods and forms by which knowledge is transferred from the supplier to the developing-country side, or the means employed to ensure that dependence on the foreign supplier is gradually reduced, in successful cases of plant sales or direct foreign investment. As an example, the South Korean bureaucracy appears to have been particularly effective in monitoring and controlling technology inflows so as to ensure that all necessary information is transferred and local engineers and managers are trained to operate and develop the technology in question (Enos 1984).

It could not be said that, by the time of the Pacific War, Japanese industry had, on average, caught up with the technical levels of the West, but in the industries of the greatest economic and military significance high levels of technology had been well assimilated and indigenous technological capacity certainly existed. The means, and degree of success, with which this had been achieved varied from industry to industry, with some cases involving undoubtedly 'appropriate' technical choice and labour-intensive adaptation of imported equipment and others illustrating various kinds of joint venture and technical tie-up with developed-country firms, all against a background of varying degrees of state intervention and protection. As a result, nonetheless, Japanese businesses and the organs of the Japanese state gained the experience which enabled them, in the much more favourable post-war climate, so quickly and cheaply to catch up with and in many fields surpass the technology of the West.

The industry of developed economies is undoubtedly characterised by its heavy reliance on machinery and equipment which needs to be operated under what must be called factory conditions. Factories do not necessarily have to be large or to be located in urban areas alongside other factories, but nonetheless they frequently are, since they require sources of power, labour and infrastructural back-up which are usually only available on a suitable scale in urban concentrations. The superior efficiency of machine technology depends on the ability to break production processes down into separate operations and to co-ordinate the results of these operations on a reasonably large scale within a factory or at least within an area of relatively close communications, and it thus demands a kind of timed and disciplined work schedule rather different from that of agriculture or 'craft-type' manufacturing activity. Industrialisation has therefore generally called for the recruitment of men and women willing and able to move to urban centres and to learn to work at new sorts of tasks according to the timing and organisational discipline of the factory.

As we saw in part II, in the early two-sector development models it was assumed that underdeveloped countries were blessed with ample resources of 'surplus' labour which would straightforwardly move to work in modern-sector industry as and when required, on the offer of wages marginally higher than the subsistence level provided in agriculture. In practice, however, the experience of developing countries seems rarely to have conformed to this model. Although very rapid rates of population growth ought to have presented industrial employers with 'unlimited' supplies of labour at low wage rates, the kinds of constraint on technical choice outlined above appear to have prevented modern-sector enterprises from taking advantage of this. Instead, the kinds of project carried out have resulted in the creation of a relatively limited number of jobs offering relatively high pay and secure conditions, a tendency sometimes reinforced by factors such as minimum wage legislation, fear of labour unrest, the need not to appear to be exploiting local labour, and so on. On the other hand, the limited prospects of obtaining employment in the modern 'formal' sector of industry and the bureaucracy do not seem to have acted as much of a deterrent to migrants leaving their villages to go to try their luck in the towns, and the Third World has witnessed rapid urbanisation combined with rising levels of un- or under-employment among city-dwellers.

More recent work on the present-day Third World has therefore concentrated less on the creation of an industrial labour force and more on the analysis of rural-urban migration. The most influential migration theory, that of Todaro, explains the decision to migrate to the city in terms of the balance between the push of low standards of living and limited economic prospects in rural areas and the pull of the chance of employment in the high-wage urban modern sector. The rate of migration is seen as a function of, on the one hand, the urban-rural income differential and, on the other, the probability of being able to secure a modern-sector job. Such a model can be used to show, for example, how the creation of more high-wage, modern-sector employment may only exacerbate the problem of urban unemployment by increasing the probability of obtaining a job and thus encouraging more people to take their chances in the towns, and it offers the improvement of rural living standards as the most likely means of discouraging migration.[2] Empirical studies of migration suggest that other factors, such as education or social relationships between particular urban and rural areas, also play a part in the decision to move, and by no means all migration takes a one-way rural-urban form. Nonetheless the dominant theme of work on this topic has been the economic motivation on the part of the migrant to move to what may be a prolonged period of unemployment in the city.

In the Japanese case, on the other hand, the focus has largely rested on the side of the industrial employer and on his methods of recruiting and maintaining an industrial labour force. Analysts of the Japanese experience have had to try to explain the contradiction between, on one side, the supposedly unlimited supply of labour available from agriculture and, on the other, the apparent difficulties experienced by industrial employers in recruiting and maintaining work forces, which eventually led them to adopt the kinds of employment practice generally held to characterise 'Japanese management'. The higher level of agricultural development and the greater range of alternative employment possibilities in the Japanese case, combined with slower population growth than in the present-day Third World, resulted in a process of interaction between industrial employers and employees within which the incoming rural migrant was able to exert greater influence over the terms of employment than his or her present-day counterpart. Out of employers' responses to this were to emerge the institutions of the segmented labour market which still prevails in Japan, differentiating recruitment practices, educational qualifications and subsequent wages and conditions between the secure, modern-sector labour force and the many who still work elsewhere in the industrial sector.

Industrial workers who make their livings outside the secure conditions of modern large-scale industry have been a feature of the Japanese economy long enough for them to be well recognised as a 'problem' and a fit subject for economic theorising. In the present-day Third World, on the other hand, the realisation that, despite rapid urbanisation, modern-sector industry could only provide quite limited employment possibilities has only relatively recently given rise to consideration of the question of how the rest of the urban or non-agricultural population survives on the economic front. In the basic dual-economy model, there were assumed to be only two forms of livelihood: existence on the family farm or wage employment in modern industry. Yet large numbers of people have been migrating to Third-World cities without the prospect of immediate modern-sector employment, and, in societies with no welfare provision for the unemployed, must be making some kind of a living somehow. Students of development have therefore become increasingly interested in analysing the activities by which such livings are earned and have coined the term 'urban informal sector' to describe the economic world in which they are carried out. Informal-sector economic activity ranges from more-or-less criminal operations, such as gambling, prostitution, begging and so on, through small-scale, transient forms of retailing and service industry (street trading, shoe shining, etc), to relatively stable family businesses in fields such as construction, transport, and household services. Unlike formal-sector employment, informal-sector activity is easy to enter (and leave), operates on a small scale using labour-intensive methods, does not require skills learnt through formal education, and is organised on the basis of family or other close personal relationships. The output and employment generated by the informal sector are frequently unrecognised and unreported, so that their scale and contribution to GNP are often largely unknown.[3]

There are basically two ways of looking at the part played by the informal sector in a developing economy and both are reflected in work on Japan. It can be seen as a reservoir of low-income workers, living in frequently degrading and insecure conditions, unprotected by the state or by trade unions or by the village community. The informal sector has no access to the sources of technical improvement or education which would enable it to modernise and develop, and the squalor of the urban slum has become the typical and symbolic image of underdevelopment. Equally, though, a more positive picture of its role can be painted. Whilst the modern sector may of necessity employ inappropriate technology to produce products which the majority of consumers cannot yet afford, it is in the informal sector that labour-intensive methods create employment producing what consumers really need. Successful small-scale businessmen save and invest, expand output and generate much more work than modern-sector enterprises, and the informal sector is the route through which both entrepreneurs and potential industrial employees can find their way into the modern economy, acquiring skills in, for example, the maintenance of vehicles and machinery, sales techniques or financial operations which may lead to success in the wider world.

In the Japanese case, what is known as the 'small and medium enterprise' sector has continued to represent such an important part of the economy that economists and economic historians were studying it long before development theorists discovered the 'urban informal sector'. Much of the early Japanese work took the pessimistic view outlined above, stressing the markedly lower incomes and much worse employment conditions of workers in small businesses and regarding the small-scale sector in general as the reservoir of exploited workers on whose backs modern industry grew. However, glimpses of a more positive assessment have also appeared in studies of small-scale businesses as sources of labour-intensive technical and institutional adaptations to imported models, and as producers of import-saving consumer goods which helped to maintain traditional tastes and consumption patterns. Many well-known entrepreneurs and inventors began their careers in the informal sector, trying their fortunes or tinkering with machines. Moreover, what is perhaps most significant about the Japanese case in this respect is that, contrary to expectations, the small-scale sector has failed to wither away and continues to provide such a significant share of employment and output in the highly developed contemporary economy that its existence can no longer be regarded as a symptom of underdevelopment (Patrick and Rohlen 1987).

Part of the explanation for the survival of the active small-business sector in Japan must lie in the emergence of institutional forms within which large and small firms were linked together in complementary ways. Most notable among these are the 'industrial groups' known as *zaibatsu* before World War II and *keiretsu* now, but the list would also include the general trading companies which dominated large areas of Japan's pre-war domestic and international trading activity, and the practice of sub-contracting which has come to play a greater role in the lives of large and small businesses in Japan than elsewhere. These institutions are often viewed as the means whereby big business controls and exploits those outside its exclusive world, but can alternatively be seen as mechanisms which enable the informal sector to change and grow and contribute to the overall development of the economy.

Observers of the technology and industrial organisation in operation in the economic giant that Japan has now become are almost always struck by the marked differences between Japanese practice and that prevalent in the West. These differences are often ascribed to the peculiarities of Japanese culture and social organisation, and are generally credited with playing a large part in Japan's economic success. In what follows, the analysis of Japanese economic history in the three areas described above will seek to reveal the striking features of Japan's industry as, rather, the products of her pre-war 'catching-up' industrialisation process, yet at the same time as factors contributing to the relatively rapid and successful absorption, into a very different economic and social environment, of the alien technology and institutions of the then-developed world.

11 Technical change and industrial growth

The popular conception of Japan in the contemporary world is undoubtedly now one of a 'high-tech' economy. Given the frequently-cited difficulties experienced by post-war developing countries in the choice of technology and the creation of indigenous technological capacity, the acknowledged achievement of mastery over the technological bases of modern industrial production is by no means the least remarkable aspect of Japan's rise to economic superpower status. When nineteenth-century Japan first encountered the wonders of Victorian industrial technology, its forms – the steamship, the railway, the telegraph – appeared as miraculously alien as late twentieth-century information technology is to much of today's Third World. Yet soon after the turn of the century Japan's military technological capacity had developed to the point of enabling her forces to achieve their first victory over a European power; by the time of World War I Japanese shipyards had the capacity to meet the bulk of domestic demand for steamships (Blumenthal 1976: 137), and the diffusion of the most up-to-date cotton-spinning technology was much wider in Japan than in Britain (Saxonhouse 1985). By the time of the Pacific War, of course, Japan had much of the technological capacity, if not the resources, to wage a long-term air, sea and ground war with the greatest world powers, and the speed with which the remaining technological backlog was absorbed during the '50s and '60s is evidence of the accumulation of scientific and engineering skills and technical experience built up over preceding decades.

There can be no doubt that the sources of the technological knowledge on which Japan's development was based lay in the industrialised West. It is possible to list certain discoveries made by Japanese inventors even before World War II, but in general the view popularly held, both in Japan and the West, that the Japanese cannot invent reflects the fact that, just as for today's

developing countries, importing technology represented the quickest
and cheapest route towards 'catching up'. Japan's nineteenth- and
twentieth-century history of technology acquisition therefore presents
us with one of the first, and certainly one of the most successful,
cases of the transfer and absorption of imported technology. Yet,
as Western engineers and scientists nowadays queue up to gaze
upon and learn from the wonders of Japanese technology, it has
become clear that, as Eleanor Westney puts it (Westney 1987: 224),
'emulation produces innovation', generating technological systems
different from, and in some respects superior to, the models on which
they were once based. It is this process of acquiring, reproducing
and ultimately improving on imported techniques which concerns
present-day development economists seeking to analyse the creation
of indigenous technological capacity.

The first, and still widely held, interpretation of Japan's early and
successful utilisation of imported technology reflected the theoretical
approaches to technological choice generally prevalent in the '50s
and '60s, as outlined earlier. These were concerned firstly with the
capital intensity and later more broadly with the 'appropriateness' of
techniques to the economic environments in which they were to be
used. The sudden opening up of the country to the outside world in
the 1850s could easily be interpreted as presenting Japanese industry
with a 'technological shelf' equivalent to a range of techniques of
varying capital and labour intensities, from which to choose the forms
most appropriate to Japanese conditions. The early Meiji business
and government elite, setting out to search Europe and America
for the best technical and institutional models to copy, neatly filled
the roles of the 'rational shoppers' (again Westney's term) in this
picture of the process of technical choice. On the assumption that
mid-nineteenth century Japan differed from the developed world
from which technology was to be imported mainly in the relative
availability and price of labour and capital, the 'rational shopper'
approach would suggest that entrepreneurs should have selected the
relatively more labour-intensive techniques which would be expected
to be most profitable in a 'labour-surplus' economy. However, when
we come to look at industrial examples, we shall see that the economic
and institutional forces and constraints making for particular technical
choices were more complex and varied than allowed for in this
standard, production-function approach and in significant cases led to
the adoption of the most up-to-date and capital-intensive techniques
then available.

The argument of those who see Japan's success in utilising imported technology as depending essentially on the ability to make use of her apparently abundant supply of labour does not rest solely, however, on the assumption of the availability and selection of labour-intensive technical choices. Rather, the adaptation of imported technology in a labour-using direction is also seen as a key element in any explanation of her industrial growth. Such adaptation took place, first of all, at the level of the techniques employed in individual industries, a prime example given being the use of double-shift working in textile factories, which enabled given items of capital equipment to be combined with larger quantities of labour. But in addition it is argued that the continued co-existence of sectors of the economy utilising largely traditional, labour-intensive methods with 'modern' sectors necessarily employing more capital-intensive techniques represented another form of adaptation, within Japanese industry as a whole, to the relative availability of capital and labour. Terms such as 'capital-shallowing' or 'capital-stretching' are employed to describe this wider process of adapting imported techniques to a different pattern of resource endowments.

This line of argument has found a more recent parallel in current interpretations of the economic success of the East Asian Newly Industrialising Countries. In the same way, their 'economic miracles' are attributed to the choice of appropriate labour-intensive techniques and products, particularly in the export sector, which resulted in the growth of employment and incomes on a much wider scale than would have been the case had similar resources been devoted to more capital-intensive forms of production.[1] It is hard, however, in the cases both of pre-war Japan and of the NICs in recent years, to use this interpretation to explain the concurrent absorption of advanced technology in other sectors of the economy where labour-intensive technical choices were either not available or, at least, not made. More detailed case-studies of NIC examples (e.g. Luedde-Neurath 1985 or Enos 1984) have revealed complex interactions of economic and institutional forces which, along with the protection and guidance of the bureaucrats of the developmental state, have generated the conditions enabling managers, technical staff and workers in the receiving industries to master imported technology. In the Japanese case studies which follow, similar interactions can be observed, as entrepreneurs and bureaucrats sought to acquire and absorb the advanced technology of industrial processes which they considered of strategic importance for the achievement of national goals. First, however, to set the scene within which individual industries operated, some consideration needs to be given to the overall impact on the use of resources and the structure of the industrial sector of the varied range of technical choices made in the course of Japan's industrialisation.

TECHNICAL CHOICE AND CAPITAL INTENSITY

In the 1960s, it was fashionable to try to measure the part played by technical progress in generating economic growth by means of 'growth accounting'. The extent to which any given increase in output could be correlated with increases in measured inputs was estimated, but in most cases input increases could not fully account for observed output growth and the unexplained growth, the 'residual', had to be attributed to other, as yet unmeasurable, causes, one of which was technical change. Calculations of this sort raised enormous conceptual and statistical problems and the spuriously exact estimates of the size of the residual which they produced have to be taken as 'measures of our ignorance' in Richard Nelson's famous phrase. Nevertheless, they did demonstrate what now seems obvious, namely that, historically speaking, increases in output have been the result of a much more complex process than simply one of using more people and/or machines than before. Moreover such calculations using Japanese data did provide evidence that the relatively fast-growing pre-World War II Japanese economy exhibited a significant unexplained 'technical change' residual, in line with the view that the backlog of technical improvements available to Japan as a result of the prior, slower, process of change elsewhere represented an important potential and actual source of output growth.[2]

A first step in disaggregating and explaining the residual was to consider, at the macro level, the characteristics of the technical change which had occurred, as exhibited in observable changes in the combinations of inputs used. This reflected the prevailing view that the key characteristic of a technology, form the point of view of its ability to raise the overall productivity of inputs in a given economic environment, was its relative labour- or capital-intensity, although it did increasingly become possible to deal mathematically with other characteristics, such as the extent to which techniques involved economies of scale. Given the relative abundance of labour and scarcity of capital overall in the pre-war Japanese economy, the selection of relatively labour-using techniques of production ought to have offered the greatest scope for achieving increases in output from the available inputs and it was therefore to be predicted that, as new technology was adopted and output grew, the ratio of capital to labour used in production in the economy as a whole would decline.

There was, however, considerable controversy as to whether or not this 'capital shallowing' could be demonstrated from the statistical material available. Estimates of changes in the capital/labour ratio using the best available data (the LTES series) do not appear to provide evidence of it and indeed seem to reveal a continuous trend towards 'capital deepening' (Ohkawa and Shinohara 1979: 185, 189). Despite the apparent existence of a labour surplus, Japanese businesses, throughout the period of Japan's industrialisation, seem to have selected relatively capital-intensive techniques which resulted in rising capital/labour ratios, and the absorption of labour into modern industry was therefore not much greater than the relatively low rates achieved by present-day developing countries (Blumenthal 1980: 554). There is no doubt that Japanese businesses found methods of adapting capital-intensive technology imports to local economic conditions, both in the ways in which machinery was utilised and in the juxtaposition of high technology in some processes with more traditional and labour-intensive techniques in other areas of activity. But nonetheless the effects of this appear to have been offset by entrepreneurs' continued willingness to invest heavily in the acquisition of capital goods embodying relatively capital-intensive methods, as a result of which the average employed worker in 1940 had at his or her disposal more than five times the value of capital with which an 1885 counterpart would have worked (Ohkawa and Shinohara 1979: 189).

The explanation for this has to be sought in the economic and institutional environment facing late-nineteenth and early-twentieth century Japanese businesses and in the process of technological borrowing from abroad. Although the extent of knowledge about what was going on in the outside world during the Tokugawa period may in the past have been underestimated, nonetheless it is substantially true that 'catching up' with the West meant going abroad and buying items from the range on the newly-available Western 'technological shelf'. However, although the buyers and sellers in these transactions may have been in some sense free to choose, they were still businesses and individuals operating within particular economic and institutional constraints. On the Japanese buyers' side, the official missions and individual students who went abroad to study advanced techniques were influenced by a whole variety of factors including the languages they spoke, the particular contacts they made, the programmes arranged for them, their personal prejudices and chance encounters. The foreign engineers and technicians who went to Japan to teach and introduce new technology were similarly influenced by their own personal circumstances and national concerns. Although a technological shelf might have existed in theory, there were practical limits to the degree of shopping around that was feasible and to the likelihood of discovering, or being told about, more labour-intensive, and presumably largely superseded, methods.

Moreover, even had it been possible to discover and utilise more labour-intensive versions of the techniques currently employed in the most advanced countries, their selection might not necessarily have met the objectives of the Japanese businesses concerned or of the state which, in important respects, supported and protected them. In many fields, the objectives of technology acquisition had to be viewed in terms of the capacity to produce particular products within quite rigidly defined specifications and quality ranges. This was not always the case – as we shall see, the success of Japanese textile producers relied to a considerable extent on adaptations to their products which fitted the particular market demands of relatively low-income Asian consumers – but in many fields, including iron and steel, automobile production, shipbuilding, machine-building, and so on, the scope for technology choice was limited by the nature of the products required. Consequently, like their counterparts in today's developing countries, the early Japanese heavy industries sought out the most advanced technology, even if it needed a large investment to acquire and a considerable time to master, because only in that way could the products of modern industry be produced.

Nevertheless, in a situation in which capital funds were relatively scarce and yet the acquisition of the desired technology required a considerable investment and a long learning period, private businesses operating in freely-working markets and subject to international competition would be unlikely to find such investments profitable. The fact that Japanese firms did acquire large-scale, capital-intensive, heavy-industrial technology must therefore be explained, in part at least, by reference to an institutional environment which offered them some protection and support and limited their exposure to market forces and international competition. On the one hand, as part I showed, various organs of the Japanese state utilised an assortment of more-or-less *ad hoc* and pragmatic means to encourage the establishment of the industries and the technological capacities which they deemed essential to Japan's economic and military needs. On the other hand, however, the major firms involved in such areas also enjoyed advantages which depended on their powerful positions in relationships with other firms. The organisational structure which linked these two forms of support was that of the *zaibatsu*. The *zaibatsu* were essentially hierarchical groups of companies, separate from each other in a legal and accounting sense, but linked by close personal, financial and trading relationships. Each group was dominated at the top by one or more of the major heavy industrial firms of the pre-war economy but each also included a bank and a trading company and a large number of interlinked medium- and smaller-scale businesses. Their role in Japan's industrial organisation is analysed in greater detail in chapter 13 (pp. 000–00) but it is important to point out here that, from the point of view of the acquisition and absorption of capital-intensive technology, membership of a *zaibatsu* group provided private-sector firms with the advantages and protection they needed to overcome the obstacles to such investments. It gave privileged (cheap) access to the loanable funds of the *zaibatsu* bank and it offered a relatively safe market and supply of inputs on good terms from among the other members of the group. Since *zaibatsu* firms were able to recruit the cream of those with special training and knowledge (the engineering graduates, the linguists, and so on), the services of scarce specialists were concentrated within the *zaibatsu*-dominated sectors of the economy, principally heavy industry, where the need for them was greatest. *Zaibatsu* firms could make use of the information-gathering and bargaining skills developed by their group's specialist trading company, and of course membership of a *zaibatsu* group helped to ensure the political influence and bureaucratic connections on which state support depended.

On the other hand, however, the need to secure the kind of skilled and committed labour force necessary to operate expensive and technologically-advanced imported capital equipment led major heavy industrial firms to begin to have to provide better wages and conditions and long-term employment guarantees to their skilled managerial and, gradually, blue-collar employees.[3] The labour-market conditions they faced did not therefore present them with an abundant supply of 'cheap' labour. When taken alongside the institutional framework which gave *zaibatsu* firms access to capital funds on relatively advantageous terms, it would follow that the acquisition and adoption of relatively capital-intensive technology was not only feasible but also an economically appropriate response to the factor supply conditions they faced.

Smaller firms were not without their own devices for improving their access to new technology. Some belonged to the lower echelons of the *zaibatsu* hierarchies and would receive technical advice, financial assistance, second-hand equipment and so on from the larger firms in the group with which they had relationships. But smaller firms outside the *zaibatsu* network also made use of their own mechanisms for the discovery and diffusion of technical knowledge. In the textile industries, as we shall see shortly, the industrial association to which most firms belonged acted both as a powerful pressure group securing advantages for its members (e.g. reduced freight rates) and as a disseminator of technical information. Trading companies, with their specialised expertise in acquiring technical and economic information abroad, could serve small companies as well as the large members of their group, as long as their interests did not conflict. Nonetheless, smaller firms did experience higher costs and less easy availability when seeking capital funds and were unlikely to be able to recruit the more skilled and committed, higher-cost, male industrial workers employed by the big companies. Smaller firms outside the heavy industrial sector therefore had to make the best use they could of the more labour-intensive technologies and products for which markets could be found in the face of international competition.

It is in the micro-level organisation of resource allocation and inter-firm relationships, therefore, that we must seek the explanation for the fact that the technical transformation of Japanese industry does not appear, at the macro level, to have involved a particularly different or 'appropriate' use of available capital and labour resources. Chapter 13 will describe this organisation in more detail and its significance for technology acquisition and for the overall development of the economy will be assessed in the conclusion to this Part. In the meantime, however, the next section presents case studies of the organisation in action in the field of technology acquisition in three different kinds of industry.

TECHNOLOGY ACQUISITION AND ABSORPTION IN PRACTICE

Cotton-spinning

Earlier sections have revealed textiles to be the most significant and rapidly-growing manufacturing industry of late nineteenth- and early twentieth-century Japan. Moreover, the cotton industry, in particular its spinning branch, was the first modern factory industry in which Japanese firms achieved international competitiveness, securing first of all much of the domestic market for cotton yarn from the imports which had flooded in once trade began, and moving on to capture major export markets in Asia. As we saw in chapter 2 growth in cotton output was a response to favourable market conditions at home and abroad and improved availability of imported raw cotton, but it depended on a rapid expansion in the number of firms and factories in the industry making use of the imported technology of the mechanised cotton mill. Cotton-spinning in the late nineteenth century was an industry in which a degree of technical choice did exist and Japanese firms were in fact able to select and develop relatively labour-using alternatives. As a result, the capital/labour ratio in the industry did decline until after the turn of the century, but although employment increased rapidly, at the same time labour productivity rose (Ranis and Saxonhouse 1985: 139–40). The industry is therefore seen as providing a good example of the adoption and adaptation of relatively labour-using technology, in line with the prevailing factor-supply situation and the general economic conditions of a 'labour surplus' economy (Otsuka, Ranis and Saxonhouse 1988: 43). However, the emergence and rapid diffusion of what did turn out to be an appropriate and successful choice can be seen to have been the result of a complex convergence of economic and institutional forces, relating not just to the relative prices of factors of production, but also to the qualities of inputs, the nature of market demand and product characteristics, and the historical roles of the various institutional actors in the story.

Cotton spinning and weaving using handicraft techniques were well-established rural industries in Tokugawa Japan, producing narrow-width cloth of traditional patterns and colours to meet Japanese tastes. There were indeed advances made in this traditional technology during the Meiji period, and water power, and later small electric motors, were applied to it, so that small-scale handicraft spinners and, more importantly, weavers continued to supply certain areas of the Japanese market even after the influx of imported cotton goods and the establishment of the domestic factory industry (Otsuka, Ranis and Saxonhouse 1988: 47–9).

Nevertheless, the traditional producers could not in general compete with imports of machine-made cotton yarn and cloth, which steadily increased through the 1870s and 1880s (Sugiyama 1988: 66). The only answer to this drain on the balance-of-payments lay in the introduction of power-driven spinning technology from abroad. Hence, during the 1870s, when the government was actively promoting and itself sponsoring the import of technology, it attempted to set up two imported spinning mills of its own and to sell imported spinning eqiupment on easy terms to private enterprises. However, although these projects were clearly in part aimed at introducing advanced Western technology which could make the spinning industry competitive in international terms, they were also constrained by other elements of government policy at the time. They were expected to contribute to import-saving objectives and thus to run on water power, rather than steam power generated from imported coal. They were also to make use of domestically-produced raw cotton, assistance to the hard-hit Japanese cotton growers being a major aim behind government policy for the industry. As a result, they proved neither technically nor commercially viable: domestic cotton supplies were unsuitable for use given the spinning technology selected (see below) and water wheels were both unreliable and incapable of generating sufficient power to achieve the necessary economies of scale. The projects were thus eventually all abandoned or sold off, victims of the contradiction between import-substitution aims, not to mention the adoption of an apparently more appropriate water-powered technology, and the requirements of technical and economic survival (Minami 1987: ch. 9).

It thus transpired that the first successful modern mill was in fact a private-sector one, the Osaka Spinning Mill, set up in 1882 as a joint-stock company by the well-known Meiji entrepreneur, Shibusawa Eiichi. This was a copy of a Lancashire mill, much larger in scale than the failed government mills, and despite earlier plans otherwise, it was steam-powered and could thus be located in Osaka, the centre of the cotton trade. It also used imported raw cotton. Platt Brothers of Manchester supplied the equipment and gave technical advice, thereby establishing themselves as the almost exclusive supplier of machinery and technology to the early Japanese textile industry.

Technology choice in the nineteenth-century cotton-spinning industry involved questions not only of power source and the quality of cotton inputs but also of the spinning mechanism itself. The technology employed by the Osaka Mill, as by the earlier government mills and by the private-sector ones built during the 1880s in the wake of the success of Shibusawa's venture, was what was known as 'mule-spinning', as opposed to the alternative 'ring-spinning' method.[4] The mule was the spinning machine on which the development of large-scale factory production of cotton yarn in Britain had been based and it dominated the technology of the British industry. As its name implies, it was a hybrid machine which improved on previous techniques by being able both to spin yarn and to wind it into a cone shape on a paper tube, but it could not perform both operations simultaneously. It required skilled and fairly heavy labour, but it could produce relatively fine yarn from not particularly high-grade raw cotton. The ring spindle, on the other hand, could spin and wind yarn simultaneously, making it faster and simpler to operate, but the extra strain placed on the thread meant that it was suitable only for coarser yarn and needed better-quality raw cotton inputs. It wound the yarn on to wooden bobbins holding less than the cone-shaped 'caps' produced by the mule. These therefore had to be changed more often, and were harder to transport to separate weaving premises. Ring-spinning was the more labour-intensive alternative and could be carried out by unskilled female workers rather than the skilled and stronger male workers required for mule-spinning, but its use had many other implications for the kind of product produced, the inputs used, the transport and energy costs created, and so on. While Britain was the home of mule-spinning, major advances in ring-spinning were made in America, where good-quality raw cotton was easily available but skilled male workers were not, and eventually, as its technical drawbacks were overcome, ring-spinning became the dominant world technology.

When the Japanese Ministry of Agriculture planned its projects for the introduction of mechanised cotton-spinning technology and when, later, the Osaka Mill was being considered, it was naturally from the leading machinery producers, which were British firms, that advice was sought. The assumption was that the new mills would use locally-grown cotton which was of poor quality, would employ male labour and would be producing yarn to supply to scattered hand-loom weavers. Mule-spinning was therefore the natural choice, as well as being the technology with which the British manufacturers were most familiar.

During the 1880s, however, the economic conditions surrounding cotton spinning in the Osaka area changed significantly. The government abandoned its policy of trying to support the domestic cotton-growers through tariff protection, and imports of better-quality raw cotton from China and India, facilitated by developments in shipping services, became available to Japanese mills. Moreover, as chapter 12 will show, industrial employers were finding it difficult to recruit male workers prepared to stay with them and acquire skill and experience, and the textile companies sought rather to be able to recruit female workers from rural areas who could be persuaded to work in the mills on a short-term basis for relatively low wages. As a result of these changes, ring-spinning became a much more attractive alternative and experimental purchases of ring spindles were made by Japanese mills in the mid-1880s.[5] Thereafter, purchases of mules ceased almost completely and the rapid expansion of production capacity in the Japanese cotton-spinning industry from the 1890s onwards was based on ring-spinning technology.[6]

The complex of forces within the changing economic environment which faced the emerging Japanese cotton-spinning industry can thus reasonably be said to have resulted in an appropriate and, as it turned out, successful technological choice. However that success also depended on subsequent adaptations which Japanese producers made in the light of the particular market conditions they faced on both the input and output sides. Ring-spinning produced relatively coarse yarn which could be used to make cloth suitable for the lower-income consumers of Japan and other Asian countries and appropriate to the Japanese climate, but, as developed in America and elsewhere, it did require higher-quality and more expensive raw cotton inputs. Japanese spinners, however, devised ways of operating it with significantly poorer-quality raw cotton through the application of more labour to the preparation of the cotton for spinning and, in particular, the mixing of high-quality and low-quality material. Nonetheless, the resulting inputs still produced more breaks in the thread under the strains of ring-spinning than would have been the case with mule-spinning or with high-quality American cotton. As a result, the average Japanese spinning operative, mending breaks in the thread as they occurred, was able to attend to fewer spindles than were British or American spinners. Since it was possible in Japan, however, to employ young female workers at relatively low wages, the greater use of labour which this implied was not enough to offset the competitive advantages of the faster-working ring-spinning technology.

Under these circumstances, the Japanese cotton-spinning industry switched to ring-spinning almost uniformly in a remarkably short space of time during the 1890s. In an industry dominated by relatively small-scale firms and operating a newly-imported factory technology, this rapid diffusion of information and of best-practice technology itself needs some explanation. Saxonhouse (1976) argues that the answer lies in the institutional actors on the Japanese scene. Central to these was the Association of Cotton-Spinners (Bōren), the industry's representative organisation, to which almost all firms belonged since membership entitled them to the freight-rate rebates offered by Japanese shipping companies (see pp. 50–1). Bōren operated as a cartel, restricting production when necessary, but it also served as a collector and disseminater of a great deal of information about the industry, which was made freely available to member firms. It published a monthly report, giving technical and economic news of relevance to cotton-spinners, and foreign visitors observed, as Saxonhouse notes (1976: 116), that, as a result of both written and personal intercommunication among them, there were essentially no secrets between firms in the Japanese industry.

The resulting tendency for all to adopt what were regarded as the best practices and innovations was intensified by the industry's almost total reliance on one machinery supplier, Platt Brothers. Platt Brothers employed the Mitsui Trading Company (Mitsui Bussan) as its exclusive agent in Japan and the trading company made use of the connections it possessed as a member of the Mitsui *zaibatsu* to obtain privileged access to Bank of Japan funds. Through this, it was able to keep down the capital cost of Platt Brothers' equipment to its Japanese customers (Otsuka, Ranis and Saxonhouse 1988: 72). Platt Brothers' engineers and technicians built up substantial experience of their Japanese market and a number of them remained based in Japan to advise their customer companies. There was also considerable mobility among the Japanese engineers and technicians in the industry, most of whom had been trained in government-funded technical colleges and universities and who developed a professional identity and ethos as textile engineers unusual in the Japanese context, where technical skills are more commonly acquired through training and experience within one firm (Otsuka, Ranis and Saxonhouse 1988: 73–6). These forces contributed further to the flow of information throughout the industry and meant that innovations which worked in one firm were liable to be quickly recommended to others. Technical practice was thus generally regarded as by and large uniform throughout the industry.

Platt Brothers had to withdraw its engineers from Japan during World War I, however, and the disruption to machinery imports gave impetus to the development of the domestic machinery and parts industry. By the inter-war period, Japanese machinery producers were able to supply a considerable and growing share of the market for textile machinery in Japan and were beginning to make their own adaptations and innovations. The most famous of these was the Toyoda automatic loom which, ironically, Platt Brothers were subsequently to license from the Japanese company (Otsuka, Ranis and Saxonhouse 1988: 89, 91–6). The boost to import-substitution provided by the war thus promoted the growing indigenous mastery of textile technology which the activities of Bōren were also fostering.

The history of technological change in the Japanese cotton-spinning industry, when viewed as a whole, reveals a story of the speedy and uniform adoption of an appropriate, labour-using technology and of subsequent adaptations to it in line with prevailing factor-supply conditions. However, our tracing of the process whereby this was achieved has revealed it to have been the result of a complex interaction of economic and institutional forces, operating within the generally favourable environment in which Japanese textile producers found themselves in the late nineteenth and early twentieth centuries. This happy configuration meant that the Japanese industry was the pioneer in using the subsequently dominant ring-spinning technology in combination with relatively low-grade cotton inputs and relatively unskilled female labour. This gave it the competitive edge which it was able to exploit so successfully in low-income Asian markets around the time of World War I. Elsewhere, different configurations of forces, as regards labour and other input supplies, systems of management and recruitment, and industrial structure and organisation, produced different choices which were to prove, in the long run, less favourable in the evolving world economic climate of the first half of this century.[7]

Heavy industries

Although the cotton-spinning industry described in the previous section must count as Japan's first modern factory industry, the technology which it employed was still a relatively small-scale and divisible one. The initial need for steam power[8] placed a limit on the minimum size of factory which would be economic, and the machinery necessary to equip a mill required a substantial outlay of capital, but nonetheless cotton mills did not have to be particularly large-scale enterprises to survive and prosper. However in the industries which concern us in this section – iron and steel, chemicals, machinery and shipbuilding – economies of scale operate strongly. Of course alternative, smaller-scale, more labour-using methods of production do exist in these industries, but as the demand for industrial raw materials increases with economic growth, the technical and economic problems of expanding the output of such processes generally limit their applicability, and commercial production of the quantity and quality of output demanded in a growing economy appears to require large-scale, capital-using production facilities. Japan relied on imports as the source of most of her supplies of capital equipment and industrial raw materials until at least the turn of the century, but thereafter, especially during and after World War I, there began a process of import-substitution which depended on the acquisition and absorption of large-scale, capital-intensive technology from abroad. This process differed in important respects – in the economic conditions under which it took place, in the institutional actors involved and in the degree of success it achieved in establishing internationally competitive production – from that taking place in cotton spinning and suggests that the relatively successful establishment of these industries did not depend on the adoption of technologies appropriate to relative input supplies and prices, but rather on factors such as the role of the state and the institutions of industrial organisation.

Attempts to acquire foreign technology in these heavy industrial fields began some time before the Meiji Restoration. A number of *han* governments sponsored projects to learn about Western production methods, mainly using the medium of Dutch books, and to construct the machinery described in these sources. The first blast furnaces for the production of pig iron, for example, were constructed in this way (Ono 1985: 237). By the 1850s, Dutch and other foreign engineers were being utilised for their knowledge of Western technology. The stranded crew of a Russian ship rebuilt their vessel, training the Japanese carpenters with whom they worked and leaving behind their blueprints (Blumenthal 1976: 133). By the 1860s, more organised efforts were being made to educate engineers and technicians in Western technology in fields such as iron and steel and shipbuilding, with training centres being set up, foreign instructors hired and Japanese students sent abroad.

It is generally argued that a considerable basis of technical knowledge and experience was acquired through such contacts with foreign teachers and engineeers, in Japan and abroad, during the latter half of the nineteenth century, and through efforts to reproduce machinery and production systems.[9] However, it must also be said that few of the resulting early ventures into technology transfer were very successful as production enterprises. Attempts to build iron ships in Japan foundered in the face of the poor quality of domestically-produced raw materials, and large-scale ships could not be constructed because of lack of suitable dockyards and appropriate technical skills (Blumenthal 1976: 151–3). Government efforts to set up blast furnaces using imported British plant were also unsuccessful, with the large-scale, up-to-date equipment proving unusable under Japanese conditions of input supply and labour skills. The furnaces were sold off and one was eventually successfully fired by its private-sector purchaser in the 1890s, by which time rather more expertise had been acquired (Ono 1985: 238–40). Efforts by late-nineteenth century electrical engineers to copy foreign models of machinery such as alternators and generators similarly failed to produce anything to match the levels of design and reliability of imported machines, at a time when technical progress in this area was especially rapid (Uchida 1980: 149–50). In the chemical industry, where reliance on imports was almost complete until supplies were disrupted by World War I, the Asahi Glass Company was the first to try to construct a plant for the production of alkali (soda-ash) for use in glass-making. But although the underlying chemical principles were well understood, the plant, completed in 1917, was badly designed and did not function well as a mass-production unit. It produced usable output but at very high cost and could not compete with imports once conditions returned to normal after the war (Daito 1980: 183–5). Moving into the early 1920s, attempts by the newly-formed Mitsubishi Heavy Electric Machinery Company to produce various kinds of electrical machinery were far from successful, as a result of what the company history described as 'the meager level of our technological competence' (Yamamura 1986: 74). All these examples suggest that, until the turn of the century and beyond, neither the private nor the public sector had the resources to overcome Japan's lack of technical knowledge and industrial infrastructure, in the face of unrestricted competition from imports, in industries in which alternatives to large-scale, capital-intensive technologies do not appear to have existed.

Two sets of forces changed this situation. On the one hand, as part I showed, after the turn of the century the state became increasingly committed to the subsidy and protection of the heavy industrial sector, in the light of what it saw as the demands of national security. This drive towards import-substitution was intensified by the effects of World War I, which gave temporary protection to high-cost Japanese producers, and subsequently by the development of the Empire and the military and economic build-up to the war in China. On the other hand, however, the means to the creation of technological capacity in these strategic industries of necessity lay in closer technical tie-ups with the foreign companies which owned and controlled advanced technologies, and the process thus also depended on the growing ability of Japanese recipients to select and operate the institutional mechanisms through which technology transfers could be achieved. In conjunction, these forces led to the acquisition by Japanese firms of, at the least, a reasonable degree of technological competence in key heavy-industrial fields by the time of World War II.

In both iron and steel and shipbuilding, the government took major steps, around the turn of the century, to establish production facilities which would utilise the most advanced, large-scale technology. The Yahata iron-works, the first large-scale integrated iron and steel production plant in Japan, was entirely a government venture and required protection and subsidy throughout the pre-World War II period. In shipbuilding, as early as 1885, the government, having just sold off most of the state-owned shipyards at prices which represented a considerable subsidy to shipbuilders, attempted to ban the production of Japanese-style wooden boats in order to promote Western shipbuilding methods. However Japanese ship-buyers, including the navy, continued to rely on imports until subsidies were introduced, from 1896, for the purchase of large-scale iron or steel ships from Japanese yards. Thereafter, the private-sector Mitsubishi and Kawasaki dockyards, as well as the naval dockyards, began to produce large ships, benefiting both from heavy government subsidies and, after 1911, tariff protection against imports (Blumenthal 1976: 136–7). By 1930, Asahi Glass, in conjunction with the other domestic producer of soda ash, was in a position to put pressure on the government for protection against foreign competition and succeeded in obtaining subsidies and, perhaps more importantly, permission to import directly one of its main inputs, salt, at a lower price than that charged by the government salt monopoly. The resulting growth in its market enabled Asahi Glass to operate its plant at an economic scale and at last begin to show a profit (Daito 1980: 188–91).

The aim of the state in these cases was essentially a technological one: to establish in Japan the technical capacity to produce the products required by an economically and militarily advanced nation. The attempt to stop the production of Japanese-style wooden ships followed from this and the Yahata Works, like steel plants constructed in a number of present-day developing countries, was designed as the vehicle for the introduction of the world's best iron and steel technology, regardless of its 'appropriateness' to Japan's factor supplies or level of economic development. State protection func-tioned, therefore, as the means whereby Japanese firms were enabled to skip stages of technological evolution and take advantage of their country's 'late-comer' status, in industries in which the acquisition of technical competence and the build-up to economic scales of production took time and large-scale investments. The emergence of the *zaibatsu*, however, meant that the protected heavy industries, with the exception of iron and steel, could be left in private hands, receiving assistance as required through the operations of bureaucratic industrial policy, but at the same time making use of *zaibatsu* firms' privileged access to private-sector finance and their favoured market positions within networks of companies supplying inputs, technical skills and trading services.

The technology which the state saw as vital to Japan's economic security was, however, still largely owned or controlled by foreign companies. Once it was accepted that methods such as copying imported models or trying to pick up information from textbooks and visits to factories overseas were generally inadequate as a means of acquiring mastery of more sophisticated technologies, Japanese firms had to seek arrangements with foreign technology-suppliers for the transfer of information.[10] In the nineteenth century, the import of technology embodied in plant and equipment and in the services of the foreign engineers who set it up, was the most common method employed. Ships were constructed from kits of parts imported from Britain (Blumenthal 1976: 151); Yahata was essentially a 'turn-key' plant import built by German engineers, and so on. However, by the time of the major development of industries such as machine-building and chemicals from around World War I, Japanese engineers and scientists had sufficient technical expertise to consider the possibility of joint ventures, licensing agreements and other kinds of technical tie-ups with foreign firms as the means of acquiring technological knowledge, and the Japanese market had become significant enough for foreign firms, on their side, to consider how best to take advantage of the technological knowledge which they owned.

Such arrangements took a number of different forms. The major shipbuilding companies were in a position, after the turn of the century, to acquire the technology of, first, the turbine and, later, the diesel engine through the purchase of patent rights from various American and European companies, resulting in domestic production in due course (Blumenthal 1976: 153). In the electrical machinery industry, there were several major, long-term tie-ups between Japanese and American firms (Uchida 1980: 152–8). In 1899, Western Electric set up the Nippon Electric Company (NEC) as a joint venture with its Japanese agents, but continued to hold a majority of the shares and transplanted its technology and management methods, lock, stock and barrel, into the telephone equipment plant which it set up. In 1905, General Electric bought a majority shareholding in the Tokyo Electric Company, a firm which had been struggling, against competition from superior imports, to produce electric light bulbs according to methods described in foreign literature. General Electric supplied all the equipment necessary to set up a lamp factory, which was designed by an American engineer and embodied mechanised mass-production techniques developed in the United States. The tie-up also enabled Tokyo Electric to gain access to subsequent technical advances made by General Electric, including, most importantly, the tungsten filament for light bulbs. In the field of electrical machinery, General Electric had a rather looser technology tie-up with Shibaura, a Mitsui-group company which later merged with the Tokyo Electric Company to form Toshiba. The agreement was negotiated by Mitsui and Co., Shibaura's parent company, and involved the transfer of information, designs, patents, and so on, from General Electric. It also enabled Shibaura employees to go to work in General Electric factories in America. Mitsubishi Heavy Electric overcame its 'meager' technological competence by means of a tie-up with Westinghouse, which provided for a wide range of technical assistance, including the exchange of personnel, and a similar sort of agreement existed between Fuji Electric and Siemens.[11]

From these examples and others mentioned elsewhere, it is clear that foreign companies were heavily involved in the supply of advanced technology to the Japanese heavy and engineering industries through the kinds of joint venture and technology transfer agreement which have become common in the post-World War II period. However, the ability of Japanese recipients to set up and make the most of these relationships was also influenced by the particular institutional environment in which they operated. Trading companies, or other fellow-members of *zaibatsu* groups, often provided interested affiliated companies with technological information and helped to negotiate agreements. Mitsui and Co. was instrumental, as we have just seen, in setting up the Shibaura/General Electric relationship and Mitsui Shipbuilding's operations had their origins in research into foreign shipbuilding industries and their technologies carried out by the Mitsui Trading Company (Blumenthal 1976: 154). Mitsubishi Trading arranged technology imports for a number of major steel companies (Lynn 1982: 51). The state also played a part in regulating dealings between Japanese and foreign firms, thereby strengthening the hand of the Japanese side, and in encouraging the diffusion of the information acquired. The Ministry of Communications, for example, as the major purchaser of telephone equipment, ordered other domestic manufacturers to copy NEC's Western Electric-derived equipment where patents allowed (Uchida 1980: 160).

For many present-day developing countries, the central issue in considering technology transfer through arrangements of the kinds described above has come to be that of the extent to which the recipients are able to learn, absorb and master the technology, thereby generating their own technological capacity. By the time of World War II, Japanese firms in a number of major industries had clearly made considerable progress in acquiring the capacity to produce products of the standards and qualities required by a modern industrial power, and in developing the necessary scientific and technical infrastructure. The ability to produce quite a wide range of machine-tools had emerged by the late '30s and reliance on imports had substantially declined (Yamamura 1986: 82–3). However, Japanese companies had achieved this state essentially through copying the technology of their Western partners and their capacity to carry out their own R & D work was still limited. They thus remained on the whole dependent on their foreign partners for technological innovations. Some examples of Japanese engineers' improvements or adaptations to imported techniques can be cited and Tokyo Electric Company did set up its own research laboratory, against the wishes of its American partner (Uchida 1980: 161–2). But the weakness of Japanese 'indigenous technological capacity' was revealed by the widening technology gap which emerged as Japan became increasingly cut off from her sources of foreign technology prior to and during World War II.

This weakness was quite widely recognised in government and academic circles and Ministries such as Commerce and Industry and Communications pursued conscious policies, as we have seen, to try to remedy it. One well-known academic scientist-turned-businessman, Ōkochi Masatoshi, pursued his own personal campaign during the 1930s to create a distinctively Japanese technological capacity, setting up an Institute of Physical and Chemical Research (*Rikagaku Kenkyūjo*), directed and staffed mainly by academic scientists, which was to develop and patent industrially useful innovations. These were then to be manufactured by newly-established small companies, often located in rural areas, so that gradually a *zaibatsu*-type industrial group was created. Although several of Japan's post-war 'high-tech' companies, most notably the camera and copier producer Ricoh, had their origins in the group, Ōkochi's mission nonetheless largely failed to overcome the preference of large-scale companies for imported technology, since his companies' products were rarely of comparable quality (Cusumano 1989).

By the time of World War II, therefore, Japanese private- and public-sector organisations had learned how to acquire technology successfully from abroad, an art which they were able to exploit yet more fully in the post-war period, but they had yet to create the capacity for their own independent technological advance. In the terms often used to describe the stages in the acquisition of indigenous technological capacity in today's developing countries, they had achieved 'know-how' – knowledge of products and processes and the capacity to adapt and even improve on them in the light of local conditions – but not 'know-why' – the ability to conduct basic research and to innovate beyond existing technology.[12] The real technological advances made by Japanese companies in areas such as consumer electronics had to await the phenomenal development of her market and her technical capabilities during the economic miracle period.

Automobiles

The economic and institutional history of the Japanese vehicle industry has already been described in some detail (see ch. 3), but some mention of its experience in the technological field is worth making here for two reasons. First, vehicle production represents an example of a different kind of technology – assembly production – from those utilised in the industries described earlier, a technology which, despite its dependence on a sophisticated range of supporting industries and skills, many present-day developing countries have sought to introduce. Second, the differing strategies adopted by the two major pre-war Japanese vehicle-producers nicely illustrate alternative approaches to the acquisition of technology from foreign-owned multinational companies and consideration of these Japanese examples presents the opportunity to trace the longer-term effects of different choices of technology-transfer mechanism on the subsequent development of the industry.

Vehicle production in Japan did not begin on any scale until the late 1920s and was dominated by the Japanese subsidiaries of American companies (Ford and General Motors) until the Ministry of Commerce and Industry and the military began, in the later 1930s, to make serious efforts, through the use of protection and subsidy, to reduce reliance on foreign suppliers and establish a domestic industry. The Japanese firms selected for development, principally Nissan and Toyota, had at this stage only very limited experience of designing and manufacturing automobiles and were quite unable to produce anything comparable, in quantity or quality, with the output of market and technological leaders such as Ford and General Motors. The successful establishment of the companies and the achievement of the goals set by the state therefore depended on acquiring and learning the technology on which the superiority of the American industry was based. For reasons largely relating to their company origins and the characters and interests of their respective founders, Nissan and Toyota chose different paths towards this goal, with results that have continued to influence the nature of their production methods up to the present.[13]

Nissan, as we saw in chapter 3, was largely the creation of Aikawa Yoshisuke. His decision to try to establish a vehicle production company arose from his connections with the military establishment, which had made him aware of the demand for Japanese-made military vehicles, and from his efforts to establish a 'new *zaibatsu*' centring on the Empire and on areas of activity outside the control of the old *zaibatsu*. His interests and his connections were wide-ranging, at home and abroad, and once he had created Nissan out of the merger of his automobile parts production facilities with the design and engineering experience of his newly-acquired DAT Motors, he was able to employ the shortest route to technology acquisition, direct transfer from foreign companies. Thus Nissan used the Mitsubishi Trading Company to import from America the machinery and machine tools necessary to equip a new factory embodying up-to-date American mass-production techniques. DAT Motors already employed an American engineer and Nissan recruited others to direct the design and construction of its plant and to teach the workforce how to operate it. The American engineers advised the use of an automated assembly-line and the adoption of the most advanced metal-working techniques for the manufacture of the vehicle bodies, and the resulting production facilities were comparable to those used in the American plants from which they were derived.

The method of direct transfer of advanced American technology set the pattern which Nissan followed in its technology acquisition strategy into the post-war period. In 1935, Aikawa decided to move into the production of lorries for military use and dispatched company managers to Europe and the United States to investigate the technical possibilities. Through its connections with General Motors, to whose Japanese subsidiary Nissan supplied parts, contact was made with an American company which had a complete plant for sale. Nissan bought this and had all the equipment shipped to Japan along with blueprints for the design of a lorry. Mitsubishi Trading was involved in this transaction and also made other large-scale purchases of machine tools for Nissan. Despite initial problems, the plant was successfully producing on quite a large scale by 1938. Considerable modifications had to be made to the design of the lorry to overcome the problems it encountered under driving conditions in Manchuria, but the resulting engine continued to be used in Nissan lorries until the late 1950s.

After the war, Nissan continued its strategy of direct technology import, entering into a technical tie-up with Austin in 1952 under which Austin A40s were assembled, at first from kits and gradually from domestically-made parts. Nissan's engineers were by this time well able to cope with the blueprints and to use the technology they learned in their own later designs. Nissan's lead in the establishment of mass production assembly-line technology in the Japanese car industry was consolidated, but a price was paid in terms of its own independent R & D capacity in which, as we shall see, it lagged behind Toyota, its main domestic rival.

Toyoda Kiichirō, the founder of Toyota, resembled Aikawa in being a qualified mechanical engineer, but he retained much more of an interest in the practice of science and engineering than did the business-empire-building Aikawa. With the engineering resources of the Toyoda Loom Company behind him, he decided that the route to the achievement of his father's goal of a Japanese car industry lay not in the wholesale transfer of complete technologies from abroad, but rather in the development of his company's own capacity to select and adapt from the range of what was available. He believed that Toyota had access to the necessary engineering skills, augmented by the recruitment of Japanese-trained experts, including academics and former employees of the Ford and General Motors Japanese subsidiaries, and that the technology of car production was sufficiently widely known to be acquired without the purchase of patents or licensing rights. Toyota therefore followed a strategy of buying what its engineers believed to be the best machine for the job and then dismantling, studying and copying it in-house. Their early car designs were based on a Chevrolet model which had been disassembled, but they also embodied components adapted from Ford models and the engine which they developed was an improvement on the Chevrolet's in some respects. As far as possible, components were made within Toyota or the Toyoda Loom Co., but many smaller parts were manufactured by Japanese sub-contractors producing copies of imported items.

In this way, Toyota engineers developed much greater experience of independent design and innovation than did their Nissan counterparts and of necessity created their own in-house machine-making capacity. The machine tools they produced tended to be universal and adaptable, to allow for the design alterations they expected to have to carry out, as compared with the specialised mass-production equipment used by Nissan. Toyota's technology was also better suited to production for the smaller Japanese pre- and post-war market and much more flexible in responding to demand changes. Thus, while Nissan remained locked into the pre-war designs and models embodied in its imported equipment, post-war Toyota engineers were developing the so-called 'just-in-time' or *kanban* flexible manufacturing system which Western management consultants suddenly discovered in the 1980s and proclaimed as the secret of Toyota's brilliant combination of the benefits of mass production with the ability to respond to the particular demands of the Japanese market for a variety of products and design modifications. This system depends on flexibility within production systems and on rapid change-overs in adaptable machine tools and its roots in Toyota's pre-war experience of the mechanisms of technology transfer are easy to see.

The experience of Japanese automobile manufacturers in the immediate post-war period revealed that they had not, by then, achieved the level of technological capacity necessary to generate products competitive with imports. They had, however, reached a level at which, once some protection was offered from imports and once the domestic market began to grow rapidly with the rise in Japanese household incomes, they were able to respond to demand and to go on to develop their own distinctive technological abilities. The roots of the technology to which British and American car manufacturers now seek access through technical tie-ups and investment from Japanese companies thus lie in the processes and methods of technology transfer utilised by the nascent Japanese industry in the pre-war period.

12 The emergence of an industrial labour force

Whatever the neglected significance of family farms and other kinds of small-scale household business in the process of economic change, it remains true that no cases of development exist in which the factory did not emerge as the increasingly dominant form of industrial organisation. The direction which technical change in manufacturing industry has taken over the period since the first industrial revolution, involving, as it has done, subdivision and specialisation in the stages of production, the application of mechanically-generated power, and the use of ever larger-scale equipment, has necessitated larger units of production, employing greater numbers of workers and requiring increasingly specialised management. In anything other than a full-scale command economy, workers for such factory enterprises must be recruited through offers of wages in some kind of market for labour, in return for the performance of tasks within an institutional organisation which operates according to different kinds of rule and practice from those of the family-based enterprise. Factories can thus be thought of as economic organisations in which a number of generally unrelated employees work for wages, using plant and equipment in which, in most cases, they do not own an interest, as directed by specialist managers.

As this suggests, there is a degree to which factory organisation is necessitated by the characteristics of industrial technology and this has led some to argue the 'technological determinist' case for 'convergence' in the forms of industrial organisation as development proceeds. In this view, a car factory will operate in much the same way, as regards production organisation and relations among workers and between workers and management, wherever it may happen to be located, because of the demands of the assembly-line techniques it employs. However, in 1958, James Abegglen first published his discovery of 'the Japanese factory' and introduced to an eager audience of sociologists, management theorists and businessmen the practices of 'lifetime employment', 'payment by seniority' and 'paternalistic management' which have since been seen as characterising 'the Japanese employment system' and as providing a key element in the explanation of Japan's post-war economic success. What Abegglen's study suggested was that large-scale factories in Japan had not, by that stage, 'converged' towards British or American practice, and while some argued that they still would, their peculiar features being 'feudal remnants' not yet discarded by a late-comer to industrialisation, Abegglen himself saw them rather as evidence that culturally-determined social characteristics could influence the nature of factory organisation. He thus interpreted the particular practices of Japanese factories, contrary to the technological-determinist view, as manifestations of 'traditional' Japanese attitudes to group organisation, hierarchies and status structures, family relationships and such like.

An implication of this was that, since the nature of the contemporary Japanese factory was a reflection of 'traditional' Japanese culture, Japanese factories must also historically have incorporated the same aspects of earlier forms of social organisation, and Abegglen went on to argue that the use by early factory owners and managers of, for example, the ideas and practices of the Japanese family group eased the transition to industrial work for early factory employees.

> It would seem from this study, then, that the very success of the Japanese experience with industrialisation may well have been a function of the fact that, far from undergoing a total revolution in social structure or social relationships, the hard core of Japan's system of social relationships remained intact, allowing an orderly transition to industrialisation continuous with her earlier social forms.
>
> (Abegglen 1958: 134–5)

In the years since Abegglen's ideas were published, studies of the history of the Japanese industrial labour force have very largely undermined this view, to the point at which Andrew Gordon, in his large-scale study of the history of labour relations in Japanese heavy industry, was able to argue that Japanese industrial workers more closely resembled their Western counterparts in the early stages of industrialisation than they have come to do since (Gordon 1985: 5). Such studies see the emergence of Japanese management practices as the outcome of a long process of interaction and conflict between the needs and demands of recruits to the industrial labour force, the requirements of managers operating new forms of technology, and the political environment created by the goals of the state.

The picture which such studies present is also of considerable significance for our understanding of the inter-sectoral movement of labour, a process which post-war development models have treated as a crucial aspect of industrialisation. As we saw in part II, the Japanese case was frequently cited as an example of the successful transformation of 'surplus labour' from agriculture into an effective factory work force. Lower rates of population growth, combined with diversification and technical development in agriculture and other small-scale businesses, meant that potential Japanese migrants faced greater demand and a wider range of opportunities for their labour than do their counterparts in today's Third World. Even allowing for these differences in situation, however, the difficulties experienced by early Japanese industrial employers in creating a stable labour force with industrial skills, and the adaptations and concessions on wages and working conditions which had to be made in the light of the actions and attitudes of industrial recruits, further undermine the idea that Japanese labour can simply be regarded as a 'surplus' or passive resource in the development process. Workers brought with them into the new factory environment the economic strength they derived from their 'traditional-sector' bases and they sought recognition of the attitudes, ideas and skills they had previously absorbed or were to acquire, although many of these were not, as it turned out, those generally associated with present-day Japanese workers. By the time of the Pacific War, a relatively stable and experienced industrial labour force was in existence in Japan,[1] but the link between the emergence of this force and the successful establishment of factory industry, both in textiles and other light industries and in heavy industry, is not a straightforward one. However successful 'Japanese management' may now be, the simple picture of the movement of surplus labour to industry, eased by managerial application of traditional or culturally-based approaches to social organisation, can no longer be offered as a model of the process of labour transfer for contemporary developing countries.

Despite the steady progress towards industrialisation achieved in Japan during the second half of the nineteenth century and the first half of the twentieth, workers who could be defined as factory employees remained a relatively small, though undoubtedly growing, proportion of the total manufacturing labour force. Probably only a few thousand workers could have been described as employed under factory conditions in the 1870s and although this number had risen to almost four million by 1940 (Taira 1978: 168), 'factories', categorised as organisations employing five or more workers, continued to account for less than half of the manufacturing labour force until well into the 1930s (Taira 1978: 168; Lockwood 1968: 203). The textile industries consistently accounted for the largest share of this factory employment: of the 2.3 million factory (five or more employees) workers in Japan in 1934, 41 per cent were engaged in textile production (Lockwood 1968: 178, 183). Of these the great majority were women: females represented 80 per cent or more of the labour force in cotton textiles throughout the pre-World War II period and over 50 per cent of all factory workers into the 1930s, and Saxonhouse's figures suggest that the early Japanese industrial labour force was more predominantly female than those of other developed or developing countries at the time (Saxonhouse 1976: 99–100). The female textile worker therefore represented the typical factory employee during the process of the creation of the early industrial labour force and it is the recruitment and employment of such workers that we shall consider first.

Male factory workers were to be found more predominantly in the heavy industrial sector and their numbers began to increase with the growth in industries such as metal-working, engineering and shipbuilding during the inter-war period. Male workers brought a different tradition and ethos with them into the factory and their recruitment and retention posed somewhat different problems for industrial employers. It was the strategies used to try to overcome these problems, and the responses of the workers involved, that provided the foundation for the management practices of large-scale Japanese enterprises and hence, although male employees in larger factories remained only a relatively small proportion of all those employed in the manufacturing sector, their contribution to the emerging characteristics of labour relations in Japan must also be considered in what follows.

WOMEN WORKERS IN THE TEXTILE INDUSTRIES

The production of textiles had always been part of the work of women in rural households, in Japan as elsewhere. With the development and diversification of the economy during the Tokugawa period, however, opportunities began to open up for the commercial sale of the products of such work outside the household. The weaving of silk and cotton was sometimes carried out in the factory-like establishments of weaver-entrepreneurs, but putting-out systems, under which women undertook weaving on looms set up in their rural homes, also became widespread and well-established as market demand grew and production spread away from the traditional urban centres of textile work. The spinning of cotton and the reeling of silk were also most commonly carried out within rural households using the labour of women.

With the opening up of the country to trade in the 1850s and the rapid increase in the demand for Japanese silk for export, growing numbers of silk filatures were set up using water, and later steam, power to process the fast-increasing cocoon output of farmers in sericultural regions. Such filatures were for the most part quite small and were located where power sources were available in and around their sources of cocoon supply. They relied on recruiting labour from the surrounding rural areas and the majority of their employees were women from local farm households, often with previous experience of silk-reeling techniques. Unlike later women workers in larger-scale cotton mills and silk filatures, such workers were generally able to commute to work from their farm homes, often using the expanding local rail network (Smethurst 1986: 167–8), and were paid daily wages graded according to their skill and the quality of their output. Those who did travel further afield to work in more distant filatures found their own accommodation and workers appear to have been relatively free to come and go and look for work as they pleased. Wage *rates* remained among the lowest recorded for the various kinds of employment available, since silk-producer employers were able to tap a source of relatively abundant labour in the generally underused time (at least as regards cash-earning opportunities) of the daughters of farm households. But as the amount of such employment on offer steadily increased and the number of hours worked rose, the *earnings* of silk-reelers grew substantially and the contributions they were able to make to the total income of their families became highly significant (Tussing 1969: 213–6).

As the application of mechanical power sources and other technical changes spread, however, larger-scale silk filatures began to appear, making use of employment systems similar to those coming to be established in the cotton-spinning industry. From the mid-1880s the number of large-scale cotton-spinning mills began to increase rapidly and their total workforce rose from 2,330 in 1887 to 25,448 in 1893 (Taira 1978: 180). These mills were usually located in urban areas, in particular around Osaka, and at first looked for recruits among the local city-dwellers. However, the rapid expansion of the industry led to fierce competition among employers for the available workers, and particularly for those with some experience since, docile and dextrous as traditional Japanese girls might have been on entering the factory, operating large-scale spinning machinery under factory conditions proved to be an occupation in which experience undoubtedly raised productivity (Saxonhouse 1976). Poaching of experienced workers became common and labour turnover among mill workers was high.

Employers responded in various ways to this difficult situation which was continuing to result in relatively low levels of labour productivity in the Japanese industry, as compared with its Indian and Chinese competitors, up to the turn of the century (Saxonhouse and Kiyokawa 1985: 196).[2] In the effort to prevent workers leaving mills, dormitories were established and considerable restrictions placed on workers' movements outside the factory. The provision of residential facilities also enabled employers to recruit workers from further afield and mill-owners increasingly came to rely on girls brought from rural areas, where networks of recruiting agents began to operate for each mill. The agents, who were not normally employees of the spinning company but rather middle-men working on their own account and receiving commission from the mill, were empowered to offer advances on wages to the families of girls contracted to work for a given period in a particular mill. Agents painted a rosy picture of factory life, stressing to parents that their daughters would be housed and cared for by their employers (Hunter 1984(a)), and indeed it seems plausible that the prospect of leaving home and going to the city, while at the same time contributing to family finances or building up savings in preparation for their own marriages, might not have been unattractive to girls otherwise faced with life and work on small family holdings in the country.

Needless to say, conditions in the mills when the girls got there rarely lived up to the picture that had been painted. Twelve-hour shifts were the rule, so that the mills could operate twenty four hours a day; living conditions were cramped and crowded, leading to high incidences of diseases such as tuberculosis, and the restrictions placed on the girls' lives were severe. Employers were prepared to pay for experience and the higher productivity it brought, so that it was possible for girls tough and persistent enough to see through their contracts to earn incomes which made a considerable difference to their families' livelihoods. But nonetheless, and despite efforts among companies to collude against poaching and to divide up recruiting areas among themselves, the commitment of mills to the employment of young girls[3] on contract from distant places meant that labour turnover remained high.

This situation did not prevent the Japanese cotton-textile industry from establishing its dominant position in Asian markets, but its causes and consequences have been widely discussed and are important for an understanding of the emerging characteristics of industrial labour in Japan. Saxonhouse and Kiyokawa (1985: 197, 203) have shown that mills in India in the late-nineteenth and early-twentieth centuries employed a much higher proportion of men than their Japanese competitors and experienced lower rates of labour turnover. Saxonhouse argues elsewhere that the competitive nature of the Japanese industry, and the almost identical technology employed in the various mills, discouraged firms from investing in workers who might so easily go to work in rival mills and from offering the wages and conditions that might have reduced labour turnover (Saxonhouse 1976). Instead, they opted to go further and further afield and to pay more and more for dubious recruiting services, in search of the young and unknowing workers who alone might be prepared to come to the mills for all that the employers believed themselves able to afford. The productivity improvements resulting from better training and greater experience among workers who were, by international standards, relatively well educated would, Saxonhouse estimates, have yielded a substantial return on the investment required, but a return which, under prevailing market conditions, might well have been reaped by competitors in the industry. As it was, workers continued to come and go and the shady methods of recruitment and control, infiltrated on the fringes by gangsters and the underworld, persisted.[4] The costs of acquiring training and experience continued to be borne by the worker, in the form of initial wages too low to compensate for the disutilities of mill life or to compare with other possible sources of income once these were known.

As the industry matured, however, and despite continuing high rates of turnover among new recruits, a growing core of experienced workers inevitably began to develop. Furthermore, employers, particularly the emerging large spinning companies, did eventually, from the 1910s, begin to experiment with methods of improving life in the mills and encouraging a long-term commitment from workers (Taira 1978: 201–5). These included purely monetary incentives, in the form of pay scales related to length of service and grades of skill and experience, together with the abandonment of the use of middle-men as recruiters. But they also involved efforts to develop social and moral values which, it was hoped, might help girls to adapt to factory life (Sugihara 1986). Thus, some educational and cultural activity was organised and management preached and encouraged, on the one hand, loyalty on the part of the worker and, on the other, respect for a worker's dignity and her efforts on the part of the company. Although female textile workers probably did not enter the factory with either the traditions or the economic strength possessed by early male industrial workers, textile-industry employers were still obliged to come to terms in these ways with a labour force which was not without other employment alternatives and whose members, and their families, were not without their own ideas as to how workers should be treated.

Japan's textile industries were in many respects phenomenally successful in establishing themselves during the latter part of the nineteenth century and the early twentieth century. A great many factors, relating both to the internal structure of the industry and to external markets, transport costs and so on, can be cited in explanation of this, but a stable, experienced and committed factory labour force does not seem to have been one of them. Nevertheless, the productivity of Japanese workers in the silk and cotton industries began to rise after the turn of the century as technology and factory organisation changed and also, as Saxonhouse and Kiyokawa (1985) argue, as the educational levels of workers increased and factory conditions were improved through shorter working hours and the implementation of factory legislation. It would, however, be hard to present the experience of the early Japanese textile industries in creating their factory labour force as a model of the transformation of surplus labour resources into productive industrial workers. Neither does it suggest that the attitudes and approaches of early Japanese industrial workers and employers embodied traditional values which, in any immediate or straightforward sense at least, eased the transition into factory work. Employers were obliged to work long and hard developing the management practices, payment systems and working conditions which would generate the experience, attitudes and values required of a disciplined work-force. By the inter-war period, the transformation had been achieved and a relatively skilled and high-productivity female labour force, managed by trained and experienced supervisory staff, was in existence in the textile industries, but the historical process of transition had been by no means a smooth or costless one.

MALE WORKERS IN HEAVY INDUSTRY

Workers in heavy industries, such as shipbuilding, metal-working, mining and engineering, constituted only a small proportion of the Japanese industrial labour force until well into the inter-war period. Nonetheless, they represented a highly significant force in the history of Japanese industrial labour, not only because of the crucial role of the industries in which they worked, but also because it was their experiences which largely shaped the characteristics of labour/management relations as they developed through into the post-World War II period. Although it remains the case that a large part of the present-day industrial labour force does not work under the conditions of the 'Japanese employment system' as it has come to be defined in the post-war period, the outlines of the system, which first began to emerge out of the interactions between workers and managers in heavy industry in the first half of this century, represent an ideal or a model which still significantly conditions the attitudes of Japanese workers and managers throughout the industrial sector.

During the Tokugawa period, the kinds of heavy industrial activity listed above were the preserves of craftsmen, that is to say, of male workers trained, generally through relatively long periods of apprenticeship, in the arts of their trade, and themselves then able to operate their own independent businesses, with their own apprentices learning in their turn through observation and experience. During their apprenticeships, trainees lived as members of the households of their employers and all aspects of their lives fell under the control of their masters. However, it should not be inferred from this that Tokugawa craftsmen were necessarily incipient lifetime employees and paternalistic employers; rather, the ethos to which they subscribed placed a high value on mobility and independence, on spending freely and enjoying the pleasures of wine, women and song (Hazama 1976: 24). Thus it was common for such artisans, once trained, to travel around the country, hiring themselves out to employers and moving on when the fancy took them. This they could do freely, since the traditional urban craft guild organisations proved unable to exert their influence over the expanding rural industrial activity of the later Tokugawa period and provided no network of support for, or control over, the journeymen artisans who travelled the country (Gordon 1985: 24).

Whilst the independent master or journeyman remained the norm within Tokugawa industrial society, by the end of the period the small but growing number of *han*-run projects in fields such as metal-working and shipbuilding was beginning to offer some scope for employment in larger-scale enterprises. The workers recruited by such enterprises were drawn from the existing supply of traditional artisans and continued to move freely among the larger-scale *han* shipyards, arsenals, and so on, local workshops and travelling employment. It was these *han* enterprises which the Meiji government inherited after the Restoration and which constituted the starting point for state, and later private-sector, development of heavy industry, and with them were inherited their practices of labour recruitment and management. Thus although foreign engineers and technicians might be brought in to teach and direct the operation of new, imported machinery and techniques, it was traditional artisans to whom they imparted the new industrial skills and who were to dictate the patterns of employment and the life-style of the male industrial labour force until at least the turn of the century.

As early modern industrial enterprises began to expand, therefore, they were faced with the problems involved in recruiting a labour force from among the former Tokugawa artisan classes, with their traditions of high mobility and relatively lax discipline as regards, for example, working hours, not to mention their heavy drinking, gambling, and so on.[5] The only method for the recruitment and control of such workers then available depended on the traditional master/worker relationships through which employment had been regulated in the Tokugawa period. A master or labour boss, generally referred to as an *oyakata* or pseudo-parent, would recruit his own group of workers for whatever task he was contracted to perform and would take his own responsibility for paying and controlling his gang. The inexperienced and semi-bureaucratic managers of the emerging modern-sector enterprises of the early Meiji period saw no alternative but to make use of this same system as the means of recruiting and managing the kinds of workers they needed for their shipyards and arsenals. Hence direct control of the labour force continued to remain essentially in the hands of a class of foremen/*oyakata*, who stood between the management of the new plants and those workers who were beginning to acquire modern industrial skills. This form of indirect management of personnel, wages and labour relations persisted, both in government-run and private-sector plants, in heavy industry until at least the turn of the century.

As a result of the inability of management to impose new industrial practices directly on to its labour force, the 'traditional values' which early industrial workers brought to the modern sector tended to

perpetuate the high mobility and lax discipline which had characterised Tokugawa industrial society. Like their counterparts in the textile
industries, employers in the early heavy industries found that workers
who had acquired skill and experience under their management
frequently capitalised on this by moving to other employers or setting
up on their own account, and the maintenance of a stable labour
force proved extremely difficult. Furthermore, Tokugawa traditions
imbued early industrial workers with respect for the independence and
dignity which their skills gave them and modern industrial employers
had to come to terms with this as they sought to impose greater direct
control and discipline over their labour forces in later periods. The
Tokugawa craftsman had possessed some, though lowly, social status
and had augmented this with a belief in the value of the skills that
could be acquired through travel and experience. With the abolition
of the fixed Tokugawa class structure, such official social status as he
had possessed disappeared and the values of traditional crafts were
undermined by the demands of new forms of technology and industrial
organisation. One of the persistent demands of industrial workers,
therefore, as they gradually came into conflict with managements
bent on imposing greater control over them was for respect, dignity
and 'human treatment'. As both Gordon (1985) and Smith (1984)
show, such pressure from the workers' side represented a significant
influence on the nature of labour relations within companies both
before World War II and since.

In addition, the persistence of the strong *oyakata*/work gang
relationship mitigated against the development of wider, horizontal
links between workers in the same trade both within and beyond
individual plants and localities. The lack of a broad tradition of
craft guild organisation, combined with the reliance of the worker
on his *oyakata* for the protection of his interests and welfare, limited
the emergence of any sense of solidarity among workers in similar
occupations which might have fostered a labour or trade-union
movement of the European or American kind. As a result, when
union activity began to develop after the turn of the century, it was
the factory or workplace, rather than the trade, which was to provide
the obvious focus for activity.

The progress of industrialisation through the second half of the
nineteenth century brought with it both greater sophistication in the
technology employed and work skills demanded in heavy industry and
a more professional and experienced managerial class, increasingly
recruited from the ranks of university graduates. Both the need and
the capacity for greater managerial control over workers operating

expensive and complex new machinery were therefore growing and this led to efforts to limit the powers of the *oyakata*. The former *oyakata* were gradually incorporated into the layers of the management structure and traded their independence for the greater security of positions as foremen within the company. Managements continued to find it difficult, nonetheless, to maintain stable labour forces, despite their increasing realisation of the costs of high rates of movement among skilled workers. From around the turn of the century, therefore, pioneering companies were beginning to experiment with incremental wage scales, bonus systems and paternalistic benefits, applying systems modelled on those of the state bureaucratic organisations, in the first instance to their own management hierarchies, but gradually to those key skilled workers whose mobility they wished to discourage.

The boom period of 1900–20 served to intensify the problems of shortage of skilled workers and high labour turnover and at the same time saw the beginnings of the development of a labour movement influenced by Western socialist ideas. Demands for shorter hours, profit-sharing and collective bargaining arrangements were accompanied, however, by efforts to improve the social status and dignity of the industrial worker and to extend to a greater proportion of the industrial labour force the benefits of security and respect conferred by 'membership' in the company, as enjoyed by the select group of managers and white-collar workers. The individual workshop or factory remained the focus of labour-movement activity but the increased economic strength of labour, especially during the World War I boom, and the brief flowering of a wider national union movement giving rise to fears of severe labour unrest, led to management concessions in various industrial conflicts and to improvements in the conditions and status of workers in a number of major heavy-industrial companies (Gordon 1985: ch. 3; Napier 1982).

The collapse of the World War I boom weakened labour's position and enabled managements to break the strength of the national union movement and cultivate direct relations with their own workers. The worsening position of workers in the labour market discouraged 'travelling' and increased workers' concern for job security within individual companies. Although many employers had little hesitation in firing workers during the depressions of the period, and practices which emphasised status differences between white- and blue-collar employees continued to be widely enforced, the continued pressure from workers for dignified treatment and respect was beginning to bear fruit in a growing recognition of the idea that loyalty to the company should, and could profitably, be rewarded with job security, access to paternalistic benefits and 'membership' of the company.

It would undoubtedly be a mistake to conclude that the practices of the 'Japanese employment system' were widely applied to blue-collar workers, even in the most prestigious companies, before the end of World War II. It was the increase in labour-movement activity in the immediate post-war period and the greater economic strength of educated labour-market entrants during the economic-miracle period that gave rise to its widespread adoption in large-scale companies and organisations. Nonetheless, its outlines are visible in the pre-war period, emerging out of the conflicts and compromises between, on the one hand, managers experiencing the same kinds of pressure as their post-war successors to maintain and develop a skilled and committed labour force in rapidly-growing modern industries and, on the other, workers who brought with them into factory life a concern for status and respect born of their traditions as independent and roving craftsmen. Employer paternalism and the 'Japanese management system' are best viewed, not as culturally determined devices for converting surplus labour into a uniquely productive workforce, but rather as the results of the conflicts generated in the process of creating a skilled industrial labour force under the conditions of relatively rapid heavy industrialisation in the twentieth century. Furthermore, inasfar as the system was applied to the still relatively small modern-sector labour force before World War II, this was only made possible by certain other features of the wider industrial environment in which heavy industrial employers found themselves, and it is to these that we shall turn in the next chapter.

13 Industrialisation and the structure of industry

The expansion of industrial production in an economy inevitably brings forth new kinds of business organisation and different forms of relationship between firms and has almost always resulted in the growth of a certain number of large-scale enterprises differentiated, in their technical characteristics, the wages and conditions of their workers and managers, and the structure of their internal organisations, from the much larger group of small-scale businesses. To a degree, the emergence of such a 'dual structure' has been regarded as an inevitable consequence of rapid industrialisation, especially where borrowed technology is employed: if industrial enterprises comparable in scale and technology with those of the developed world are to be established in a developing country, firms with access to the large amounts of capital and skilled labour required must come into existence, and these firms must of necessity operate according to rules rather different from those applicable to the preponderant mass of smaller-scale and more traditional businesses. However, as the pace of economic and technical change has speeded up, the divergence between the experience of those inside the modern sectors of today's developing countries and those outside, in rural areas or in what has come to be known as the urban informal sector, has continued to widen and has become a recurrent theme in development-studies work, as well as an ever-growing problem for those concerned to improve welfare and lessen inequality in today's Third World.

'Industrial dualism' of this kind has long been recognised as a feature of Japan's industrial structure. Japanese scholars, from the inter-war period onwards, have been drawing attention to the dichotomy in wages and productivity, capital availability and technological levels between the large-scale businesses which have dominated heavy industry and the smaller-scale firms whose products meet demand for a whole range of consumer goods and industrial inputs.

Whilst Japanese industrial dualism has much in common with the phenomenon observed in today's developing countries, two aspects of it have attracted particular attention and might, it could be argued, lead to a rather different assessment of the part played by the small-scale, 'informal' sector in Japan's industrialisation from that generally accorded to 'traditional' sectors in models of Third World development. These are, on the one hand, the sheer persistence of small-scale business in Japan and, on the other, the, not unrelated, close economic and institutional interconnections between large and small firms within the Japanese industrial structure.

Economic theory has generally assumed that, in most industries, as technology advances and as capital becomes more abundant and labour relatively scarcer, small-scale businesses are bound to find it increasingly difficult to survive in competition with big businesses and will gradually disappear. Their continued existence could thus be seen as a symptom of incomplete development and they themselves as remnants of the 'traditional' economy which would of necessity eventually wither away. Nonetheless, in the mid-1980s, when Japan could hardly be described as less than a developed economy, small-scale firms and family enterprises continued to employ a considerably higher proportion of Japanese workers than did large-scale ones.[1] Agricultural and retailing businesses constituted the largest categories within the 'small-and-medium' sector but by no means all small firms could be said to be 'traditional' in their activities, a substantial number being engaged in industries employing sophisticated technology and fulfilling demands for 'modern' products and parts. Marked differences in wages and conditions of employment according to the scale of enterprise still exist, but it is increasingly difficult to regard this as exclusively the result of 'traditional remnants' in the economy. In some areas of activity at least, the continued presence of small businesses has to be seen as a dynamic element in Japan's continued economic growth, providing, on the one hand, innovation and flexibility which large firms are not always able to generate and, on the other, outlets for the skills and energies of substantial numbers of workers and entrepreneurs who remain, not infrequently by choice it seems, outside the world of the big-company 'salary-man'. The role which small firms now play in the advanced, late-twentieth century Japanese economy thus suggests that some reassessment of their part in past development might also be called for.

In addition to the general assumption of the long-term economic and technical superiority of large-scale enterprises, most models of dual industrial structures have also taken for granted relatively clear lines of demarcation between the large-scale modern and small-scale traditional sectors. The characteristics of firms belonging on either side of the line can be quite clearly distinguished in terms of types of industrial activity and technology, the attributes of workers, the markets supplied and even, quite commonly, geographical location, and the two sectors are generally regarded as quite separate and exclusive. It is true that, in the Japanese case, movement of firms or individuals across the inter-sectoral dividing line has been difficult.[2] This is not, however, a reflection of inpenetrable barriers to communication but rather of the existence of a complex network of interrelations among large and small firms enabling each to create its own demand and supply niche within which to try to survive in a competitive world. This, so to speak, organic economic interdependence has been created within the Japanese industrial system through the institutionalisation of barriers to competition in product and labour markets and through organisational forms such as the *zaibatsu* groups, the general trading companies and the practice of subcontracting. It could be argued that this interrelated structure, many elements of which have received a bad press as regards their impact on equality and freedom of economic competition, did generate benefits from a developmental point of view, contributing to the provision of income and employment for those outside the modern sector and lessening the severity, in the Japanese case, of the 'dualist' problem which has produced such marked 'growth without equity' in many of today's developing countries.

In what follows, some scattered evidence as to the characteristics of life and work in small businesses and the urban informal sector in pre-war Japan will be pieced together. We can then go on, first, to look at the demand-side forces which enabled informal-sector businesses to continue to find niches for their products within markets for consumer goods and a range of manufactured items, before, second, setting out the institutional arrangements on the supply side which allowed small firms to survive by complementing, rather than competing with, large ones.

SMALL BUSINESSES AND THE URBAN INFORMAL SECTOR DURING INDUSTRIALISATION

In 1982, two-thirds of Japanese private-sector employees worked in enterprises employing fewer than 100 people; 30 per cent of the labour force worked in businesses with one to four workers and a similar percentage were owners of, or family members working in, family businesses (Patrick and Rohlen 1987: 332–3, 338). On the basis of figures such as these, it is generally reckoned that no more than a third of employees work in large-scale organisations under the conditions of the 'Japanese employment system', and if Japan today is an economy heavily populated by small businesses, in the past it was all the more so. Some impression of this can be deduced from overall sectoral employment figures (taken from Ohkawa and Shinohara 1979: 392–4). While the total population was rising from just over 34 m in 1872 to almost 72 m by 1940, the number gainfully employed in agriculture and forestry marginally declined, from 15.5 m in 1872 to 13.5 m by the late 1930s. Non-agricultural employment, on the other hand, rose from 5.6 m in 1872 to over 20 m by 1940, but employment in the manufacturing sector, where we would expect large businesses to be located, had only reached 6 m by the mid-1930s. Furthermore, as table 13.1 shows, the majority of manufacturing-sector workers were themselves employed in relatively small-scale enterprises throughout the pre-war period. This tendency would appear even more striking had the surveys on which the table is based covered establishments with fewer than five workers and a census of industrial workers taken in 1930 did indeed find that over half of the industrial labour force was employed in such tiny workplaces (Lockwood 1968: 111). Thus, as Japan industrialised, the growing population and labour force were absorbed not into the kinds of big company we now associate with Japanese industry, nor indeed into agriculture, but into the world of small-scale manufacturing, commerce and services which development economists now call the urban informal sector.[3]

One of the main reasons for the neglect of the role of the urban informal sector in developing countries may well be the difficulty of assembling reliable information about the activities and characteristics of those who belong to it, and this is even more the case with pre-World

Table 13.1 The distribution of workers in manufacturing industry by size of establishment 1909–40 (%)

Number of workers	5–49	50–499	500–
1909	45.7	33.6	20.7
1914	40.0	34.9	25.1
1919	33.9	34.6	31.5
1930	37.0	37.4	25.6
1940	36.5	27.4	36.2

Source: Minami (1986), table 9.16: 318

War II Japan. However, it is possible to deduce a little about both the demographic and economic features of those who lived in Japan's rapidly-growing cities and who, for the most part, worked in the informal, small-business sector. First, as in today's Third-World cities, the majority of informal-sector dwellers were migrants, born outside the cities in which they came to live and work. In the 1880s, over 80 per cent of Japan's population lived in settlements of fewer than 10,000 inhabitants, but this proportion steadily declined to around 70 per cent by the time of World War I and just under 50 per cent by World War II (Taeuber 1958: 49, 71). The population of rural areas had ceased to rise by the inter-war period and it was the cities which absorbed the growing numbers of younger sons and daughters of rural and urban households alike. In particular, it was the great conurbations of Tokyo/Yokohama, Osaka/Kobe/Kyoto and Nagoya which grew fastest. Inhabitants of these six cities rose from 2.4 m people, or 6 per cent of the total population, in 1888 to 6.1 m, or 11 per cent by 1918, and in the even more rapid urbanisation of the inter-war period, the population of cities with over 100,000 inhabitants grew from 3,753,000 in 1920 to 21,292,000, almost 30 per cent of the total population, in 1940 (Taeuber 1958: 47, 71). A high proportion of those who found employment in the urban informal sector must therefore have been born elsewhere and were likely to have spent a relatively short time in the city. As early as 1908, a survey of those employed in Tokyo found only 35 per cent to be natives of the city (Nakamura 1983: 128).

Given this, the demographic characteristics of those who belonged to the urban informal sector can be deduced. Migrants everywhere tend to come from the younger economically-active age-groups and to have fewer dependents than average. Both men and women in Japan migrated in pursuit of work, but female migrants tended to be concentrated in the areas offering employment in textile mills, and elsewhere the single male migrant, living in lodgings or a dormitory, was more common. Substantial numbers of women and girls did migrate to the big cities, though, to work as household servants, waitresses, and so on, and over time male migrants married urban brides or brought fiancées from their villages, so that a more normal family pattern became established. Nevertheless, for much of the period of Japan's development, and especially during the inter-war period of particularly rapid urban and industrial growth, the urban informal sectors of major cities must have been dominated by the young and the relatively recently arrived, making up a population whose sex distribution was distorted by the pattern of migration and by the demands of particular kinds of urban employment, and whose social and family ties to the locality were limited.

As in urban informal sectors everywhere, the range of activities by which this population earned its living was wide. However, figures for small-scale businesses in Japan today show that, apart from farms, the largest numbers of small firms can be categorised as involved in wholesale or retail distribution, services or construction (Patrick and Rohlen 1987: 339) and this was also almost certainly the case in the past. Surveys of employment in Tokyo in the early part of this century indicate large numbers of male workers employed in commerce and communications services and of female workers as household servants, and it was also these areas of employment which seem to have expanded fastest during the rapid urbanisation of the inter-war period (Nakamura 1983: 126, 218). The nature of the work involved may have changed as the technology of city life developed: one of the commonest occupations of inhabitants of the Tokyo ghettos during the Meiji period was rickshaw-pulling, but this gradually died out as forms of transport changed (Chūbachi and Taira 1976: 408–10). Nonetheless commerce and services continued to provide the most common sources of income and employment for workers in the urban informal sector throughout the industrialisation period.

However, there were also a great many manufacturing businesses which were family enterprises or small workshops and which, given the conditions of the employment they offered and the insecurity of their existence, must be counted as belonging to the urban informal sector. Ohkawa and Rosovsky divide industries into three categories: (1) food processing, together with wood and ceramic products and a host of miscellaneous industries; (2) textiles and (3) metals, chemicals, machinery and equipment, and show that the first group, which provided over half of industrial output and employment in the second half of the nineteenth century and continued to account for 20–25 per cent of both up to World War II, was dominated by small-scale businesses (Ohkawa and Rosovsky 1961: 81–6). Much textile output came to be produced in larger-scale mills as the industry grew, but small-scale workshops continued to meet demand from significant sections of the market. Only in the heavy and chemical industries did large-scale plants reveal overwhelming economic superiority. As the next section will show in more detail, the continued and even growing employment of large numbers of workers in small-scale enterprises in Ohkawa and Rosovsky's group-(1) industries reflects the maintenance of demand for 'traditional' products, particularly in food, but also in clothing and many kinds of household goods. However, many small firms were engaged in the production of non-traditional items or of parts to supply to larger factories, and a variety of Western-style goods such as bicycles and electric lamps were widely manufactured in small factories.

Members of the urban informal sector therefore ranged from the craftsman or small-scale factory owner, employing family members and/or a few hired workers in the, relatively speaking, more secure and skilled production of food and other household products, through the small shopkeepers, restaurateurs, bar-owners and providers of all manner of personal services, to casual day-labourers, servants, prostitutes, pickpockets and beggars. Although some were long-term residents of the traditional craft-industry areas of cities like Tokyo and Osaka, many more were newcomers trying their luck with greater or lesser success. It is difficult, therefore, to generalise about their welfare and living conditions but one or two points can be made on the basis of available statistics and material such as life histories.

First of all, there seems little doubt that, as in almost all economies, a persistent correlation has existed in Japan between wage rates and the scale of enterprise, such that the smaller the business the lower the incomes it generates. For those working in manufacturing establishments with five or more workers, differentials related to scale began to be detectable by the 1900s, with those in enterprises with five to nine employees receiving approximately 20 per cent less than those in enterprises with more than a thousand workers. These differentials widened thereafter, especially in the inter-war period, so that by the early 1930s those in the smallest enterprises were earning on average only a little over 60 per cent of the incomes of those in the largest (Yasuba 1976: 258). This reflects the emergence of large-scale factories in the heavy-industrial sector, employing capital-intensive, imported technology and able to pay higher wages and to begin to offer better conditions of employment in order to retain experienced workers. Thus the disparity in wages and conditions which standardly marks the division between the 'modern' and 'traditional' sectors of industry clearly emerged as Japan industrialised.

Those with wage-earning jobs in smaller manufacturing enterprises must, however, have represented the upper end of the spectrum of income recipients in the urban informal sector. Others relied on casual earnings and the comings and goings of customers, and data on their income positions are few. Women workers, who represented a large proportion of the informal service-sector labour force, consistently earned less than men, of course, and their position in the labour market was weakened, like that of some kinds of male worker as well, by their dependence on employers for board and lodging and by the need to repay advances made to their families when they entered employment. Even those who operated as independent businessmen or craftsmen – the small-scale shopkeepers, *tatami* mat-makers, barbers, street traders, rickshaw-pullers – were frequently unable to make much more than day-labourers once they had met charges for credit, materials and so on.[4]

Given the difficulty of generalising about income levels, a better glimpse of welfare and living standards in the urban informal sector of industrialising Japan can perhaps be gained from the few general descriptions and surveys made by contemporaries of life among the poorer sections of the urban population. Chūbachi and Taira (1976) have assembled evidence which relates both to quite well-paid urban factory workers and also to casual workers living in the ghetto areas of the main cities, during the Meiji and inter-war periods. In the Meiji-period survey, the factory workers appear to have been settled with quite stable nuclear families or elderly parents, living in two or three rented rooms in tenement houses, whereas broken families and temporary accommodation were in evidence among the ghetto-dwellers. All were spending a large proportion of their household income on food, as most Japanese households continued to do throughout the period up to World War II.[5] This expenditure should, however, have bought even the casually employed rickshawman in the survey an adequate supply of rice, and more than that if he and his family ate rice extended with other grains. The factory workers were literate and recorded expenditure on, for example, newspapers, but it is difficult to know what, if anything, the ghetto families bought beyond the bare necessities. None of the families surveyed, neither the factory workers nor the ghetto-dwellers, seem to have been living sufficiently within their means to be saving anything.

By the time of the inter-war period surveys, divergences between the lifestyles of factory workers and the more casually employed ghetto poor seem to have widened. The poor families were by then spending a higher proportion of their incomes on food than factory-worker households, and a lower proportion in rent on their lower-quality housing, even where their incomes were similar. The stable worker-households also spent more on clothing, health, sanitation and education than the ghetto poor, suggesting the emergence of distinct differences in lifestyle and culture. As the incoming urban population sorted itself out, so to speak, significant numbers of those employed in the small-business sector began to develop less 'informal' lifestyles, although still living with greater independence and insecurity than big-company employees, while those who remained, for whatever reason, casually employed came to be distinguishable, whether or not living in the ghettos still to be found in Japan's major cities today, as the poor, in need of relief or correction.[6]

Despite this differentiation, however, the evidence does suggest that there was, overall, some improvement in the living conditions of the urban population which did spread to the mass of those working outside the big-company sector. Urban housing conditions gradually improved as better forms of heating and lighting (paraffin stoves, glass windows, etc.) spread. Diets became healthier and more varied as more households were able to include a wider range of vegetables and pulses in their meals. Books and magazines, travel, and newer forms of entertainment such as the cinema began to fall within the reach of increasingly settled urban households. Those who worked in the small-scale sector never attained the security or, on average, the earning-power of those with large-scale sector jobs, but nevertheless small businesses were able to secure a sufficient share of the growth of income and employment consequent on industrialisation to survive and indeed to provide improved living conditions for a significant section of the labour force.

Thus, far from fading away in the face of competition from big business, the world of the small-scale manufacturing, commercial or service-industry household became established, with its own culture and way of life, as part of the Japanese economic, social and political scene.[7] The Japanese case thus presents us with an example of the way in which the small-business sector can make the transition out of the 'informal' status it now holds in many developing countries. Research into the routes whereby households made this transition has been, however, very limited and the descriptions above are of necessity based on scattered and often impressionistic surveys covering very small samples. We do, though, know rather more about the economic mechanisms whereby small businesses became integrated within the developing structure of Japanese industry and it is these, and their implications for our understanding of the characteristics of a successful industrialisation process, which are the subject of the remaining sections of this chapter.

THE ECONOMICS OF THE SMALL BUSINESS SECTOR

Economic analysis and policy prescription, whether conventional or Marxist, have tended to assume that big is beautiful, or at least progressive. The economic advantages of specialisation and division of labour within large-scale production systems have been recognised since Adam Smith's time; powerful technological forces operate to create economies of scale in many industries, and as capital has accumulated and labour become scarcer in the advanced economies where most R & D work takes place, the direction taken by technical change has intensified the trend towards greater capital intensity and consequently larger scale. The development of mass production techniques has made possible the widespread diffusion of many consumer durables which would otherwise have remained the privileges of only the rich, and the expansion of production for the mass consumer market in many ways provides the key to the growth of the European and American economies in the twentieth century, as well as playing a large part in the post-war Japanese economic miracle.

Nonetheless, large-scale production techniques have not proved to be superior in all areas of economic activity, even in the most advanced economies. In some cases, technological or other supply-side features of production have worked against large-scale organisation; in agriculture, for example, diseconomies of scale seem to set in at quite low levels of size of enterprise. In others, the nature of the product and its market may make production on a large scale impractical; many kinds of service industry, where personal contact with the customer is required, would exhibit this tendency. Development economists have tended to concentrate on the theoretical case against large scale, arguing that large-scale production, resulting as it usually does from the choice of capital-intensive techniques, represents an inefficient use of resources in economies where labour is abundant and capital scarce. However, this supply-side argument has also become increasingly interconnected with the demand-side case for 'appropriate products': large-scale, capital-intensive techniques are adopted because little choice is available as long as products are required to meet the same specifications as their equivalents produced in developed countries. Products designed to meet the demands of the (lower-income) domestic market, on the other hand, may not need to meet the same specifications and can potentially be produced competitively on a smaller scale using more labour-intensive methods, thus generating employment and at the same time helping to meet the 'basic needs' of the mass of the population.

Theoretically speaking, therefore, there are a number of reasons why small firms might be more efficient and competitive than large in certain markets or technological niches or under certain economic conditions. They might also, of course, owe their survival to market imperfections which restrict competition between big and small firms and the next section will consider the ways in which such restrictions were institutionalised within the Japanese industrial structure. However, the Japanese case clearly does present an example of the small business sector surviving, and indeed developing, at least in part through the exploitation of the economic advantages of smaller scale outlined above. The analysis which follows of the activities of small businesses over the course of industrialisation reveals them as able, on the one hand, to tap relatively cheap sources of labour, skill and entrepreneurial drive (those of women, for example) not utilised by larger firms and, on the other, to meet demand for products which large firms could not competitively produce. To some extent, this ability must be put down to good fortune and historical circumstances, in particular to the absence of the developed-country mass producers of consumer goods whose attractive and highly-advertised products create new patterns of wants in today's developing countries. Deliberate policy certainly also played a part, and Japanese government leaders and economic bureaucrats were aware of the import-substitution potential of the small-scale sector from the Meiji period onwards (Shinohara 1970: 9). But the persistent ability of small firms to carve out a changing and complementary role for themselves, alongside large firms, within the industrial structure suggests that the trend towards bigness may not be as inevitable as once thought and that the demand for the variety of products and skills which small businesses can meet may not be something that necessarily disappears over the course of development.

The range of activities in which small and family businesses have typically been engaged over the course of Japan's industrialisation has been very wide.[8] Table 13.2 gives some indication of this, by illustrating the types of economic activity in which self-employed and family workers, as compared with hired workers, tended to be found in the inter-war period. As would be expected, far and away the most important area of employment was agriculture and much of Part II has already been devoted to analysis of the survival of the small farm. However, significant numbers of family workers were also to be found in various kinds of service activity, particularly the provision of wholesaling and retailing, transport and other services, such as catering. These sorts of occupation are largely the province of small enterprises in most economies, although the greater persistence of the small shop in Japan does contrast with experience in Britain and America at least. As we have seen, expansion of employment in these kinds of service industry was a major factor in the growth of the urban informal sector, particularly in the period up to World War I, and there is nothing unusual about the large role of small and family businesses in this. What these industries do clearly illustrate, though, are some of the most important characteristics distinguishing the areas of economic activity in which small businesses do have advantages over large:

- their products are frequently differentiated in some way, giving them a degree of monopoly power (for example, they cater, literally very often, to particular locations in which they have little competition);
- they employ relatively labour-intensive technologies, capital requirements generally being limited to premises and/or stocks and small-scale equipment;
- they do not require a great deal of formal education on the part of the work force, although organisational ability and other kinds of entrepreneurial skill are necessary to survival and success, as are the personal qualities needed to provide service and attention;
- they are areas of activity in which women often make up a large

Table 13.2 The distribution of hired and family workers by type of industry 1920–30 (numbers of employees, thousands)

| | 1920 | | 1930 | |
	Hired workers	Self-employed and family workers	Hired workers	Self-employed and family workers
All industries	7842	18698	9578	19824
Major categories of which:				
Agriculture, forestry and fishing	657	13782	710	13778
Mining	405	15	301	13
Construction	539	178	471	493
Manufacturing	2781	1657	2841	1860
Wholesale and retail	641	2021	1289	2835
Transport and other public utilities	797	336	1078	211
Services	1310	622	1855	616
Civil Service	544	35	733	–

Source: adapted from Nakamura (1983): table 8.4: 219

part of the labour force, working part-time or combining labour in, for example, the family shop or restaurant, with the running of the household.

In the service industries, therefore, small Japanese businesses, like their counterparts elsewhere, have continued to be able to exploit these advantages, making use of otherwise underutilised sources of labour through their application of labour-intensive techniques and creating niches in markets through product differentiation.

What is perhaps more interesting about the Japanese case, however, is the extent to which, as table 13.2 also shows, small businesses maintained their foothold in areas of manufacturing, as opposed to service, activity in which they were able to exploit these same advantages. It is convenient to divide these areas of manufacturing into broadly two categories, the first of which might be labelled, following Ohkawa and Rosovsky, the production of indigenous goods. These are defined as final products of types generally in use before 1868, meaning largely, therefore, food products and household goods associated with the 'traditional' Japanese lifestyle. These include numerous edible products often unfamiliar to the Western consumer, but also items of Japanese-style clothing and many household goods made of pottery, bamboo, laquer, straw, and so on. Using data for 1955, Ohkawa and Rosovsky show that, even well into the post-World War II period, about a half of total consumer expenditure went on indigenous consumption goods, and given their nature as 'basic-needs' items, the proportion in earlier periods must have been higher. Furthermore, over 80 per cent of the value of assets (not including buildings) acquired by households before 1941 was accounted for by indigenous items such as silk kimono and Japanese-style bedding (Ohkawa and Rosovsky 1961: 488, 492–3).

This persistence in the demand for indigenous goods reflects the fact that, despite the novelty-value of the various Western-style goods which began to appear in Meiji Japan, the lifestyles and consumption habits of the majority of the population were slow to change in any fundamental way (Hanley 1986). Diets improved, but mainly as a result of the wider diffusion of what had formerly been considered high-class Japanese-style cuisine, centring on white rice, vegetables, pulses and fish products. The consumption of Western-style foods like bread, milk and meat did not begin to increase significantly until after the Russo-Japanese War, when many ordinary army recruits encountered such food for the first time. Western-style clothing began to be worn during office hours by urban white-collar workers from the Meiji period onwards, but the majority of the population, particularly women, limited their concessions to Western fashion to hats, hairstyles and cosmetics, and continued to wear Japanese-style clothes (which are in many ways more practical within Japanese-style houses) at least until experience with Western-style military uniforms became widespread. Western-style buildings, constructed with non-traditional materials, were erected in growing numbers, but most were public buildings, factories, department stores and so on, and Japanese-style housing, with its accompanying furniture and fittings, remained the norm for most people.

From a developmental point of view, the significance of this continued demand for Japanese-style, indigenous goods lies partly, of course, in the limits thus imposed on the import of Western goods. But for present purposes, Ohkawa and Rosovsky's research can also be used to show that both the technology and the markets of the indigenous-goods industries possessed characteristics conducive to small-scale organisation and that small and family enterprises did indeed dominate production in these areas. On the supply side, their data show that indigenous-goods production is on average more labour-intensive and less subject to economies of scale than the production of 'modern' goods (484–7). The workers employed may possess considerable training in traditional skills, but do not on the whole require high levels of formal education. Women and family workers are much more likely to be employed in indigenous-goods production than in modern, and Ohkawa and Rosovsky estimate (478) that 79 per cent of all women workers in 1930 were engaged in indigenous occupations (here including agriculture). On the demand side, indigenous goods tend to be quite highly differentiated as products. Many, for example, are regional varieties of goods, making use of particular local inputs. Traditional building styles, textile patterns and so on show considerable regional variation and the traveller on today's Bullet Train will be well aware of the abundance of local food products, now sold primarily as gifts and souvenirs but once part of the ordinary family's diet, reflecting local agricultural conditions and tastes. Taking all these factors together, small businesses, with their capacity to tap underutilised and cheaper sources of labour, particularly that of women and family workers, and their advantages in meeting particular, differentiated, local demands, might therefore be expected to be heavily represented in indigenous-goods industries and Ohkawa and Rosovsky's findings confirm this (483–4). The maintenance of demand for indigenous products throughout the pre-World War II period and the continued importance of the small-scale sector in total production and employment are thus intimately connected phenomena of considerable significance in determining the pattern of Japanese industrialisation.

Nonetheless, since indigenous products of these kinds were generally 'basic needs' goods, demand for them was likely to fall proportionately as incomes rose and for a full explanation of the long-term survival and development of the small-scale sector in Japan we have to look to the second broad category of its activities. This covers the areas of non-indigenous manufacturing in which small-scale businesses managed to establish themselves, principally in the production of parts and components for Western-style producer and consumer goods. During the inter-war period particularly, the number of small-scale factories and workshops engaged in this type of production, generally under subcontract to larger firms, began to increase and we shall be considering in more detail in the next section the institutional forces which led larger-scale firms to develop the subcontracting system in this way. On the technical and economic side, however, a major factor was the ability of small businesses to tap cheaper sources of labour than those utilised by larger-scale employers. This made it possible to operate, more-or-less profitably, with more labour-intensive methods than the skill- and capital-intensive imported techniques adopted by large firms. Nonetheless, the 'non-indigenous' small business sector should not be regarded as necessarily 'traditional' or stagnant from a technological point of view. The subcontracting system itself put pressure on small firms to upgrade their technical capacity to meet the needs of their big-company customers and they were assisted in this by the spread of the electric motor, which made the mechanisation of small-scale factories feasible in a way which the steam engine, the only mechanised power source available in earlier-industrialising countries and a large-scale and indivisible capital item, did not (Minami 1987: 324–5). Estimates of the number and growth of small firms engaged in the production of 'non-indigenous' goods before World War II are almost impossible to make but, as the next section will show, the subcontracting system did become widely established in industries such as machine-building during the inter-war period and this continued to provide the basis for the development of small businesses during the later economic-miracle period.

The developing role which small firms played in the production of machines and other non-indigenous goods is perhaps best illustrated by an example (from Ishikawa 1981: 384–6 and 404–6). Bicycles were first imported into Japan soon after the Restoration, and their numbers proceeded to grow thereafter. The only models available at this time were expensive British bicycles which only relatively high-income purchasers could afford. They did, however, need repairs and spare parts which small-scale Japanese workshops were able to provide and it was out of this experience that the domestic bicycle-manufacturing industry was to grow. Eventually, Japanese-made bicycles, assembled from the parts made in small workshops in the Osaka area, came on to the market and by 1920 the value of domestic production exceeded that of imports. Exports of Japanese bicycles to China and other parts of Asia also began to grow. Within the industry, the production process was broken down into a great many small stages, most of which could be carried out in small workshops using general-purpose equipment and particular labour skills. The results were lower-quality products than the competing imports, but they sold at much lower prices and reached a much wider market of potential bicycle-users at home and abroad. As with 'indigenous' consumption goods, the use of relatively labour-intensive techniques resulted in a production system appropriate for small-scale enterprises manufacturing a product for lower-income purchasers, but this time what had originally been an imported technology was adapted to produce a non-indigenous good.

In such ways, in the manufacture of new, Western-style goods as in the production of indigenous ones, small businesses discovered areas of activity in which they were able to make use of their economic advantages. What these areas had in common was, on the supply side, the application of relatively capital-saving technology, exhibiting few scale economies and making use of available sources of lower-wage labour (e.g. that of women), and, on the demand side, their production of generally quite highly differentiated products meeting the demands of lower-income consumers. This economic account of the comparative advantages which enabled small businesses to survive cannot, however, altogether explain their persistence in fields where, in other economies, larger-scale organisation has resulted in lower costs of production and the gradual eclipse of the small firm as industrialisation proceeded. We must now turn to consideration of the institutional arrangements which limited competition between large and small firms in Japan and thereby helped to preserve the small business.

THE INSTITUTIONS OF INDUSTRIAL ORGANISATION

Developing countries, almost by definition, are endowed with only limited supplies of capital for investment in new industries and of workers and managers with the formal education and experience necessary to operate new forms of technology. At the same time, though, the establishment of 'modern' industries is generally seen as a national goal which the state is heavily involved in trying to achieve. In this situation, the allocation of the scarce resources required in abundance by growing modern industries is rarely left to the uncontrollable forces of the market and there frequently emerge institutional arrangements which ensure preferential access to capital and educated manpower for enterprises whose existence and growth is seen as contributing to the national goal of industrialisation. Such arrangements include the formal procedures of state planning organisations but may, in addition, or alternatively, involve the development, on the side of modern-sector enterprises themselves, of structures through which the political and economic strength necessary to maintain access to scarce resources can be mobilised. The initial need, if new industries are to be established and survive, for, for instance, protection from imports or the provision of investible funds from banks results in the establishment of close links between the state and its bureaucracy on the one hand and the leaders of modern-sector businesses on the other, and the institutionalisation of such links creates market imperfections which in turn limit the access of businesses outside the system to scarce resources. In such a situation, large-scale modern-sector businesses exercise influence which is not available to small-scale firms and which enables them to obtain cheaper investment funds, to be granted licences to import, to be protected from foreign competition and to pay higher wages to a privileged labour force. The dual economy has thus become institutionalised within the political and social structures of many present-day developing countries.

In late nineteenth- and twentieth-century Japan, this process resulted in the appearance of the large-scale industrial groups, known as *zaibatsu*, which came increasingly to dominate the modern and heavy-industrial sectors of the economy and to exercise significant political and social influence. Analysis of the role of the *zaibatsu* in Japan's industrialisation reveals, however, that their development depended, at least in part, on the interrelationships which grew up between the large-scale *zaibatsu* enterprises and the much greater number of small-scale businesses, surviving and adapting, as earlier sections have described, within the industrialising economy. These interrelationships were themselves institutionalised in arrangements, in particular concerning the recruitment of labour and the subcontracting of parts of production processes, through which the division of economic responsibility between big and small firms was maintained and through which competition for resources was restricted. Frictions within the system were also substantially reduced by the activities of the so-called general trading companies which grew up in response to the needs and demands of both large and small firms as Japanese business became increasingly enmeshed in the world economy.

Industrial groups

In the period between the late nineteenth century and World War II, the 'modern sector' of Japan's economy, that is to say heavy industries, such as mining, shipping and shipbuilding, and the manufacture of machinery, metals and chemicals, as well as the leading financial institutions and trading companies, was dominated by companies belonging to one or other of four large-scale conglomerate industrial groups or combines known as *zaibatsu*.[9] This term is written with Chinese characters meaning 'financial clique/faction', as are the words for the rather similar sorts of organisation which exist in some of the present-day Newly Industrialising Countries.[10] The common feature of these organisations lies in the fact that they are composed of a number of legally distinct companies, each leading its own production and accounting life but linked to the other companies in the group, with varying degrees of strength, through some combination of personal, historical, economic or financial interrelationships. As a rule, such groups tend to have interests in a wide range of industries and although many have been and still are giant economic organisations, they should not be thought of in the same way as large corporations of the British or American type whose strength lies in their domination of one particular area of production.

The four great pre-war Japanese *zaibatsu*, known after their founders or their founder's company as Mitsui, Mitsubishi, Sumitomo and Yasuda, differed to some extent in their histories, as in their organisational structures and industrial specialisations, but all could be said to have originated in the activities of Meiji-period entrepreneurs who learned to operate successfully in the economic and political climate of the first stages of industrialisation.[11] We have already encountered Iwasaki Yatarō who laid the basis for the Mitsubishi *zaibatsu* as he diversified away from his original shipping interests in the late nineteenth century. Like him, the founders of the other major *zaibatsu* used their personal connections with members of the Meiji government to gain the kind of protection and patronage necessary for the establishment of new kinds of industrial venture, at a time when capital and modern industrial skills were especially scarce, foreign competition was fierce and the state was heavily involved, at first directly and then through more indirect means, in promoting economic development. The privatisation of the government-owned enterprises in the 1880s, for example, provided the initial opportunity for a number of future *zaibatsu* founders. As their early ventures succeeded, and as their ability to raise funds, using their economic strength and their personal and political connections, improved, they acquired or set up enterprises in new fields and so came to control growing but diversified industrial empires.

As these empires grew, and as their founders aged and handed over to their successors, the typical organisational structure of the groups took shape. At the apex of each group was a holding company, largely owned by the family of the original founder, and this company operated as the major shareholder in the most important production and trading companies belonging to the group. These generally included a bank and a general trading company, along with a number of major manufacturing and mining companies. These companies were in turn linked through interlocking shareholdings and directorships and through personal ties such as marriage alliances. The major companies themselves then branched out through acquisitions and the establishment of subsidiary companies, each of which also developed its own affiliates within the group. This process was intensified by the effects of the post-World War I depression which led to bankruptcies among companies not enjoying the protection of *zaibatsu* membership and drove others to enter subordinate relationships within the groups. As a result, by the inter-war period, the *zaibatsu* had established themselves as pyramidal organisations containing hundreds of companies, often engaged in widely different industrial, financial and trading activities. When added together, the turnovers or the assets of companies belonging to each of the groups amounted to massive totals and the Mitsui and Mitsubishi *zaibatsu* in particular were able to exercise great influence over the economic and also political life of the country.

Despite the size and influence of each group taken as a whole, however, the extent to which the internal organisation of the *zaibatsu* permitted central control or co-ordinated activity was to a degree limited. Companies within each *zaibatsu* group depended on finance from the group's bank; they used the group's trading company to market their output and secure their inputs; their boards of directors interlocked with those of other companies and knew one another personally through frequent social contact, and by preference they traded with one another, offering each other better terms or easier credit than would be available to outsiders. But as the pyramid spread out, these ties lessened and relationships among the hundreds of smaller companies on the edges of the group were much more fluid. Furthermore, although the major groups did specialise to some extent in particular areas of industry or trade, few *zaibatsu* companies were in a position to exercise monopoly power over the supply of any individual product. Rivalry between *zaibatsu* groups was intense and in many major industries oligopolistic competition between two or more firms was the rule.[12] Economic rivalries spread over into political differences and 'big business' in pre-World War II Japan was a far from monolithic interest group.

Nevertheless, the economic and political power and influence of the *zaibatsu* meant that they acted as the channels whereby capital and scarce educated manpower were directed towards the modern industrial sector and it is in this that their chief contribution to the speed and pattern of Japan's industrialisation lay. A later section beginning at p. 233–8 will describe how this operated in the labour market, but control over sources of finance was in many ways the key to *zaibatsu* organisation and to the ability of group companies to expand in capital-intensive areas. The growth of share-ownership among the wider public was very limited and the role of the stock exchange as a source of business capital has remained relatively small until quite recent times. Savings were for the most part deposited in banks, giving the *zaibatsu* banks at the apex of the financial system dominant influence over the allocation of funds and the provision of credit, especially after the demise of many smaller banks in the post-World War I collapse. This influence was further strengthened by the close links between *zaibatsu* banks and government financial institutions. The system made it extremely difficult for businesses outside *zaibatsu* control to obtain investment funds on anything like the same terms as those within and inhibited the spread of capital ownership outside the groups. On the other hand, however, it did ensure that available capital was directed towards the development of the heavy industrial base, much as has happened in more fully planned developing economies. Similarly, the *zaibatsu* structure concentrated and shared the use of technology imports, foreign exchange and other scarce 'modern' inputs within organisations which were able to make effective use of them.

The price which was paid for this contribution to development goals took the form of the institutionalisation of a degree of inequality and imperfection in the economic system, the effects of which on the lives of those living and working outside the 'modern' sector we have glimpsed in earlier sections. The limits placed on the diffusion of the ownership of capital and the management of modern-sector resources also influenced the long-term development of Japan's political and social structure in ways which have been much criticised. Furthermore, by the inter-war period the major 'old' *zaibatsu* had become sufficiently entrenched and conservative to wish to avoid branching out into some of the more risky areas of modern technology and fields such as vehicle production, as we have seen, were left to more enterprising 'new' *zaibatsu*-founders to open up. Nevertheless, looking back with hindsight from the dualist world of many of today's developing countries, the boundaries created by the existence of the *zaibatsu* between the modern, capital-intensive and 'traditional', more labour-intensive sectors look far from watertight. As subsequent sections will now illustrate, the *zaibatsu* depended on and made use of a complex network of interrelationships between business organisations within and outside the modern sector and the pre-war Japanese industrial structure as a whole appears considerably more interdependent than modern technology, labour and management practices, and international trading conditions will allow in today's developing world.

Subcontracting

Many firms in most economies buy in from outside a substantial proportion of the parts and services they need to produce their final product, rather than make the investments of time and money necessary to supply them in-house. Major automobile producers everywhere, for example, make use of specialist parts-producers for many of the individual components they assemble into vehicles. Nonetheless, in Japan, subcontracting of this sort is regarded as something of a national institution, viewed either as embodying all that is exploitative in the 'dual structure' of Japanese industry or alternatively as an expression of the hierarchical but personalised long-term relationships of trust and patronage that make Japanese business culturally unique and inpenetrable to foreigners. The practice of larger firms' subcontracting elements in the production process to smaller firms became widespread in the Japanese economy in the inter-war period, although it remained understandably more common in assembly-type industries, such as machine-making and electrical-goods and vehicle production, than in process industries like metal-manufacture or chemicals. It was a major factor in the survival and growth of the small-scale sector in non-indigenous manufacturing and in the development of interrelationships and interdependencies between large-scale and small-scale enterprises. As such, it gave the industrial structure distinctive characteristics which in their turn affected the speed and pattern of Japanese industrial growth.

There seems no doubt that subcontracting has come to be a more common practice in the Japanese economy than is typical elsewhere. Historical data on the extent of the practice in the pre-war period are hard to find, but according to one estimate, by 1934 78 per cent of factories in the machinery industry employing more than 30 people were buying in products from outside (Nakamura 1983: 224). By the late 1970s and early 1980s, 82 per cent of firms with more than 300 employees used subcontractors, the average large firm in manufacturing employing 68 different subcontracting firms, and subcontracting remains the key to existence for the smallest manufacturing enterprises (one to three workers), two-thirds of whom engage in it (Uekusa 1987: 503, 347). Although some forms of subcontracting (e.g. the employment of gangs of workers under a labour-boss) had been utilised in pre-World War I industry, it is generally agreed that the system spread during the period of economic fluctuations in the 1920s and became well established as manufacturing industry expanded more rapidly in the '30s. It allowed large-scale, modern-sector firms, burdened with heavy overheads of equipment and skilled and experienced workers they did not wish to risk laying off, to increase their flexibility through hiving off the production of parts which could be manufactured by smaller firms using cheaper and more dispensible labour. For the small enterprise, entering a subcontracting relationship provided some guarantee of a market in the difficult inter-war economic climate and potentially some protection, through a link, however distant, with larger-scale companies and perhaps a *zaibatsu* group. Despite the much more rapid growth of the economy in the post-World War II period, the conditions which gave the system its advantages, to some extent to both sides, have not disappeared and, as a result, typical Japanese firms in many industries continue to rely on subcontractors for many items which British or American companies would produce for themselves.[13]

Furthermore, where British or American firms do purchase parts from outside, they generally make use of specialist component-makers who in their turn supply many other firms in the industry. Such firms exist equally in Japan and indeed it would be the goal of many small-scale businesses to develop into such a parts-supplier. However, when subcontracting is being discussed in the Japanese context, it is frequently a rather different kind of inter-firm relationship that is meant and one which is undoubtedly more common in Japan than in many Western economies. Many Japanese subcontrators, and especially the smallest ones, rely on orders from one major purchaser alone and produce to the design and requirements of the larger firm. They are thus particularly dependent on one buyer and vulnerable should the larger firm decide to cut back on orders, and it is this sort of vulnerability and dependency which has given rise to the argument that subcontracting has been the means whereby large-scale business has exploited small-scale. Through its indirect employment of the work forces of dependent small firms, the large firm, in the pre-World War II period as since, was able not only to continue to pay its workers substantially more than workers in small firms could earn, but also to off-load on to its subcontractors the risk to employment caused by business fluctuations, thereby offering much greater security to its own employees.

On the other hand, however, the dependent subcontractor's close relationship with its customer firm did provide it with access to resources and services which small firms cannot as a rule afford. As the technology of the main firm was up-graded, so had to be that of its subcontractors producing component parts, and the main firm would need to provide technical guidance and assistance with the purchase of machinery to enable its subcontractors to meet its changing requirements. The large firm was responsible for the marketing of the final product and it might provide credit and support with financial institutions. It was, on the whole, in the interests of larger firms to be able to rely on a network of high-quality subcontractors, so that, although the small firm bore risks on behalf of the large firm and was ultimately vulnerable, it was not without its own ability to gain from the mutual relationship.

The close ties between larger firm and subcontractor also need to be seen in the context of the wider network of inter-firm relationships of which they formed a part. Thus, major firms had subsidiaries who employed larger-scale subcontractors who in their turn used smaller subcontractors and so on. Lines of communication and of credit therefore reached down from the great *zaibatsu* companies and their banks and trading companies to the small workshop in the back yard. This meant that, when the great company sneezed, as during the banking crises and depressions of the inter-war period for example, the backyard workshop caught cold, but it meant also that, as the economy grew, big business used the subcontracting system as a means of expanding employment and output without the high degree of risk this would otherwise have implied, given the capital-intensity of their technology and their heavy overheads. As a result of the use of subcontracting therefore, the small firm was not completely cut off from the modern sector, as the dual-economy picture might suggest, but was to some degree integrated into it in ways which promoted the growth of employment and output in the industrial sector as a whole.

The segmented labour market

This somewhat positive view of the role of small businesses and subcontracting in Japan's development is not the one which emerges from many of the available Japanese studies of employment and the labour market in pre-World War II Japan. The striking feature which these studies tend to bring out is rather the divergence in wages and employment conditions between those who worked in large-scale enterprises and those employed in small businesses, and more broadly the marked correlation in the Japanese economy between wage rates and the scale of enterprise. Such inequalities exist in most economies: large-scale enterprises tend to adopt more capital-intensive technology, thus generating the higher labour productivity which justifies the payment of the higher wages required to secure the more stable and better-educated labour forces needed to operate expensive machinery. However, it has generally been accepted that differentials have been wider in Japan than in other industrialised countries, with large firms paying higher wages and offering very significantly better and more stable employment conditions for broadly similar kinds of work than small ones.[14]

In a perfectly competitive labour market, competition among workers and between large- and small-scale employers would be predicted to result in an equalisation of wages paid for the same kind of work. That this has happened even less in Japan, as industrialisation has occurred, than elsewhere has led to the search for 'imperfections' in the labour market and particular institutional arrangements which limit labour-market competition in the Japanese case. From this has emerged the idea of the 'dual' or 'segmented' Japanese labour market: the institutional arrangements governing the recruitment and employment of labour enable large firms to pay higher wages to their own workers, while at the same time ensuring the existence of a pool of lower-paid workers outside the large-scale sector, to be drawn on (e.g. through sub-contracting) as required and available to be exploited by small-scale businesses as a cheaper source of labour. The key to the mechanism behind this system lay in the undoubted differences in recruitment and employment practices between large and small firms, which limited competition for labour between them. At the same time, however, as we have already begun to see, large firms and small firms remained in many ways intertwined and analysis of the pattern of changes in wage differentials and of the nature of the labour-market mechanism shows that the fates of workers in the large-scale and small-scale sectors were not as completely independent of each other as the idea of the dual labour market might imply.

Yasuba's calculations of the changing pattern of wage differentials according to the size of enterprise, using available national-level survey data, are shown in table 13.3. and suggest that differentials already existed in the early years of this century and thereafter generally widened. Where it is possible to trace changes in more detail, however, the evidence suggests that movements in differentials around this trend followed a pattern similar to those of other kinds of occupational and regional wage differentials, narrowing during the boom years of the 1910s, widening during the more depressed period through the '20s and early '30s, and then narrowing again as the economy picked up in the later '30s (Yasuba 1976: 254–62; Taira 1970: 31–6). In this respect, wage differentials by size of firm can be said to have been driven by the economic forces of the market, declining during the World War I boom period when demand for labour was high and large- and small-scale employers competed for workers, and widening again in the '20s, when employment growth in the modern industrial sector slowed down, expanding the supply of workers available to the small-scale sector. This sort of evidence has led a number of writers to argue that the 'modern' and 'traditional' sectors of the labour market were linked by competitive forces such that expanding demand for labour on the part of large-scale firms did lead to generally rising wage rates throughout the economy and that therefore large firms never faced an 'unlimited supply of labour' held in the small-scale sector.

Nonetheless, although the fates of employees throughout the economy were linked together through the forces of overall supply and demand for labour, the fact remains that a structure of differentials did emerge, especially in the inter-war period, and has continued to exist, even in post-war Japan, to a greater extent than elsewhere. When large firms are seeking to expand their work-forces, pressure is placed on wages throughout the gradations of this structure and differentials

Table 13.3 Wage differentials by size of establishment (indices of standardised average wage rates where largest scale of establishment = 100*)

1909 Workers per establishment		1914 Workers per establishment		1932/3 Workers per establishment		1951
5– 9	82.3	78.5	5– 10	61.2	4– 9	47.1
10–29	87.6	83.1	10– 50	74.0	10–19	52.0
30–49	92.7	87.5	50–100	81.0	20–29	56.5
50–99	96.5	91.9	100–500	89.2	30–49	61.5
100–	100.0	100.0	500–	100.0	50–99	68.2
					100–	100.0

* Computed from national surveys of factories for 1909, 1914 and 1951. 1932/3 data cover major cities only. For details of methods of calculation, see Yasuba 255–8.
Source: Yasuba (1976), table 5: 258

narrow, but the nature of the structure still means that limits exist to the degree of competition for labour between larger- and smaller-scale employers. The three major characteristics used to segment the labour force and limit competition between employers have been sex, age and educational attainment, and the history of the segmentation of the labour supply on the basis of these characteristics shows how it operated as a key element in the interlocking structure of large and small firms. We saw in chapter 12 how the use of the 'Japanese employment system', including 'lifetime' employment, age-related wage payments and employer paternalism, was beginning to spread from white-collar to blue-collar employees of major companies in the inter-war period, as employers sought the means to secure stable and experienced labour forces. Those who have attempted to disaggregate the sources of wage differentials between large and small firms in industrialising Japan have shown how the gradual application of these employment practices interacted with the increasing segmentation of the labour supply on the basis of sex, age and education to facilitate the payment of higher wages in large firms than in small.

First of all, large firms, apart from the relatively few operating in the textile industry, in general employed a far lower proportion of women in their labour forces than did small. A number operated in the kinds of industries deemed unsuitable for women workers throughout the world (e.g. mining, shipbuilding), but equally, whatever the technology, where a stable, skilled or experienced labour force was required, women were generally considered ineligible on the grounds that their employment was expected to be temporary, and women workers have never been offered the 'lifetime guarantee' of employment. The practices of large-scale firms in this respect therefore left small-scale firms free to recruit the labour of much of the female workforce at lower wages, free of the competition of high-wage, 'modern-sector' employers, and large male/female wage differentials, widening with the age of workers as men receive their age-related wage increases, have continued to prevail in the Japanese economy to this day.[15]

Secondly, the chief criterion, apart from sex, according to which labour market entrants are categorised for potential employers in Japan today is the level and nature of their educational qualifications. Prestigious employers, such as the bureaucracy and 'top-class' industrial firms, limit their white-collar recruitment to graduates of what are considered the best universities and their blue-collar recruitment to those with the best school records. The origins of these practices clearly go back to the time when higher-education establishments were being set up expressly to provide the trained manpower needed by the state and by new modern industries and when the still-limited provision of secondary schooling restricted the numbers leaving school with more than the minimum years of education behind them. Although big businesses in the pre-World War II period could not apply the practices of educational segregation as rigidly as their postwar successors do, nonetheless accepted paths through the education system leading to recruitment by large-scale firms gradually became institutionalised, placing limits on the degree of competition between large and small firms for labour-market entrants. Smaller businesses were thus left free to recruit, without competition from high-wage employers, those lacking the educational qualifications required for consideration by larger firms.[16]

The third characteristic on which labour-market segregation has been based is related to the spread of the practices of age-related wage determination and employer paternalism through which managements began to seek, in the pre-World War II period but more markedly since, to try to reduce labour turnover and industrial unrest. To the extent that these practices succeeded in their objectives, leading to workers' developing a sense of belonging, staying with the company and building career experience, wages and salaries tended to rise as labour turnover fell and the average length of service of company employees rose. Large firms increasingly came to recruit only from among immediate graduates of the educational system, who received relatively low starting salaries in the expectation of future increases and who represented clean sheets on which to imprint company experience. Smaller firms did not offer the same increases in wages and salaries as length of service increased, but were at the same time left to recruit at lower wages, free from the competition of larger firms, those older workers who had never entered employment in the large-scale sector or who had left it, voluntarily or through more-or-less obligatory early retirement.

Labour market segregation operating in the above ways, while enabling large firms to build more stable and experienced labour forces, clearly resulted in their having to pay higher wages than they would have done had their potential employees had to compete in the labour market with the large number of women, older people and less formally-qualified workers who were increasingly segmented off from them. It should not be forgotten, therefore, that the ability of larger firms to sustain the system depended on their relatively strong position in the industrialising economy, which was based on both their economic and their institutional power. Their more advanced and capital-intensive technology, their privileged access to investment funds, their ability to secure imports and foreign exchange as required, their close connections with the politically and bureaucratically powerful and their often oligopolistic position in the markets for their products all enabled them to secure the long-run economic success which allowed higher wages to be paid. Meanwhile, though, the segregation of labour supply prevented the full force of these higher wages from making itself felt in the areas of the labour market in which smaller firms recruited, enabling the small-scale sector to continue to offer lower wages than would otherwise have been the case to women, to older workers, to the less formally educated, the less settled and the more independent who, through choice or necessity, were ruled out of employment in the high-wage modern sector. Thus the survival and success of the two sectors were interconnected through their mutual dependence on the segmented structure of the labour market.

At the level of individual firms too, the fortunes of large and small businesses were linked together, not just by macro forces and the institutional structure of the labour market, but also by interrelationships based on *zaibatsu* membership, subcontracting and other kinds of long-term ties, so that the recruitment and utilisation of labour in a larger firm affected employment in the particular smaller companies with which it was linked. If labour costs rose for small companies, this affected their ability to meet the demands of their larger-scale customers and, on their side, larger companies, whose interests lay in maintaining a stable set of subcontractors under their patronage, might not, for example, impose the whole burden of employment risk on them in times of lowered demand. As in dual economy models, the modern sector was able to maintain its own higher-paid, more stable labour force, while the small-scale sector provided employment for other elements in the labour supply, but the interdependence between large and small firms meant that, although they rarely competed directly for the same labour, what happened to workers in one sector affected those in the other, and neither was without influence on the pattern of economic change.

General trading companies

As we saw in Part I, the progress of Japan's industrialisation in the late nineteenth and early twentieth centuries involved increasing integration into the world economy. The demand for imported raw materials and capital equipment grew along with industrial expansion and Japanese goods increasingly found export markets in Asia and beyond. The business of dealing with foreign suppliers and customers is one which requires special expertise (e.g. knowledge of foreign languages) and it involves considerable risks and the long-term tying-up of capital. Businesses in developing countries might be expected to lack access to the necessary expertise and to be unable to bear the risks involved in organising and financing international trading of their products. The smaller the firm, moreover, the greater the difficulties and barriers. As a result, either the government must step in to organise the provision and marketing of imports and exports, by establishing, for example, state marketing boards for primary-product exports, or foreign trade is likely to fall into the hands of advanced-country or multinational companies large enough and experienced enough to supply the expertise and take the risks. At any rate, aside from the export of staple primary products, overseas trade is likely to remain the preserve of the modern sector, whether in the hands of large-scale domestic institutions or foreign ones.

From the time of the opening-up to trade in the 1850s until the late 1880s and 1890s, Japanese trade largely conformed to this pattern. Primary products (mainly raw silk and tea) constituted the bulk of exports, imports were chiefly made up of manufactured textiles and machinery and other capital goods, and almost all trade was handled by foreigners, either Western or Chinese. However, thereafter the pattern changed, with the growth of exports of both cotton textiles and a widening range of other manufactured goods and with an increasing proportion of foreign trade conducted by Japanese organisations. Chief among these were the so-called general trading companies (*sōgō shōsha*[17]), who succeeded in bridging the gap between the outside world and both large-scale *zaibatsu* companies and the smaller-scale businesses which produced much of what was exported as industrialisation proceeded. General trading companies thus represented that link in the interlocking industrial structure which served to integrate Japanese businesses, both large-scale and small, into the world economy.

Japan's major trading companies are today massive multinational organisations through whose hands pass not only a high proportion of Japanese imports and exports but also a great deal of international business in financial and information-gathering fields. General trading companies raise credit, organise transport, insurance and foreign-exchange transactions, and provide marketing information, assistance in negotiations and a whole range of services facilitating international trade and finance.[18] To do this, they maintain a network of branches throughout the world, staffed by a corps of employees who build up a detailed knowledge of the products and regions in which they specialise. In the cases of the most important of today's general trading companies, however, the experience on which their present-day multinational status is built goes back to the early stages of Japan's economic involvement in world trade and to their important role both in enabling Japanese trade to develop under the control of Japanese companies and in providing smaller businesses with access to export markets.[19]

The prohibition on foreign contacts imposed under the Tokugawa system meant that when, in the 1850s, the country was re-opened to trade, no Japanese citizen had any real knowledge or experience of business transactions with the outside world. Consequently foreigners were able to monopolise the business of transporting and marketing Japan's early exports of silk and tea and arranging her imports. The 'unequal treaties' under whose provisions trade was conducted also strengthened the position of the Western traders who settled in the ports designated for the handling of trade. Merchant houses were set up by foreigners (Western and Chinese) who possessed both the market information and the capital to engage in the risky business of buying and selling abroad in foreign currencies, and it was through these that Japanese buyers and sellers had to operate. These merchant houses, colluding among themselves and protected by the diplomatic strength of their governments, the immunities granted them under the treaties, and the necessity of using Western shipping and insurance companies in the movement of goods to and from Japan, were able to manipulate prices and commissions and to profit at the expense of the helpless Japanese buyers and sellers. Ensconced in this profitable and comfortable world, however, the Western merchant houses failed to adapt and develop their trading networks as the economy changed through the late nineteenth century and were in due course to see their positions undermined by the rise of competing Japanese institutions.[20]

Government and business circles in Meiji Japan could not but recognise that both profits and the national interest could be served by breaking the stranglehold of the merchant houses on Japanese trade. Nevertheless, given the risks involved, the substantial capital required and the combined forces of Western economic and diplomatic pressure, early efforts in this direction met with little success. Even the Mitsui Trading Company (Mitsui Bussan), formally established in 1876 and backed both by the strength of the Mitsui organisation and by excellent connections with the government,[21] remained unimportant in the overall management of Japanese trade until the 1890s and its efforts to set up branches in New York and Hong Kong, to add to its one in Shanghai, came to nought. Other future founders of general trading companies were in the process of accumulating capital and domestic trading experience, but none was in a position to by-pass the established merchant houses as far as international dealings were concerned (Yamamura 1976: 169–72).

From around the turn of the century, however, a number of developments in the Japanese economy came together to improve the situation for Japan's fledgling international traders, putting them in a position to grow rapidly once the favourable conditions of the World War I boom emerged. On the one hand, the unequal treaties were gradually being repealed and the political and military balance of power between Japan and the Western nations was shifting in Japan's favour. On the other hand, Japanese institutions were beginning to establish themselves in the areas of business which facilitated international trade and to be able to provide Japanese importers and exporters with credit, foreign exchange, shipping and insurance. The financial system had been stabilised by the establishment of the Bank of Japan and the control of inflation in the 1880s; the semi-governmental Yokohama Specie Bank was by now able to conduct foreign exchange transactions, and Japanese shipping companies were by this stage operating on the international routes travelled by Japan's imports and exports.

Against this background, it was Mitsui Trading's entrepreneurial initiative in responding to the growth of demand for imported raw cotton in the 1890s by developing, in collaboration with the NYK shipping company, its own direct access to new sources of supply in India that established it as the first major Japanese general trading company. Its contacts and experience in the textile industry also enabled it to act as exclusive agent to Platt Brothers, who supplied most of the capital equipment for the expansion of the Japanese cotton-spinning industry, and as the quality of Japanese textile products improved, it was Mitsui Trading which opened up the export market in China. Other areas of business began to develop and, by the eve of World War I, around a fifth of Japan's exports and a sixth of her imports were handled by Mitsui Trading (Yamamura 1976: 176). The Mitsui group's great rival, Mitsubishi, soon similarly recognised the value of a specialised trading company. In 1918, when the Mitsubishi companies were reorganised into *zaibatsu* form, their trading interests were separated off to create the Mitsubishi Trading Company (Mitsubishi Shōji), which went on to develop and diversify its foreign and domestic trading activities, acting mainly as agent for Mitsubishi companies in their overseas dealings. Other trading companies, such as C. Itoh and Iwai, whose domestic business in textile wholesaling and other lines was prospering during the 1910s, still found it hard to break into international trading, but their more-or-less unsuccessful efforts in this period gave them the experience needed to be able to take advantage of the boom in Japanese overseas trade during World War I. With the expansion in demand for Japanese exports and with Western shippers and agents out of action because of the war, profits rolled in, new lines of business were established and overseas offices were set up world-wide.

The collapse of the boom ushered in harder times for trading companies, but those which had been reasonably well established in domestic and international business before the war were able to weather the storm and to grow rapidly as Japan's exports and colonial trade took off again in the 1930s. By the late '30s, the two giant general trading companies, Mitsui Trading and Mitsubishi Trading, between them handled around 30 per cent of Japan's total import and export trade and had outgrown the Western-based trading companies which had initially dominated Japanese foreign trade. Other major trading companies by then handled a further 20 per cent of imports and exports, although none really rivalled Mitsui and Mitsubishi in the scale and range of their business (Yoshihara 1982: 86).

The survival and growth of the major general trading companies through the '20s and '30s was based on the role they had created for themselves within the Japanese industrial structure and the economic functions they fulfilled in a rapidly industrialising economy moving relatively late into the world of international trade. Essentially, as Yamamura (1976) argues, their strength lay in their ability to provide credit to their client firms. Whilst *zaibatsu* companies could rely on credit and protection from their group's bank, smaller firms were frequently driven, in the uncertain conditions of the 1920s, to tie themselves into relationships with *zaibatsu* firms and/or, if they depended on export markets, with larger-scale trading companies. The trading companies themselves, as a result of the volume of their business and their consequent ability to assess and spread risks, were in a stronger position to obtain credit from the banking system on reasonable terms than their individual clients. They were therefore able to act as suppliers and guarantors of credit in return for commissions on trading business. Like the subcontracting relationships within *zaibatsu* groups at the domestic level, general trading companies thus acted on the international level as institutional mitigators of the effects of the 'dual structure'. They channelled credit and other resources and services, such as foreign trade expertise, from their modern-sector preserves towards the small-scale and more labour-intensive sectors of the economy which were thus able to provide a large share of Japan's pre-war exports.

General trading companies are not perhaps quite such 'uniquely Japanese' institutions as they are sometimes made out to be: somewhat similar, Western-based multinational trading organisations do exist and the East Asian Newly Industrialising Countries now have their own home-bred versions (Hofheinz and Calder 1982: 76–8). Nonetheless, the Japanese general trading companies were the first to profit from and grow out of the large-scale provision of specialised trading services and to build up the credit lines, information-gathering networks and specialist linguistic and other skills which constitute their resources. The need for such services was greater in Japan, suddenly opened up to trade across large-scale linguistic, cultural and geographical barriers, than it had been in the more slowly-developing and cosmopolitan West, yet few domestic businesses were in a position to lay out the resources required to supply such services for themselves. The general trading companies discovered and exploited the scale economies inherent in these operations and over the long term accumulated the trading and negotiating skills and the techniques of acquiring information which make them such formidable business organisations today. However, although the economic basis for their growth can be explained in this way, their emergence and survival in the face of competition from initially much more experienced and powerful foreign trading agencies must owe a great deal to the surrounding development of Japanese industry and business and to the state's promotion and protection at strategic points. By contrast with, for example, China in the past and many other developing countries today, it was the links forged between trading companies and the emerging domestic banking, shipping, cotton-spinning, mining and iron and steel industries, to name but the most important, that resulted in the 'marginalisation' of Western trading interests. Today's multinational companies are not so easily marginalised and it is probably true that only the state trading organisations of planned economies could match, in the developing world today, the scale and the scope achieved by the private-sector, and quite competitive, general trading companies of pre-war Japan.

14 Conclusion

Industrialisation, involving the transfer of the forms of technology and organisation associated with industrial production in the now-developed world, has seemed to offer to developing countries the key to prosperity and economic independence. And yet, in the experience of many Third World countries since World War II, the establishment of new industries producing new kinds of product has resulted in structural changes in their economies which have generated new, and perhaps greater, degrees of external dependence and internal inequality than had existed in their previous 'underdeveloped' states. The technology of developed-country industries has not proved easily adaptable to the conditions of less developed economies and the difficulties experienced in absorbing and controlling technical change within developing-country enterprises have led to reliance on external sources of technological input. Meanwhile, the marked dichotomy in technology and managerial organisation between the implanted modern industrial sector and the indigenous rural and urban manufacturing sector has intensified the inequalities in income and employment conditions observable in the dual economies of many Third World nations. The lure of possible employment in the high-wage modern sector has drawn migrants to cities in great numbers and fed the growing 'urban informal sector' in which they have sought to gain a living. All in all, while industrialisation today has in general generated faster rates of growth than those experienced in developed countries in the past, its benefits have often failed to trickle down and transform technology and industrial organisation throughout the economy, and it has at the same time created new inequalities and divisions of its own.

The major exceptions to these generalisations, it is often suggested, are the Newly Industrialising Countries of East Asia. Here, the argument goes, the abandonment of import-substitution policies and trade restrictions led businesses to make economic and technical choices (including choices as to products to produce) in line with world market prices and the relative availability of factors of production within their economies. This meant the selection of relatively labour-intensive methods of production, mainly for export goods, and resulted in rising industrial employment and, eventually, relatively higher wages, which in turn led to shifts towards more capital-intensive methods and products. Opponents of this 'free-market' interpretation of the NIC phenomenon would point rather to the various ways in which the state in these countries sought to assist in the establishment of the more capital-intensive industries on which economic growth ultimately depended, and to forms of protection and subsidy which helped modern-sector industries overcome the problems of acquiring and absorbing technology. Nonetheless, most would argue that South Korea, for example, had successfully overcome the first stages of industrialisation, absorbing and mastering the imported technology of capital-intensive and sophisticated forms of production in industries such as iron and steel, shipbuilding and electronics, while generating growth in employment in more labour-intensive areas such as textiles. In the Japanese case too, although the technological gap to be bridged may not have been as great as it is for today's developing countries, the same transition had been achieved by the time of World War II and the same questions arise as to the nature of the economic and institutional mechanisms whereby advanced technology was mastered while at the same time growing industrial employment was being generated.

As we saw in chapter 11, the existing macro-level evidence does not support the argument that the explanation lies in the selection by Japanese industry of the labour-intensive path of technological development which would have been appropriate to the relative supplies of labour and capital. Industrial production, taken as a whole, became broadly more capital-intensive over the course of the pre-World War II period and few attempts seem to have been made to search out labour-intensive alternatives in the major industries for which technology was acquired abroad. There is evidence that in some industries, notably textiles, imported technology was where possible operated in a more labour-intensive way than that for which it had been designed, and important innovations were made which enabled cheaper sources of less-skilled labour to be employed. This resulted in the production of a more 'appropriate' product, better suited in both price and quality to the markets which Japanese producers served. However, in other industries such as vehicles and iron and steel, where domestic competition was undoubtedly less intense and where the defeat of overseas competitors was the goal of both business and the state, it seems clear that mastery of the technology, rather than adaptation to local conditions, was the primary objective. In general, therefore, the choice of technology and product specification depended on both the market and the institutional conditions faced by producers in individual industries, but the overall result was to incorporate increasing inputs of capital, embodying up-to-date forms of technology, in the establishment of new industries.

If the key to Japan's successful pre-war industrialisation does not lie in the widespread choice of particularly appropriate new technology, then, as in the case of the NICs, it is to the successful adoption and mastery of imported techniques that we must look for a better explanation. Here again, however, it is hard to generalise, since the institutional and market conditions under which new technology was introduced varied widely from industry to industry and from time to time. In textiles, it was industry-wide organisations, most notably the cotton-spinners' association, Bōren, which provided the communications network through which information and training were supplied to the many relatively small firms in the industry. This resulted in the uniform adoption of similar technology, made available through one foreign-technology supplier (Platt Brothers), and hence the rapid dissemination of improvements and solutions to technical problems and the relatively free movement of skilled labour throughout the industry. Through Bōren, through the use of general trading companies, through the services of Platt Brothers' technicians and in general through the fairly open and competitive structure of the industry, relatively small-scale firms were able to overcome the problems of acquiring and successfully adopting technology developed overseas.

In other industries, however, where scale economies were greater and the number of firms smaller, technology was transferred through direct relations between foreign suppliers and incipient Japanese producers. The mechanisms for this ranged from full-scale joint ventures through plant imports and technology transfer deals to reverse engineering and other efforts to copy patented processes. Even within one industry, vehicles, substantially different methods of acquiring technology were employed by the two major producers, both ultimately successful but resulting in different paths of long-term technological development. Firms in these heavier industries also benefited from the services of general trading companies, and membership of *zaibatsu* groups facilitated the exchange of technology and skilled personnel between companies. But, most significantly, it was these firms who were the major recipients of the various types of support and assistance which the state was able to provide. Even judging only from the examples we have encountered, the range and variety of the forms of institutional assistance were considerable: the state directly provided the funds for the initial acquisition of modern iron-and-steel technology; laws and regulations encouraged, and provided subsidies for, the purchase of large-scale ships from Japanese yards; the MCI and other ministries used their links with major businesses to disseminate information and strengthen the hand of the Japanese side in technology transfer negotiations; it was the demands of the army which promoted the establishment of vehicle production in Japan and the MCI which made life too difficult for the Japanese subsidiaries of foreign vehicle-producers. At a broader level, it was the state's provision of education and training in engineering and science that generated the supply of scientifically educated entrepreneurs like Aikawa and Toyoda and the class of engineers and technicians who, at a lower level, learnt how to operate machinery and to overcome its teething troubles.

Thus the bureaucratic developmental state began, from the turn of the century onwards, to employ the range of weapons at its disposal at any given time to aid the acquisition of technology and to provide a supportive environment for modern-sector businesses. The progress made was, in many fields, considerable and put Japanese firms in a position to take advantage of the much more favourable conditions for technology transfer after World War II. Nonetheless it should not be forgotten that Japanese modern-sector industries, while often in command of pre-World War II technology, generally remained high-cost producers, unable to compete at an economic level with advanced-country producers, and without their own independent R & D capacity, well into the post-war period. Rather than mastery of individual technologies themselves, it was the institutional capacity, in both the private and public sectors, to translate technological goals into practice that was the most important legacy of pre-war experience.

For developing countries, industrialisation involves the introduction not only of new technology but also of new forms of work and organisation. New enterprises must recruit workers and accustom and train them for life under different conditions of employment from those with which they have been familiar outside the modern sector. It is generally assumed that, under the conditions of abundant labour supply generally prevalent in developing countries, recruitment presents few problems, but the difficulty of adjusting to the disciplines of factory life may lead to high labour turnover and lower than necessary labour productivity. Those who have observed factory life in present-day Japan, with its 'permanently-employed', hard-working and devoted company labour forces, find it hard to believe that such problems were ever experienced there and argue that the 'culturally-determined' attitudes to work and to group organisation which are observed today must have smoothed the transition to factory life for early industrial workers too, thus contributing to an apparently easy and successful industrialisation process. However, the historical evidence now available reveals the 'Japanese employment system' more plausibly as the product than as the cause of Japan's experience of industrialisation.

In our consideration of both agriculture and industry, we have seen that early Japanese industrial employers rarely found themselves facing conditions which conform to the idea of an unlimited supply of labour. When they sought to expand their workforces, they faced competition from other sources of employment, and when demand for labour was high, wages rose and differentials narrowed. Moreover, those whom they recruited, including both the young girls who went to work in textile mills and the male workers employed, in fewer numbers, in heavy industries, did indeed bring with them attitudes and experiences which they applied to their new work, but these included not only skills in traditional occupations like spinning or metalwork but also values and beliefs about the life and treatment of workers which were not always conducive to the employers' goal of a stable labour force. Thus labour turnover among both girls in the textile mills and male heavy-industrial workers was initially high. Many workers proved unwilling to bear, in the form of low wages and poor working conditions, the costs of acquiring the skill which would eventually lead to high productivity and either sought to capitalise on their experience by moving to another employer or left modern-sector employment altogether. It was as a result of the conflicts and compromises which this situation brought about that the outlines of the 'Japanese employment system' began to emerge, with employers attempting to retain workers by relating pay to length of service and by creating conditions which gave greater meaning and dignity to their work and recognition to their part in the company. Nonetheless, the application of the full Japanese employment system to the blue-collar, as opposed to the white-collar, workers of large-scale organisations was by no means complete by the time of World War II and it was the labour unrest of the immediate post-war period which led to its widespread adoption as a means of creating and maintaining a stable and committed labour force.

Although the system of employment in the modern sector thus moved only slowly towards the characteristic post-war model, nonetheless divergences in wages and conditions between those who worked within it and those outside it were a consequence of the industrialisation process in Japan as they are in today's Third World. Moreover, as in present-day developing countries, only a relatively small proportion of those who, as a consequence of the economic and social changes brought about by industrialisation, no longer found employment in agriculture or rural industry could be categorised as modern-sector factory workers. The majority of those who moved to the cities of industrialising Japan derived their livelihoods from the 'urban informal sector', from small-scale manufacturing businesses, services and other even less secure and often less reputable sources of work and income. Industrialisation, and its accompanying urbanisation, thus generated new forms of poverty and inequality resembling in nature, if not perhaps in scale, those to be found in many of today's Third World economies.

Looking back from the vantage point of the highly effective economic system of today's Japan, however, it is striking to note that Japan was not only the first country to achieve a high level of economic development on the basis of a rice-growing agriculture but also the first to industrialise while preserving such a large and, in many ways, dynamic small-scale business sector. The small-scale sector contained the new urban poor and the mass of those whose incomes and conditions of work would never match those of the white-collar and blue-collar modern-sector elite. Nonetheless, the survival, and indeed growth, of the small-scale sector depended on the survival of relatively labour-intensive production methods and of demand for labour-intensively produced products and it maintained employment on a scale which investment in the modern sector could never have generated. Thus, if adaptation did take place in the face of a situation in which capital was in shorter supply and labour more abundant, relative to the best available technology, than had been the case in earlier-developing countries, it is to be found less in the choice of the technologies employed in individual industries and more in the overall structure of production and in the pattern of demand for more or less labour-intensively produced goods.

The survival of the small-scale sector can be traced to a combination of interrelated economic and institutional factors. On the one hand, the market for goods for which viable labour-intensive production methods existed survived and grew within Japan and elsewhere in her Asian export markets. The domestic consumer market remained dominated by traditional, highly differentiated, food products and other consumption goods, for which only relatively labour-intensive production methods (perhaps with the addition of an electric motor) were known and in which large-scale advanced-country producers had no interest. Labour-intensive Japanese producers, aided by general trading companies, by developments in Japanese shipping and by the fortunate withdrawal of Western competition at crucial times, found a ready export market in Asia for their lower-quality but cheaper consumer goods. Meanwhile, large-scale Japanese firms, with their easier access to investment funds and their ability to meet the demand for heavy industrial products and capital goods, concentrated on supplying the markets for products for which more capital-intensive production techniques had come to be developed in the advanced economies.

In the parts of their production processes where viable labour-intensive techniques could be utilised, however, large-scale producers were able to take advantage of the cheaper sources of labour available to smaller firms through institutional arrangements which gave them greater flexibility and a reasonable degree of control over the output of their small-scale suppliers. These institutional innovations in industrial organisation, epitomised by *zaibatsu* groupings but also including the general trading companies and the wider subcontracting relationships which intermediated between smaller firms and their potential markets, functioned through their ability to segment markets for inputs and output. Yet paradoxically, their effect was also to create channels of communication between larger and smaller firms along which were transmitted credit, technical information and a certain degree of mutual reliance. Thus, although wide divergences existed between the 'modern' and 'traditional' sectors in Japan as in other industrialising countries, the picture of a dual economy composed of two distinct and unconnected parts is inappropriate in the Japanese case. Furthermore, it is through these interconnections, imprinted on the economic and institutional structure of Japanese industry as it grew, that the small-scale sector has been able to survive and, it is now argued, to play a dynamic part in late-twentieth century Japan's economic success.

It can be argued (though it is more frequently simply taken for granted) that behind these forces facilitating the survival of small firms lay the two hundred years of seclusion from the world during the Tokugawa period, which consolidated an essentially Japanese lifestyle and pattern of consumption too deep-rooted for subsequent contact with the West to undermine. However this may be, whether we attribute the survival of traditional consumption habits to the resulting depth of Japanese attachment to traditional cuisine, clothing and housing, to pre-war state protectionism and nationalism or to the limitations placed on the 'demonstration effects' of Western goods by the absence of today's sophisticated and world-wide communications technology, the result was that Western borrowing proceeded much faster in heavy and producer-good industries than in consumer-goods production. This has meant that post-war industrialised Japan has been left with much more of a cultural identity of her own, embodied in saké, raw fish, futons, tatami mats and so on, than can perhaps be retained by the nations of today's Coca-Cola-drinking, hamburger-eating (or at least -desiring) Third World.[1] Whilst Western businessmen may now rail against this cultural identity as a non-tariff trade barrier, its part in Japan's economic growth (and also, perhaps, in her political history and past international relations) is something that the student of development cannot ignore, and it was essentially the small-scale sector which preserved that tradition and adapted it for survival in a late-twentieth century post-industrial society.

'Development is', in Gavin Kitching's plain words, 'an awful process. It varies only, and importantly, in its awfulness' (Kitching 1989: 195). No-one can deny that there were awful aspects to Japan's development and that some, notably those who struggled to find a living in the urban informal sector or the early factories and mills, bore a disproportionate share of the cost, in terms of dislocation and decline in the quality of their lives uncompensated by any substantial improvement in their material standard of living. Nonetheless, what is important about the Japanese case is that those costs were not borne in vain and over time both the productive capacity of the economy and the consumption standards of the majority of the population have grown steadily and even, since World War II, miraculously. Part III has sought to show how some elements in Japan's industrialisation process resemble elements to be found in the experience of earlier-developing countries and of today's Third World, while others do not, and that the single 'keys' to explaining Japan's economic success in terms of pre-existing or culturally-determined prime movers turn out to be, for the most part, the products rather than the determinants of the effort to establish modern industry. What can however be said is that the distinctive combination of elements which went to make up the emerging structure of Japanese industry was largely determined by the indigenous (though not necessarily 'traditional') economic, political and social forces which, from the turn of the century at least, were able to influence the terms on which dealings with the outside world were transacted, in a way which many other developing countries, both before and after World War II, have found impossible. Eclectic borrowing and the addition of distinctive local elements are possible only under conditions of reasonable political strength and independence and in a relatively favourable world economic environment. The success of the NICs suggests that, under these conditions, the cultures of many nations may in fact be conducive to successful industrialisation.

General conclusion

It has not been the objective of this book to distinguish new 'lessons' for today's developing countries from Japan's past experience or to produce a new 'Japanese model' of development. If study of Japan's economic history, as it has proceeded over recent years, tells us anything, it is that her path to development was by no means a straightforward, unidirectional, progressive one, but rather one composed of many divergent lanes, as well as some dead ends and some bypasses, and a detailed map is required to plot a way along it. Our task has simply been to translate Japanese economic history into the language of contemporary development economics and thereby to try to bring out, for the illumination, it is hoped, of students of both development and Japan, such 'family resemblances' and interesting differences as may exist between the past experience of Japan and the present experience of today's developing world. Nonetheless, such an exercise is pointless unless it is the case that knowledge of Japan can broaden and improve our understanding of the ways in which economic development takes place, and it was the general failure to use the Japanese case in this way, resulting from the inaccessibility of even much of the English-language work on the subject and the difficulty of preserving a comparative or theoretical framework in research on Japan, that have provided the motivation and justification for this book. Hence it is perhaps useful to conclude by bringing together what have seemed to me to be the most significant overall points of difference and similarity between Japan's experience and that of other developing countries, in terms of the major issues with which development studies has been concerned in recent years and the contribution which understanding of Japan's case in particular can make to the analysis of the past and future of the developing world.

The strategies followed by the nations setting out after World War II, newly independent in many cases, on the road to economic development have not been adjudged altogether successful. Experiences have of course varied in significant ways, but much of the work in development studies over recent years has been concerned to analyse why many developing countries, despite achieving quite rapid rates of measured economic growth, continue to suffer from such a range of problems. Dualism and inequality have continued to characterise the development paths of a great many Third World nations; dependence on developed countries for capital, technology and other crucial resources has even intensified, and despite the potential of new agricultural technology, rural development programmes have persistently failed to provide for the food and other basic needs of many people. Japan's development path was by no means a smooth one: there were clearly winners and losers and sections of the population who bore the costs of industrialisation more heavily than others, and the frictions and contradictions which arose in the course of her relatively rapid industrialisation can be seen as contributing significantly towards bringing her so disastrously into conflict with the Western powers in Asia. Yet the major problems besetting post-World War II developing countries seem not to have emerged with anything like the same intensity, while the base was being laid on which Japan was successfully to become one of the world's major economic powers. There is no single factor lying behind this contrast, and this book has only been able to bring together a limited number of the strands of an explanation, but it would be ducking the issue not to attempt a general summing-up.

To some extent, of course, the causes of the contrast lie in outside forces unrelated to policy or circumstance within Japan. The world in which Japan developed was undoubtedly one dominated, economically and militarily, by the industrialised West, but the ability of developed-country states and businesses to influence or control events, both within their own borders and further afield, was, for technological reasons, not as great as it was to become in the post-World War II age of mass communications and the powers of mass destruction. Equally, the technological gap between the industrialised and developing worlds, though large, was not as wide as it is now. Hence the ability of the developing-country side to control the transfer of knowledge was greater and the internal dichotomy between those adopting imported technology and consumption patterns and those not was less marked. Furthermore, inasfar as the industrialised nations were able to dominate and exploit the then-underdeveloped world of their colonies and spheres of influence, Japan remained, from their point of view, on the periphery of the periphery, its potential, relative to the costs of 'incorporating' it, dwarfed by that of the vast markets and resources of China, India and Africa. During the crucial period of the late nineteenth and early twentieth centuries when her industrial base was being laid, Japan's head remained for the most part below the parapet as far as the West was concerned, appearing only now and then to take advantage of outside circumstances, above all of the import-substituting and export-promoting possibilities opened up by the effects of World War I. Nevertheless, a great deal of work remains to be done on the ways and means whereby Japanese businesses interacted with the outside world and succeeded in retaining a degree of independent control over their resources and their technological capability.

This being said, however, such a dependency-theory argument does not provide a complete explanation as to why Japan, and not other similarly placed nations before and since, achieved industrialisation while avoiding many of the problems currently associated with it. For those following other schools of thought, it was natural, in the light of much of the development-studies work of the '50s and '60s, to begin to look for an answer in the actions of the state and in whatever could be discerned as the strategy it had adopted. The dramatic political and institutional changes resulting from the Meiji Restoration provided a focal point in the effort to delineate that strategy and there is no doubt that Japanese governments from that time onwards saw economic development as a national goal and tried to do what they could to promote it. Nonetheless, it has not proved easy either to attribute specific developmental results to the assortment of actions taken by the various organs of the state or to fit the totality of those actions into any of the recognised categories of development strategies used in development-studies analysis. The Meiji state was keen to promote both import-substitution and the growth of exports, but its capacity to control the inflow of imports was severely constrained by its treaties with the Western nations and it is hard to attribute much of the growth of Japan's main exports directly at least to anything the state did. Inter-war governments were converted to the virtues of freer international trade, but the potential of a strategy based on comparative advantage could not be realised given the conditions of the world economy at the time and the domestic political situation. The import-substitution policies clearly being pursued in the 1930s, within the context of an increasing degree of state planning and control, laid the industrial basis on which war could be fought and on which, it might be argued, the post-war economic miracle was founded, but did not create industries capable of competing efficiently with developed-country rivals. All in all, officials and bureaucrats intervened in the economy in all sorts of ways, but no consistent strategy or co-ordinated planning of resource allocation is really discernible, even though the forces of free competition were clearly not accepted as the driving force for the achievement of developmental goals.

The fact that the activity of the Japanese state was clearly pervasive and yet not apparently consistent with recognised approaches to the roles and strategies of states in economic development gave rise to the 'developmental state' as a third model, alongside the fully-planned and free-market ones, of the relations of government to the economy. Chalmers Johnson's exposition of this idea (Johnson 1982) and its subsequent use in analysis of present-day developing countries represent perhaps the best recent example of the value of studying Japan's historical experience as an aid to understanding the development process in general. The ability to conceptualise a state (or bureaucracy) which intervenes in *ad hoc*, pragmatic forms to promote industrialisation, but which allows competitive forces to operate where it deems them appropriate or cannot avoid them, is a clear result of the study of Japan in contrast to Western European nations and the United States. Nonetheless, the microeconomic work on Japan's industrialisation presented here warns us against over-enthusiastic use of the idea in two ways. The history of governmental involvement in the Japanese economy, including the results of Johnson's own work, reveal the Japanese 'developmental state' to have been, first, a product of trial and error, political conflict, successes and failures, conditioned by historical experience rather than by any model or strategy, and, second, only one, and not in itself a monolithic one, among a number of different economic and institutional actors who played their parts in the growth and development of modern industry. The 'developmental state' is a fruitful and useful concept for understanding government/business relations in Japan and in other societies, but it is neither a model nor the single key to explaining Japanese development.

If we cannot, therefore, take the strategy of the state as the ultimate cause of Japan's successful industrialisation, then perhaps the explanation lies rather in the changing economic and institutional structures which underlay her industrialisation process. In a sense, the argument of this book has been that it does, but again no simple model appears adequate to describe the interrelationships involved. Dual-economy, surplus-labour models of the resource-transfer relationship between agriculture and industry, for example, can be seen to have concealed, in an over-simplified picture of a passive and exploited 'traditional' sector out of tune with later developments in the analysis of 'peasant' farming, the active role of farm households themselves in intensifying the utilisation of the resources they controlled and adapting to the demands of the industrialising economy. The institutional and technological characteristics of Japan's industrialisation cannot be explained without taking account of the moves made by farmers, individually and in groups, to protect their interests and secure and raise their incomes in the face of changing national and international circumstances. It was the technological and economic arrangements resulting from the process of mutual conflict and adaptation between agricultural and industrial employers which precluded the emergence in Japan of the extremes of dualism and the neglect of agriculture, of rural industry and of 'basic needs' besetting present-day developing countries.

On the other hand, however, Japan's development path in no sense involved 'putting agriculture first'. The most up-to-date, capital-intensive technology was imported into a relatively privileged modern industrial sector; urbanisation and the growth of the industrial labour force proceeded at a relatively rapid rate, and although agrarianism and the values of a disappearing rural culture were preached by nationalists and romantic populists in Japan as in other industrialising societies,[1] the distribution of developmental resources continued to be heavily biased in favour of industry. However, the introduction of factory industry took place within an environment in which it was impossible to ignore the economic and technological strengths of informal-sector producers and farm households, and in its institutions and its technology, modern industry adapted to take account of this and to exploit the resources of the rest of the economy as best it could. The resulting institutional adaptations – the 'Japanese employment system', the *zaibatsu* groups, subcontracting, general trading companies, the division of labour and product markets between the high-technology, capital-intensive modern sector and the more labour-intensive small-scale sector – maintained employment growth and resulted in an industrial structure more integrated than that prevailing in more strictly 'dualistic' present-day developing countries, although at the same time remaining based on more personalised hierarchical interrelationships than those which link businesses in the Western developed world. As was the case with the role of the state, the apparently bemusing characteristics of the contemporary Japanese industrial structure, so often held to be 'culturally' determined, can be seen to have their roots in a historical process of conflict and adaptation, with its winners and losers, its successes and failures, in the context of particular economic and political forces.

If Japan's development process can only be explained and analysed as the result of particular historical forces and circumstances and cannot, therefore, be taken as a model, we return to the question of what, if anything, is its relevance to the present-day practice of development studies. The answer, I would reiterate, lies in the modifications which knowledge of the Japanese case must lead us to make in our understanding and interpretation of a whole range of aspects of the development process. Furthermore, precisely because Japan's environment, culture and historical circumstances are significantly different from those of other now-developed countries, these modifications are likely to be all the more important and valuable. The development experience of the post-war Third World has resembled, and will continue to resemble, that of Japan in a great many important respects more closely than it resembles that of the Western industrialised world. Much has been found wanting in the models and prescriptions based on Western experience which have been presented to developing-country states in the post-World War II period and which have profoundly affected the strategies they have adopted. The activities of the Japanese state provide a different kind of example which has already begun to offer bureaucracies in some developing countries a model more appropriate to their needs and to their own natural modes of operation in a world of multinational companies, high-technology transfer and world-wide mass communications and trade. Given present rates of population growth and the inability of modern industry to absorb growing labour forces at an adequate rate, small-scale agriculture and informal-sector activity will survive in the developing world and their influence on technology, on patterns of demand and consumption, on group activity and inter-enterprise relationships, not to mention their potential for contributing towards employment growth and the spread of technological change, will be clear to anyone familiar with the features of Japan's experience.

The failure of those who work on Japan to relate Japanese experience to the wider concerns of development studies, and the consequent lack of relevantly presented data, have meant that this book has neglected many areas in which Japan's economic past may well have great significance for present-day development issues. Perhaps the most striking difference in the situations facing late-nineteenth century Japan and present-day developing countries lies in the absence in the Japanese case of the population explosion with which today's Third World has struggled to cope. Demographic change over the course of Japan's economic development, particularly during the Tokugawa period, has been a subject of considerable interest to Japanese and Western scholars, but its broader consequences have yet to be fully analysed. Equally, some of the major factors frequently cited as explanations for Japan's post-World War II economic miracle, including in particular the high rates of saving and capital accumulation and the massive investment in the education of the population as potential industrial workers, clearly have their pre-war counterparts, but the implications of the institutional organisation of savings mobilisation or of mass education for the pre-war industrialisation process have yet to be drawn. Most work on Japan's external economic relations during her industrialisation has focused on links with Europe or America, but just as development economists have begun to discover intra-Third World trade and investment flows and technology transfer, so Japan is beginning to be revealed as part of an intra-Asian trading network in the nineteenth and early twentieth centuries. In all these and many other areas, much work remains to be done, both in improving understanding of Japanese experience and in relating it to the comparative framework provided by the study of present-day developing countries.

Unhappily, to the extent that it is indeed true that the industrialisation process in today's developing world does generate structures and institutions which bear closer resemblances to those of Japan than to those of the West, Japan's experience also suggests that conflicts will arise. The pursuit by South Korea and Taiwan of industrialisation paths not unlike that of pre-war Japan is already generating 'trade friction' and support for protectionism in the West, fuelled by the fear of alien and apparently incomprehensible societies. The resort to easy explanations of the economic processes of other nations in terms of inherent and unique cultures only makes such conflicts more dangerous and harder to resolve. It is the failure of those who study such societies to explain to the wider world how their differing features have arisen out of historical combinations of economic, political and social forces that this book has tried, in its own limited field, to combat.

Notes

1 INTRODUCTION

1 My overview of the state of development economics, here and throughout the book, relies heavily on Colman and Nixson (1986). Hunt (1989) appeared in the course of writing and also proved useful as a reference source.

2 From the time of Japan's startling victory in the Russo-Japanese War (1904–5), her development did however provide a model and example to significant and influential thinkers and political leaders in China and elsewhere in Asia.

3 Most notably, Ohkawa Kazushi, Minami Ryōshin, Shinohara Miyohei, Umemura Mataji and others involved in the large-scale project, based at Hitotsubashi University, which established the statistical foundations for the economic analysis of Japanese development. This work has resulted in the publication of the multi-volume statistical series *Chōki Keizai Tōkei* (*Long-Term Economic Statistics*), generally (and hereafter) referred to as LTES.

4 In the late 1970s and early 1980s, for example, Singapore and Malaysia adopted specific 'learn from Japan' and 'look East' policies.

5 Exceptions to this generalisation include, most importantly, Johnson (1982) and also, for example, Moulder (1977) and Ohkawa and Ranis (1985).

6 The most up-to-date is Minami (1986). For others, see the 'Guide to further reading'.

2 THE STATE AND EARLY INDUSTRIALISATION

1 Although some private entrepreneurs certainly did borrow from abroad. See Wray 1984: 40–1.

2 The severity of the effects of the deflation on farmers has however been questioned. See Smethurst 1986: 57–60.

3 Through the rediscounting of bills issued by the spinning companies (Takamura 1982: 29).

4 See for example Wray 1984: 58 for a memo detailing the views of Ōkuma Shigenobu, one of the leaders of the Meiji oligarchy.

5 For more details about Tokugawa shipping, see Wray 1986: 250–4.

6 Although this proportion was to rise rapidly thereafter to reach over 50 per cent by the time of World War I (Yui and Nakagawa 1985: 19; Allen 1962: 92).

7 For more on Iwasaki and for an excellent study of Mitsubishi's shipping operations, on which the following relies heavily, see Wray 1984.

8 Though Wray argues that the conflict did have positive benefits in crystallising government policy and creating a specialist shipping company with Mitsubishi's management skills and structure and the government-sponsored company's ships (Wray 1984: 217–18).

3 THE STATE AND THE GROWTH OF THE MODERN INDUSTRIAL SECTOR

1 Minami 1986: 117, based on LTES figures (see Introduction note 3). Industry = mining, manufacturing, construction, transportation, communications and utilities.

2 For a fuller description of the structures and operations of the *zaibatsu*, see ch. 13.

3 Independence from the government has remained part of Nihon Kōkan's tradition. See Lynn 1982: 62.

4 See Lynn 1982: 84–5 and 186–7. Lynn's study is one of the very few to give concrete examples of the ways in which MITI's actions actually made a difference to the investment decisions taken by firms.

5 For the history of the Japanese automobile industry on which the following relies heavily, see Cusumano 1985, chs 1 and 2.

6 See for example the comments of the drivers using American- and Japanese-made vehicles in Manchuria in the 1930s, as recorded in the second episode of the television documentary series *Shōwa*, broadcast by the UK's Channel 4 in September 1987. This programme presents an excellent, and surprisingly dramatic, account of the stages of industrial policy which resulted in the removal of Ford and General Motors and the establishment of the domestic industry.

7 Aikawa had close links with the bureaucrat responsible for the drafting of the Automobile Manufacturing Industry Law, Kishi Nobusuke, later MITI Vice-Minister and Minister and ultimately Prime Minister after the war (Johnson 1982: 131).

8 The Bank of Japan and the Ministry of Transport both opposed the promotion of the car industry (Cusumano 1985: 19). According to Johnson's sources, Kishi's 1936 Automobile Manufacturing Industry Law continued in effect, even though officially rescinded, until the late 1960s (Johnson 1982: 33).

4 CONCLUSION

1 This view is rarely explicitly set out but is frequently implicit in the way in which material is presented, for example in much of the 1960s material on the 'Japanese model of development'. However, Yamamura 1974 sets out the hypothesis very clearly before challenging it.

2 However, not all of those who emphasise the key role of government

ministries in Japan's later economic growth would wish to follow this line of argument. Johnson would ascribe the bureaucracy's role less to culture or ideology and more to the imperatives of Japan's historical situation which required the state to be 'developmental' (Johnson 1982).

3 Sugiyama (1988: 74–6) argues that the 'treaty port system' as established under the Unequal Treaties itself paradoxically acted as a non-tariff barrier protecting the Japanese market for Japanese producers. By in effect confining foreign business activity to the designated ports, it discouraged foreign firms from developing their own distribution networks 'up country', through which they would have been able to penetrate the Japanese home market.

4 For more on economic change during the Tokugawa period see ch. 8.

5 INTRODUCTION

1 Alternatively, the labour transfer might to some extent be offset by harder work on the part of those remaining, or by technical improvements in agriculture, provided these did not require investment of capital and consequently a reduction in the growth of industry.

2 For a clear and simple summary of the model, setting out the further assumptions (about technology and population growth) and deductions made, see Colman and Nixson 1986: 32–8, who also point out the advance which the model, for all its faults, represented over earlier theorising about developing countries, focusing, as it did, on 'those structural elements in the process of change, concern with which is one of the key features distinguishing development economics from macroeconomics' (37).

3 For the full version of the model, and its application to Japan, see Hayami and Ruttan 1971.

4 For a fuller discussion, see Bray 1986.

5 As we shall see later, the Marxist-dominated mainstream of Japanese scholarship on pre-war economic development, while less inclined to emphasise the positive and successful elements of Japanese industrialisation, was equally engaged in an effort to fit Japan into a Western model.

6 For example using the idea of 'proto-industrialisation'. For a summary and critique, see Clarkson 1985.

6 THE MACROECONOMIC ROLE OF AGRICULTURE IN JAPAN'S DEVELOPMENT

1 Calculated from Ohkawa and Shinohara 1979: 278–80 and 392–3. See also tables 2.1 and 3.1.

2 See Introduction, note 3.

3 See Hayami and Yamada 1969: 107–8. Table 2.2 presents some of their data together with the alternative estimates discussed in ch. 6

4 See ch. 7, for detailed discussion of these changes.

5 For a full discussion of labour recruitment from the point of view of industrial employers and workers, see ch. 12 and for a wide-ranging

survey of the evidence, which challenges the notion of unlimited supplies of labour to Japanese industrial employers, see Napier 1982.

7 TECHNICAL CHANGE IN PRE-WAR AGRICULTURE

1 It has been argued against this that the failure of agricultural incomes to keep pace, relatively speaking, with industrial ones contributed to the absence of a growing mass market for consumer goods in the pre-war period, leaving modern-sector industry reliant on the state and the military for demand for its products. For further discussion of the pattern of demand for industrial products, see ch. 13.
2 For an excellent description of the characteristics of rice cultivation in general, upon which the following draws heavily, see Bray 1986: ch. 1 and *passim*.
3 By no means all fields could be drained satisfactorily and the practice of leaving the field under water through the winter because of this, and in order to conserve water supplies, was widespread in the Tokugawa period. See p. 122 below.
4 Mechanised threshers, hullers and polishers began to appear prior to World War II, but suitable small harvesters are a more recent phenomenon.
5 This point was first made in Ishikawa Shigeru's pioneering *Economic Development in Asian Perspective* (Ishikawa 1967).
6 For some examples from the Tokugawa period see Smith 1959: 87–92, and for some later sericultural cases, see Smethurst 1986: 189–94.
7 For more on the distribution of landownership, see ch. 8.
8 For this argument in full, see Waswo 1977.

8 INDUSTRIALISATION AND THE FARM HOUSEHOLD

1 This gave rise to what has come to be known as the 'Japanese capitalism debate', which continued through the inter-war period and beyond, between two conflicting schools of Marxist thought on the nature and interpretation of rural change in Japan. For a full description of the debate and its meaning for the analysis of economic development, see Hoston 1986 or Morris-Suzuki 1989: ch. 3.
2 For convenient but critical summaries of this sort of interpretation, see Hanley and Yamamura 1977: 12–19 on the Tokugawa period and Smethurst 1986: 7–19 on later years.
3 For the available estimates of the growth of tenancy, see Francks 1984: 65.
4 For a forceful, though controversial, presentation of this case, together with data on living standards, rents, and so on, see Smethurst 1986: ch. 1.
5 For the full story, see Smith 1959.
6 For a good example from sericulture, see Vlastos 1986: 99–102.
7 The area planted to mulberry trees more than doubled between the 1880s and the 1910s (Minami 1986: 93–4).
8 For a more detailed analysis of rural/urban migration, see ch. 12.
9 For the analysis on which the following is based, see Vlastos 1986.
10 See Vlastos 1986: ch. 8. For a contrary view along more conventional Marxist lines, see Bix 1986.
11 For an example, see Waswo 1977: 35–7.

12 Smethurst argues, against this line, that disputes in the 1930s were not
   fundamentally different from those in the '20s and that the apparent shifts
   in regional distribution and character may have more to do with changes
   in the methods of collecting statistics.
13 See, for example, the debate in the *Journal of Japanese Studies* vol. 15,
   no. 2, Summer 1989.

10 INTRODUCTION

1 For an excellent survey of the literature in this field, see Fransman 1985.
2 For a discussion of the Todaro model, and other theoretical approaches to
  rural-urban migration, see Colman and Nixson 1986: 118–25.
3 For definition and discussion of the urban informal sector, see Colman and
  Nixson 1986: 128–32.

11 TECHNICAL CHANGE AND INDUSTRIAL GROWTH

1 See, for example, Little 1979 or 1982: 141–13, 176–81. For more on
  the parallels between Japan and the NICs, see the conclusion to this Part.
2 For estimates of the residual see Minami 1986: 108 or Ohkawa and
  Rosovsky 1973: ch. 3. It should be noted that these estimates show a
  much higher residual growth rate in the post-war period.
3 For more on this, see ch. 12.
4 For the description of these technologies on which the following is based,
  see Saxonhouse 1985.
5 Some smaller Japanese mills had adopted ring-spinning from their
  inception in the 1870s and early 1880s, so that both technologies
  were known in Japan at the time when the major mills opted for
  mule-spinning.
6 Incidentally, or perhaps not, the two largest mule-spinning mills were
  subsequently destroyed in fires (Saxonhouse 1985: 219).
7 In India, for example, mules were chosen, on the advice of British
  engineers, for similar reasons as initially in Japan. However, since male
  workers continued to predominate in the labour force, cotton-mixing
  techniques like those used in Japan did not develop and moreover the
  finer yarns produced with the mule suited the Indian climate better. Thus
  the conditions which favoured the use of the increasingly outmoded mule
  continued to prevail. See Ranis and Saxonhouse 1985: 145–53.
8 In the 1910s and 1920s, electric motors came to be widely used, especially
  in smaller-scale plants. See Minami 1987: 197–202.
9 Many of the leading figures in the later establishment of heavy industries
  had spent time living and working in Europe or America. A number of
  examples appear later in this chapter.
10 The extent to which this was so varied from industry to industry. It was
   easier to copy machines (e.g. electrical equipment, machine-tools, etc.)
   than processes (e.g. the manufacture of iron and steel or chemicals)
   because the latter involve 'invisible' factors, such as temperatures or
   pressure levels. The leading Western producer of chemical alkalis was
   able to keep its technology almost completely secret for a long period
   (Uchida 1980: 163).

11 For these and other examples from the electrical machinery and machine-tool industries, see Yamamura 1986: 71–83.
12 For these definitions and a useful summary of contemporary Third World experience in this area, see Weiss 1990: 236–44.
13 The following relies on Cusumano 1985: 40–9, 60–72.

12 THE EMERGENCE OF AN INDUSTRIAL LABOUR FORCE

1 However, the immediate post-war period nonetheless saw substantial labour unrest.
2 In silk-reeling too, Japanese workers were considerably less productive than their European or Chinese counterparts in the second half of the nineteenth century (Eng 1986: 170).
3 The majority of girls employed in cotton mills were under 20 and typically 10–20 per cent were under 14 (Taira 1978: 184–5).
4 See Taira 1978: 184, and compare Honig 1986 on gangsters and cotton-mill girls in China.
5 See Gordon 1985: 25–38 for some examples of what would nowadays be thought of as very un-Japanese attitudes to work, saving, and so on, among Meiji-period industrial workers.

13 INDUSTRIALISATION AND THE STRUCTURE OF INDUSTRY

1 See Patrick and Rohlen 1987, an excellent survey of the place of small businesses in the contemporary Japanese economy.
2 Though there are some notable exceptions, for example Sony, to prove the rule.
3 For a more detailed analysis of the data on the distribution of employment see Taira 1988: 609–12. Taira concludes that no more than 40 per cent of the non-agricultural labour force, representing 15 per cent of total employment, worked under 'modern' conditions in 1920.
4 See Lockwood 1968: 210 for some examples.
5 The proportion of total personal income spent on food was 67.5 per cent in 1874–83, falling to 63.7 per cent in 1896–1906 and 58.9 per cent in 1917–26. It did not drop below 50 per cent until the 1930s (Hanley 1986: 465, using LTES data).
6 For Japan's ethnic minorities – principally those of Korean or Chinese origin, along with members of the Japanese outcast group, the *burakumin* – discrimination constituted a major cause of poverty and 'ghettoisation'. However, these groups make up quite a small proportion of Japan's population (probably about 3.5 per cent today) compared with ethnic minorities elsewhere, and the problem of poverty now and in the past cannot be considered as exclusively a question of discrimination.
7 The urban small-business way of life is lovingly portrayed in the ever-popular *Tora-san* films. For a description, see Buruma 1984: ch. 12.
8 Definitions of 'small business' depend on the statistical sources being used and are in any case largely arbitrary, given the graded structure of many industries. Whatever categorisation is being used, whether according to

number of employees, use of family labour, scale of turnover, value of assets, and so on, it almost always turns out that the proportion of enterprises at the lower end of the scale is higher in Japan than in most other industrialised countries. For various comparative measures using 1980s data, see Patrick and Rohlen (1987).

9 In the inter-war period 'new *zaibatsu*' began to appear, centring particularly on companies with interests in the Empire receiving patronage from the military. There also emerged a number of smaller-scale groupings at the local or regional level. Industrial groups rather like the pre-war *zaibatsu*, but different from them in certain important respects, have re-appeared since World War II, though these are generally described as '*keiretsu*', a term without the militarist and imperialist connotations acquired by '*zaibatsu*'.

10 *Chaebol* in South Korea – for example, Hyundai and Daiwoo – and *caifa* in Taiwan – for example, Tatung. See Hofheinz and Calder 1982: 73–5.

11 Mitsui was a major trading and financial concern in the Tokugawa period and helped to finance the anti-Tokugawa alliance during the Restoration period, but thereafter its fortunes came to depend on its growing interests in new industrial and mining activities, as did those of the other *zaibatsu* founded by 'upstart' Meiji businessmen. For a very clear and concise account of the origins and operation of the pre-war *zaibatsu*, see Allen 1980.

12 For an example, see the competition between Mitsui and Mitsubishi in the shipping industry described in ch. 2.

13 There is very little case-study material available in English on the subcontracting system before World War II, but for a vivid description of its operation today in a fairly traditional industry (textiles) see Dore 1986: ch. 7.

14 For some comparisons using post-war data, see Minami 1986: 315–17 and Table 9.17. As Minami points out, while differentials in wages by scale of enterprise in Japan are large by comparison with Britain and the USA, the contrast with, for example, other European countries is not nearly as marked.

15 For historical data on male/female wage differentials, see Taira 1970: 30–1.

16 For a study of the rise of the university-educated managerial class in large-scale Japanese companies, see Morikawa 1989.

17 This term was not used before World War II. Up till then, what are now called *sōgō shōsha* were called *bōeki shōsha* (foreign trade companies). See Yoshihara 1982: 9–10.

18 They also operate substantial businesses in wholesaling and credit within Japan.

19 For a straightforward account of the history of general trading companies, see Yoshihara 1982.

20 For some British examples, see Davenport-Hines and Jones 1989.

21 For example, as soon as it was established it was given the exclusive contract to market the coal from the government-owned Miike mine.

14 CONCLUSION

1 This is not meant to suggest that Japanese consumers do not eat hamburgers or drink Coca-Cola. They do so in vast quantities, but what is striking is that, alongside this, they have also retained, and even developed, their taste for 'traditional' Japanese consumer goods. Visitors to Tokyo department stores will be able to see (though probably not afford) beautifully redesigned traditional household goods and even 'designer kimono'.

GENERAL CONCLUSION

1 See Gluck 1985, in the light of the popularity of similar kinds of agrarian nationalist view in other industrialising countries, before and since, as described in Kitching 1989.

Glossaries

JAPANESE TERMS

Periods of Japanese history

Tokugawa 1600–1868, generally viewed as Japan's feudal era, sometimes called Edo period after the name of the administrative capital of the Shōguns, Edo, later renamed Tokyo
Meiji 1868–1912, initiated by the Meiji Restoration
Taishō 1912–26
Shōwa 1926–89

Tokugawa-period government

Shōgun military ruler and in practice national leader, under the nominal rule of the Emperor
daimyō feudal lord, in charge of individual domain (*han*)
samurai retainers of the *daimyō*, engaged in military or administrative duties
han domain of each *daimyō*

Economic institutions

zaibatsu pyramidal group of interlinked industrial and financial companies, dominating heavy industry and the 'modern sector' of the economy from the early part of the twentieth century
general trading company (sōgō shōsha) company specialising in the organisation of retailing, wholesaling and financial transactions, especially involving foreign trade
MCI/MITI Ministry of Commerce and Industry, later Ministry of International Trade and Industry, the ministry responsible for industrial policy

Agriculture

Meiji Nōhō package of improved agricultural techniques, centring on higher-yielding, fertiliser-responsive rice varieties, speading among Japanese farmers in the later Tokugawa and Meiji periods

ECONOMIC TERMS

Macroeconomic concepts

GNP, GDP Gross National Product, Gross Domestic Product: measures of the value of the total output of a national economy over a given time period, calculated by means of prevailing prices

economic growth rate of growth per annum of GDP or GNP

investment expenditure by businesses or the government on goods (capital goods) or services whose purpose is to increase the capacity to produce output in the future

consumption expenditure on goods for immediate use or enjoyment, that is, not investment

savings income not expended on consumption

inflation/deflation persistent tendency for the prices of all goods to rise/fall

International trade

exports goods sold overseas and paid for in foreign currency

imports goods produced overseas and sold in the domestic market, for which foreign producers must be paid in foreign currency

balance of payments national accounts showing how inflows and outflows of foreign currency were balanced in any time period, hence a balance of payments deficit (and vice versa surplus) means that outlays of foreign currency on imports exceeded receipts of foreign currency for exports and had to be met by withdrawals from national reserves of foreign currency or foreign currency borrowings

gold standard system of fixed exchange rates of currencies in terms of gold, in operation among major trading nations before World War II

comparative advantage the idea behind the theory that if all producers specialise in the production of those goods which they can produce most efficiently (or least inefficiently) relative to other producers, then the maximum possible total output will be produced. It is frequently further argued that free competition in markets, or, at the international level, free trade, will induce profit-maximising producers to specialise in those goods in which they have a comparative advantage and will therefore lead to maximum possible output

Production and technology

productivity   measure of output per unit of input; for example, labour
  productivity = output per man; land productivity = output per hectare,
  that is, yield
capital/capital goods   man-made resources for use in the production of
  output; for example, machinery, factory buildings
technical change   introduction of new methods of production, often either
  capital intensive (= increasing the input of capital per unit of output
  relative to that of other inputs) or labour intensive (= increasing the input
  of labour per unit of output relative to that of other inputs)
economies of scale   characteristic of techniques of production such that costs
  of production per unit of output fall as output increases
R & D   research into and development of new techniques, usually referring
  to expenditure by companies on such activity

Industrial organisation

oligopoly   situation in which there are only a few (usually large-scale)
  producers competing to produce a particular product
cartel   agreement among producers in an industry to restrict competition and
  share out the market between them

Terms in development theory and strategy

neo-classical   term describing economic theories based on the assumption
  that analysis of the operation of competitive market forces can explain
  economic decisions and events
structuralist   term describing approaches to economic analysis which assume
  that pre-existing economic structures and institutions play a large part in
  determining economic activity and in particular the underdevelopment of
  parts of the economies of developing countries, hence structural change is
  a necessary precondition for sustained development
dependency theory   theory that developing-country economies inevitably
  become 'dependent' on developed-country ones, and hence incapable
  of sustained independent growth, once they are involved in economic
  relations with them
import substitution industrialisation (ISI)   strategy of erecting trade barriers
  against imports of specific goods and hence creating incentives for the
  development of local-based industrial production
export oriented industrialisation (EOI)   strategy of encouraging production
  of goods which can be competitively sold as exports at world market prices
NIC   Newly Industrialising Country: one of the group of countries, particularly concentrated in East Asia, which have achieved rapid rates of
  economic growth and industrialisation in recent years

Guide to further reading

(Full publication details of the works described are given in the bibliography.)

BIBLIOGRAPHY AND HISTORICAL BACKGROUND

Macpherson, *The Economic Development of Japan* is both a concise survey of the literature on the subject and a useful bibliography. Wray, *Japan's Economy: A Bibliography of its Past and Present* is a much more comprehensive bibliography. For those unfamiliar with the general outlines of Japan's modern history, Hunter, *The Emergence of Modern Japan* is recommended and the same author's *Concise Dictionary of Modern Japanese History* is a handy reference source. *The Cambridge History of Japan* vol. 6 (ed. Duus) contains detailed surveys of the state of knowledge (as of the late 1970s) in various areas of Japanese economic history.

THE MACROECONOMIC PICTURE

Minami, *The Economic Development of Japan* provides a straightforward macroeconomic account of Japan's development. Less comprehensive but in some ways more stimulating are Nakamura, *Economic Growth in Prewar Japan* and Ohkawa and Rosovsky, *Japanese Economic Growth*. Ohkawa and Shinohara, *Patterns of Japanese Economic Development* conveniently summarises the multi-volume LTES statistical series.

THE TOKUGAWA ECONOMY

T. C. Smith's *Agrarian Origins of Modern Japan* is required reading on commercialisation and economic and technical change in agriculture, and *Native Sources of Japanese Industrialization* brings together many of Smith's influential contributions to books and journals (not only on the Tokugawa period). Also recommended are Jansen and Rozman, *Japan in Transition* which covers a number of interesting areas of economy and society in the late Tokugawa/early Meiji period, Vlastos, *Peasant Protests and Uprisings in Tokugawa Japan*, and Hanley and Yamamura's strikingly revisionist *Economic and Demographic Change in Preindustrial Japan*.

THE ROLE OF THE STATE

Smith, *Political Change and Industrial Development in Japan* gives the standard account of state involvement in the economy in the Meiji period. Part II of Yamamura, *A Study of Samurai Income and Entrepreneurship* presents challenging evidence on the respective roles of entrepreneurs and the state. Chalmers Johnson's *MITI and the Japanese Miracle* is not only a seminal work on the emergence of the 'developmental state' in Japan but is also a good read.

AGRICULTURE

Hayami, *A Century of Agricultural Growth in Japan*, especially Part I, provides a macro survey of agricultural change from 1868 until World War II. Chapters 2 and 3 of Francks, *Technology and Agricultural Development in Pre-War Japan* summarise the technical and institutional story. Ohkawa, Johnston and Kaneda (eds) *Agriculture and Economic Growth* brings together a number of useful papers on agriculture's role in the development process. Also recommended are Waswo, *Japanese Landlords* and, for the broader Asian picture, Bray, *The Rice Economies*. Ann Waswo's translation of Nagatsuka Takashi's classic novel *The Soil* gives an authentic and vivid picture of rural life in pre-war Japan and includes an excellent introduction.

INDUSTRY

Patrick (ed.), *Japanese Industrialization and its Social Consequences* and Wray (ed.), *Managing Industrial Enterprise* contain a number of valuable papers on microeconomic and institutional aspects of Japanese industrialisation. In recent years there has also appeared a series of excellent monographic studies of individual companies and industries including Gordon, *The Evolution of Labour Relations in Japan* (on heavy industry), Wray, *Mitsubishi and the NYK* (on shipping), Fruin, *Kikkoman* (on the famous soy-sauce company), and Cusumano, *The Japanese Automobile Industry*.

Bibliography

Abegglen, J. (1958) *The Japanese Factory*, Glencoe, Illinois: The Free Press.

Allen, G. (1962) *A Short Economic History of Modern Japan* (2nd edn), London: Allen and Unwin.

—— (1980) 'The Concentration of Economic Control', in G. Allen *Japan's Economic Policy*, London: Macmillan.

Barnhart, M. (1987) *Japan Prepares for Total War: the Search for Economic Security, 1919–1941*, Ithaca, New York: Cornell University Press.

Bix, H. (1986) *Peasant Protest in Japan, 1590–1884*, New Haven: Yale University Press.

Blumenthal, T. (1976) 'The Japanese Shipbuilding Industry', in H. Patrick (ed.) (1976) *Japanese Industrialization and its Social Consequences* Berkeley: California University Press.

—— (1980) 'Factor Proportions and Choice of Technology: the Japanese Experience', *Economic Development and Cultural Change* 28 (3): 547–59.

Bray, F. (1986) *The Rice Economies*, Oxford: Basil Blackwell.

Buruma, I. (1984) *A Japanese Mirror*, London: Jonathan Cape.

Chūbachi, M. and Taira, K. (1976) 'Poverty in Modern Japan: Perceptions and Realities', in H. Patrick (ed.) (1976) *Japanese Industrialization and its Social Consequences*, Berkeley: California University Press.

Clarkson, L. (1985) *Proto-Industrialization: The First Phase of Industrialization?*, Basingstoke: Macmillan.

Colman, D. and Nixson, F. (1986) *Economics of Change in Less Developed Countries* (2nd edn), Oxford: Philip Allen.

Crawcour, E. (1965) 'The Tokugawa Heritage', in W. Lockwood (ed.) *The State and Economic Enterprise in Japan*, Princeton: Princeton University Press.

Crowley, J. (1970) 'A New Deal for Japan and Asia: One Road to Pearl Harbour', in J. Crowley (ed.) (1970) *Modern East Asia: Essays in Interpretation*, New York: Harcourt.

Cusumano, M. (1985) *The Japanese Automobile Industry: Technology and Management at Nissan and Toyota*, Cambridge, Mass.: Harvard University Press.

—— (1989) '"Scientific Industry": Strategy, Technology and Entrepreneurship in Prewar Japan', in W. Wray (ed.) (1989(b)) *Managing*

Industrial Enterprise. Cases from Japan's Prewar Experience, Cambridge, Mass. and London: Harvard University Press.

Daito, E. (1980) 'The Development of the Ammonia-Soda Process in Japan 1917–1932', in A. Okochi and H. Uchida (eds) (1980) *Development and Diffusion of Technology* (Fuji Conference Proceedings, Vol. 6), Tokyo: Tokyo University Press.

Davenport-Hines, R. and Jones. G. (1989) 'British Business in Japan since 1868', in R. Davenport-Hines and G. Jones (eds) *British Business in Asia since 1860*, Cambridge: Cambridge University Press.

Dore, R. (1960) 'Agricultural Improvement in Japan', *Economic Development and Cultural Change* 9 (1) (Part 2): 69–91.

Dore, R. (1986) *Flexible Rigidities*, London: Athlone Press.

Duus, P. (ed.) (1988) *The Cambridge History of Japan, Volume 6: The Twentieth Century*, Cambridge: Cambridge University Press.

Eng, R. (1986) *Economic Imperialism in China*, Berkeley: Institute of East Asian Studies, University of California.

Enos, J. (1984) 'Government Intervention in the Transfer of Technology: the Case of South Korea', in R. Wade and G. White (eds) *Developmental States in East Asia: Capitalist and Socialist*, Bulletin of the Institute of Development Studies, University of Sussex, 15 (2): 26–31.

Fei, J. and Ranis, G. (1964) *The Development of the Labour Surplus Economy*, Homewood, Illinois: Irwin.

Francks, P. (1984) *Technology and Agricultural Development in Pre-War Japan*, New Haven and London: Yale University Press.

Fransman, M. (1985) 'Conceptualising Technical Change in the Third World in the 1980s: an Interpretive Survey', *Journal of Development Studies* 21: 572–652.

Fruin, M. (1983) *Kikkoman: Company, Clan and Community*, Cambridge Mass.: Harvard University Press.

Gerschenkron, A. (1962) *Economic Backwardness in Historical Perspective*, Cambridge, Mass.: Harvard University Press.

Gluck, C. (1985) *Japan's Modern Myths: Ideology in the Late Meiji Period* Princeton: Princeton University Press.

Gordon, A. (1985) *The Evolution of Labor Relations in Japan: Heavy Industry, 1853–1955*, Cambridge, Mass.: Harvard University Press.

Griffin, K. (1979) *The Political Economy of Agrarian Change* (2nd edn), London: Macmillan.

Hanley, S. (1986) 'The Material Culture: Stability in Transition', in M. Jansen and G. Rozman (eds) (1986) *Japan in Transition*, Princeton: Princeton University Press.

Hanley, S. and Yamamura, K. (1977) *Economic and Demographic Change in Preindustrial Japan, 1600–1868*, Princeton: Princeton University Press.

Hauser, W. (1974) *Economic Institutional Change in Tokugawa Japan*, London: Cambridge University Press.

Hayami, Y. (1975) *A Century of Agricultural Growth in Japan*, Tokyo: Tokyo University Press.

Hayami, Y. and Ruttan, V. (1971) *Agricultural Development: An International Perspective*, Baltimore and London: John Hopkins Press.

Hayami, Y. and Yamada, S. (1969) 'Agricultural Productivity at the Beginning of Industrialization', in K. Ohkawa, B. Johnston and H. Kaneda (eds) (1969) *Agriculture and Economic Growth: Japan's Experience*, Tokyo: Tokyo University Press.

Hazama, H. (1976) 'Historical Changes in the Life Style of Industrial Workers', in H. Patrick (ed.) (1976) *Japanese Industrialization and its Social Consequences*, Berkeley: California University Press.

Hirschmeier, J. and Yui, T. (1975) *The Development of Japanese Business 1600–1973*, London: Allen and Unwin.

Hofheinz, R. and Calder, K. (1982) *The Eastasia Edge*, New York: Basic Books.

Honig, E. (1986) *Sisters and Strangers*, Stanford: Stanford University Press.

Hoston, G. (1986) *Marxism and the Crisis of Development in Prewar Japan*, Princeton: Princeton University Press.

Hunt, D. (1989) *Economic Theories of Development*, New York and London: Harvester Wheatsheaf.

Hunter, J. (1984(a)) 'Recruitment in the Japanese Silk Reeling and Cotton Spinning Industries, 1870s–1930s', *Proceedings of the British Association for Japanese Studies* 9: 64–85.

Hunter, J (1984(b)) *Concise Dictionary of Modern Japanese History*, Berkeley: University of California Press.

Hunter, J. (1989) *The Emergence of Modern Japan*, London: Longman.

Imai, K. (1980) 'Iron and Steel', in K. Sato (ed.) (1980)*Industry and Business in Japan*, New York: Sharpe.

Iriye, A. (1974) 'The Failure of Economic Expansionism: 1918–1931', in B. Silberman and H. Harootunian (eds) (1974) *Japan in Crisis: Essays on Taisho Democracy*, Princeton: Princeton University Press.

Ishikawa, S. (1967) *Economic Development in Asian Perspective*, Tokyo: Kinokuniya.

Ishikawa, S. (1981) *Essays on Technology, Employment and Institutions in Economic Development*, Tokyo: Kinokuniya.

Jansen, M. and Rozman, G. (eds) (1986) *Japan in Transition*, Princeton: Princeton University Press.

Johnson, C. (1982) *MITI and the Japanese Miracle*, Stanford: Stanford University Press.

Kayō, N. (1958) *Nihon Nōgyō Kiso Tōkei* (Basic Statistics of Japanese Agriculture), Tokyo: Nōrinsuisangyō Seisansei Kōjō Kaigi.

Kitching, G. (1989) *Development and Underdevelopment in Historical Perspective*, (2nd edn) London: Routledge.

Lewis, W. (1954) 'Economic Development with Unlimited Supplies of Labour', *Manchester School* 22: 139–91.

Little, I. (1979) 'An Economic Reconnaissance', in W. Galenson (ed.) (1979) *Economic Growth and Structural Change in Taiwan*, Ithaca: Cornell University Press.

Little, I. (1982) *Economic Development: Theory, Policy and International Relations*, New York: Basic Books.

Lipton, M. (1977) *Why Poor People Stay Poor*, London: Temple Smith.

Lockwood, W. (1968) *The Economic Development of Japan* (2nd edn), Princeton: Princeton University Press.

LTES = Ohkawa, K., Shinohara, M. and Umemura, M. (1965 onwards) *Chōki Keizai Tōkei* (Long-Term Economic Statistics), 14 vols, Tokyo: Tōyō Keizai Shimposha.

Luedde-Neurath, R. (1985) 'State Intervention and Export-Oriented Development in South Korea', in G. White and R. Wade (eds) (1985) *Developmental States in East Asia*, Brighton: Institute of Development Studies, University of Sussex.

Lynn, L. (1982) *How Japan Innovates: A Comparison with the U.S. in the Case of Oxygen Steelmaking*, Boulder: Westview Press.

McCallion, S. (1989) 'Trial and Error: The Model Filature at Tomioka', in W. Wray (ed.) (1989b) *Managing Industrial Enterprise, Cases from Japan's Prewar Experience*, Cambridge, Mass. and London: Harvard University Press.

Macpherson, W. (1987) *The Economic Development of Japan c.1868–1941*, Basingstoke: Macmillan.

Magaziner, I. and Hout, T. (1980) *Japanese Industrial Policy*, London: Policy Studies Institute.

Minami, R. (1986) *The Economic Development of Japan*, Basingstoke: Macmillan.

Minami, R. (1987) *Power Revolution in the Industrialization of Japan: 1885–1940*, Tokyo: Kinokuniya.

Morikawa, H. (1989) 'The Increasing Power of Salaried Managers in Japan's Large Corporations', in W. Wray (ed.) (1989(b)) *Managing Industrial Enterprise, Cases from Japan's Prewar Experience*, Cambridge, Mass. and London: Harvard University Press.

Morishima, M. (1982) *Why Has Japan 'Succeeded'? Western Technology and the Japanese Ethos*, Cambridge: Cambridge University Press.

Morris-Suzuki, T. (1989) *A History of Japanese Economic Thought*, London: Routledge.

Mosk, C. (1981) 'The Evolution of the Pre-Modern Demographic Regime in Japan', *Population Studies* 35(1): 28–52.

Moulder, F. (1977) *Japan, China and the Modern World Economy*, Cambridge: Cambridge University Press.

Nagatsuka, T. (1989) *The Soil*, translated and with an introduction by Ann Waswo, London: Routledge.

Najita, T. (1987) *Visions of Virtue in Tokugawa Japan*, Chicago: University of Chicago Press.

Nakagawa, K. (ed.) (1976) *Strategy and Structure of Big Business* (Fuji Conference Proceedings, vol. I), Tokyo: Tokyo University Press.

Nakamura, J. (1966) *Agricultural Production and the Economic Development of Japan*, Princeton: Princeton University Press.

Nakamura, T. (1983) *Economic Growth in Prewar Japan*, New Haven and London: Yale University Press.

Napier, R. (1982) 'The Transformation of the Japanese Labour Market, 1894–1937', in T. Najita and J. Koschmann (eds) (1982) *Conflict in Modern Japanese History*, Princeton: Princeton University Press.

Ohkawa, K., Johnston, B. and Kaneda, H. (eds) (1969) *Agriculture and Economic Growth: Japan's Experience*, Tokyo: Tokyo University Press.

Ohkawa, K. and Mundle, S. (1979) 'Agricultural Surplus Flow in Japan 1868–1937', *The Developing Economies* 17 (3): 247–65.

Ohkawa, K. and Ranis, G. (eds) (1985) *Japan and the Developing Countries*, Oxford: Basil Blackwell.

Ohkawa, K. and Rosovsky, H. (1961) 'The Indigenous Components in the Modern Japanese Economy', *Economic Development and Cultural Change* 9(3): 476–501.

Ohkawa, K. and Rosovsky, H. (1973) *Japanese Economic Growth, Trend Acceleration in the Twentieth Century*, Stanford: Stanford University Press.

Ohkawa, K. and Shinohara, M. (eds) (1979) *Patterns of Japanese Economic Development, A Quantitative Appraisal*, New Haven and London: Yale University Press.

Okochi, A. and Uchida, H. (eds) (1980) *Development and Diffusion of Technology* (Fuji Conference Proceedings, vol. 6), Tokyo: Tokyo University Press.

Ono, A. (1985) 'Borrowed Technology in Iron and Steel: Brazil, India and Japan', in K. Ohkawa and G. Ranis (eds) (1985) *Japan and the Developing Countries*, Oxford: Basil Blackwell.

Otsuka, K., Ranis, G. and Saxonhouse, G. (1988) *Comparative Technology Choice in Development*, Basingstoke: Macmillan.

Patrick, H. (ed.) (1976) *Japanese Industrialization and its Social Consequences*, Berkeley: California University Press.

Patrick, H. and Rohlen, T. (1987) 'Small-Scale Family Enterprises', in K. Yamamura and Y. Yasuba (eds) (1987) *The Political Economy of Japan, Volume 1: The Domestic Transformation*, Stanford: Stanford University Press.

Popkin, S. (1979) *The Rational Peasant*, Berkeley: California University Press.

Ranis, G. (1969) 'The Financing of Japanese Economic Development', in K. Ohkawa, B. Johnston and H. Kaneda (eds) (1969) *Agriculture and Economic Growth: Japan's Experience*, Tokyo: Tokyo University Press.

Ranis, G. and Saxonhouse, G. (1985) 'Determinants of Technology Choice: the Indian and Japanese Cotton Industries', in K. Ohkawa and G. Ranis (eds) (1985) *Japan and the Developing Countries*, Oxford: Basil Blackwell.

Saitō, O. (1986(a)) 'Scenes of Japan's Economic Development and the "Longue Durée"', *Bonner Zeitschrift fur Japanologie* 8: 15–27.

Saitō, O. (1986(b)) 'The Rural Economy: Commercial Agriculture, By-Employment and Wage Work', in M. Jansen and G. Rozman (eds) (1986) *Japan in Transition*, Princeton: Princeton University Press.

Sawada, S. (1972) 'The Development of Rice Productivity in Japan – Prewar Experience', in Japan Economic Research Centre (ed.) (1972) *Agriculture and Economic Development – Structural Re-Adjustment in Asian Perspective*, Tokyo: Japan Economic Research Centre.

Saxonhouse, G.(1976) 'Country Girls and Communication among Competitors in the Japanese Cotton-Spinning Industry', in H. Patrick (ed.) (1976) *Japanese Industrialization and its Social Consequences*, Berkeley: California University Press.

Saxonhouse, G. (1985) 'Technology Choice in Cotton Textile Manufacturing', in K. Ohkawa and G. Ranis (eds) (1985) *Japan and the Developing Countries*, Oxford: Basil Blackwell.

Saxonhouse, G. and Kiyokawa, Y. (1985) 'Supply and Demand for Quality Workers in Cotton Spinning in Japan and India', in K. Ohkawa and G. Ranis (eds) (1985) *Japan and the Developing Countries*, Oxford: Basil Blackwell.

Scott, J. (1976) *The Moral Economy of the Peasant*, New Haven and London: Yale University Press.

Shimpo, M. (1976) *Three Decades in Shiwa: Economic Development and Social Change in a Japanese Farming Community*, Vancouver: University of British Columbia Press.

Shinohara, M. (1970) 'A Survey of the Japanese Literature on Small Industry' in B. Hoselitz (ed.) (1970) *Structural Changes in Japan's Economic Development*, Tokyo: Kinokuniya.

Silberman, B. (1974) 'The Bureaucratic Role in Japan, 1900–1945: The Bureaucrat as Politician', in B. Silberman and H. Harootunian (eds) (1974) *Japan in Crisis: Essays on Taisho Democracy*, Princeton: Princeton University Press.

Silberman, B. and Harootunian, H. (eds) (1974) *Japan in Crisis: Essays on Taisho Democracy*, Princeton: Princeton University Press.

Smethurst, R. (1986) *Agricultural Development and Tenancy Disputes in Japan 1870–1940*, Princeton: Princeton University Press.

Smith, T. (1955) *Political Change and Industrial Development in Japan: Government Enterprise 1868–1880*, Stanford: Stanford University Press.

Smith, T. (1959) *The Agrarian Origins of Modern Japan*, Stanford: Stanford University Press.

Smith, T. (1970) 'Ōkura Nagatsune and the Technologists', in A. Craig and D. Shiveley (eds) (1970) *Personality in Japanese History*, Berkeley: University of California Press, reprinted in Smith (1988).

Smith, T. (1973) 'Premodern Economic Growth: Japan and the West', *Past and Present* 60: 127–60, reprinted in Smith (1988).

Smith, T. (1977) *Nakahara: Family Farming and Population in a Japanese Village, 1717–1830*, Stanford: Stanford University Press.

Smith, T. (1984) 'The Right to Benevolence: Dignity and Japanese Workers, 1890–1920', *Comparative Studies in Society and History* 26(4): 587–613, reprinted in Smith (1988).

Smith, T. (1986) 'Peasant Time and Factory Time in Japan', *Past and Present* 111: 165–97, reprinted in Smith (1988).

Smith, T. (1988) *Native Sources of Japanese Industrialization 1750–1920*, Berkeley: California University Press.

Sugihara, K. (1986) 'The Transformation of Social Values of Young Country Girls', in J. Hunter (ed.) *Aspects of the Relationship between Agriculture and Industrialisation in Japan*, London: Suntory Toyota International Centre for Economics and Related Disciplines, London School of Economics.

Sugiyama, S. (1988) *Japan's Industrialization in the World Economy 1859–1899*, London: Athlone Press.

Taeuber, I. (1958) *The Population of Japan*, Princeton: Princeton University Press.

Taira, K. (1970) *Economic Development and the Labour Market in Japan*, New York: Columbia University Press.

Taira, K. (1978) 'Factory Labour and the Industrial Revolution in Japan', in P. Mathias and M. Postan (eds) (1978) *The Cambridge Economic History of Europe* vol. VII, part 2, Cambridge: Cambridge University Press.

Taira, K. (1988) 'Economic Development, Labour Markets and Industrial Relations in Japan, 1905–1955', in P. Duus (ed.) (1988) *The Cambridge*

History of Japan, Volume 6: The Twentieth Century, Cambridge: Cambridge University Press.

Takamura, N. (1982) 'Japanese Cotton Spinning Industry during the pre-World War I Period', in A. Okochi and S. Yonekawa (eds) (1982) *The Textile Industry and its Business Climate* (Fuji Conference Proceedings, vol. 8), Tokyo: Tokyo University Press.

Tussing, A. (1969) 'The Labour Force in Meiji Economic Growth: A Quantitative Study of Yamanashi Prefecture', in K. Ohkawa, B. Johnston and H. Kaneda (eds) (1969) *Agriculture and Economic Growth: Japan's Experience*, Tokyo: Tokyo University Press.

Uchida, H. (1980) 'Western Big Business and the Adoption of New Technology in Japan: the Electrical Equipment and Chemical Industries 1890–1920', in A. Okochi and H. Uchida (eds) (1980) *Development and Diffusion of Technology* (Fuji Conference Proceedings, vol. 6) Tokyo: Tokyo University Press.

Udagawa, M. and Nakamura, S. (1980) 'Japanese Business and Government in the Inter-War Period: Heavy Industrialization and the Industrial Rationalization Movement', in Nakagawa, K. (ed.) *Government and Business* (Fuji Conference Proceedings, Vol. 5), Tokyo: Tokyo University Press.

Uekusa, M. (1987) 'Industrial Organisation: the 1970s to the Present', in K. Yamamura and Y. Yasuba (eds) (1987) *The Political Economy of Japan, Volume 1: The Domestic Transformation*, Stanford: Stanford University Press.

Vlastos, S. (1986) *Peasant Protests and Uprisings in Tokugawa Japan*, Berkeley: California University Press.

Waswo, A. (1977) *Japanese Landlords*, Berkeley: California University Press.

Weiss, J. (1990) *Industry in Developing Countries*, London: Routledge.

Westney, E. (1987) *Imitation and Innovation: the Transfer of Western Organizational Patterns to Meiji Japan*, Cambridge, Mass.: Harvard University Press.

White, G. and Wade, R. (eds) (1985) *Developmental States in East Asia,* Brighton: Institute of Development Studies, University of Sussex.

Wray, W. (1984) *Mitsubishi and the NYK, 1870–1914*, Cambridge, Mass.: Harvard University Press.

Wray, W. (1986) 'Shipping: From Sail to Steam', in M. Jansen and G. Rozman (eds) (1986) *Japan in Transition*, Princeton: Princeton University Press.

Wray, W. (1989(a)) *Japan's Economy: A Bibliography of its Past and Present*, New York: Markus Wiener Publishing.

Wray, W. (ed) (1989(b)) *Managing Industrial Enterprise, Cases from Japan's Prewar Experience*, Cambridge, Mass. and London: Harvard University Press.

Yamamura, K. (1974) *A Study of Samurai Income and Entrepreneurship*, Harvard: Harvard University Press.

Yamamura, K. (1976) 'General Trading Companies in Japan – Their Origins and Growth', in H. Patrick (ed.) (1976) *Japanese Industrialization and its Social Consequences*, Berkeley: California University Press.

Yamamura, K. (1986) 'Japan's *Deus ex Machina*: Western Technology in the 1920s', *Journal of Japanese Studies* 12, 1: 65–94.

Yamamura, K. and Yasuba, Y. (eds) (1987) *The Political Economy of Japan, Volume 1: The Domestic Transformation*, Stanford: Stanford University Press.

Yasuba, Y. (1976) 'The Evolution of Dualistic Wage Structure', in H. Patrick (ed.) (1976) *Japanese Industrialization and its Social Consequences*, Berkeley: California University Press.

Yoshihara, K. (1982) *Sogo Shosha: the Vanguard of the Japanese Economy*, Tokyo: Oxford University Press.

Yui, T. and Nakagawa, K. (eds) (1985) *Business History of Shipping* (Fuji Conference Proceedings, vol. 11), Tokyo: Tokyo University Press.

Index